978 0754678533

D1795702

MEDIA, RELIGION AND CONFLICT

For Gill, Miriam, Sam and Simon

Media, Religion and Conflict

Edited by
LEE MARSDEN AND HEATHER SAVIGNY
University of East Anglia, UK

ASHGATE

Published by
Ashgate Publishing Limited
Wey Court East
Union Road
Farnham
Surrey, GU9 7PT
England

Ashgate Publishing Company
Suite 420
101 Cherry Street
Burlington
VT 05401-4405
USA

www.ashgate.com

British Library Cataloguing in Publication Data

Media, religion and conflict.
   1. Religion and international affairs. 2. Mass media--
   Religious aspects. 3. Mass media and international
   relations. 4. Mass media and public opinion. 5. Religion
   and international affairs--Press coverage.
   I. Marsden, Lee. II. Savigny, Heather.
   302.2'3-dc22

Library of Congress Cataloging-in-Publication Data

Media, religion, and conflict / [edited] by Lee Marsden and Heather Savigny.
      p. cm.
   Includes bibliographical references and index.
   ISBN 978-0-7546-7853-3 (hardback) -- ISBN 978-0-7546-9681-0
(ebook) 1. Terrorism--Press coverage. 2. War--Press coverage. 3. Islam--Press coverage.
4. Religion and politics. I. Marsden, Lee. II. Savigny, Heather.

   PN4784.T45M43 2009
   070.4'493036--dc22

                                                                      2009019978

ISBN 9780754678533 (hbk)
ISBN 9780754696810 (ebk)

Mixed Sources
Product group from well-managed
forests and other controlled sources
www.fsc.org Cert no. SA-COC-1565
© 1996 Forest Stewardship Council
FSC

Printed and bound in Great Britain by
MPG Books Group, UK

Contents

List of Figures

List of Tables

Notes on Contributors

Henrik Bødker is an Associate Professor at the Institute for Information and Media Studies, Aarhus University, Denmark.

John Bradley is a postgraduate research student at Edinburgh University.

Nick Cohen is a freelance journalist and columnist for *The Observer*.

Ivor Gaber is Research Professor in Media and Politics at the University of Bedfordshire and Emeritus Professor of Broadcast Journalism at Goldsmiths College.

Patrik Ettinger is a Researcher at the University of Zurich.

Jeffrey Haynes is Professor of Politics at London Metropolitan University.

Michael Higgins is Lecturer in Journalism and Communications at the University of Strathclyde.

Justin Lewis is Professor of Communication and Head of the Cardiff School of Journalism, Media and Cultural Studies, Cardiff University.

Lee Marsden is Lecturer in International Relations at the University of East Anglia.

Paul Mason is Director of Postgraduate Research at the Cardiff School of Journalism, Media and Cultural Studies, Cardiff University.

Kerry Moore is a Lecturer in the Cardiff School of Journalism, Media and Cultural Studies, Cardiff University.

Heather Savigny is Senior Lecturer in Politics at the University of East Anglia.

Lisa Thomas is a Research Assistant at the University of Bedfordshire.

Linards Udris is a Researcher at the University of Zurich.

Acknowledgements

The works included in this volume are from scholars at the leading edge of their respective disciplines and represent a reflection of the diversity of the ways in which the intersection between media, religion and conflict may be debated. We would like to thank the chapter authors not only for their impressive array of contributions but also for their timeliness and promptness in submitting their chapters, making our job far much easier than it could have been! Our appreciation is extended to Nick Cohen for his permission to use his Isaiah Berlin memorial lecture as the foreword for this book. We would like to thank Simon Gerrard, John Greenaway and John Street, in particular, for their insightful comments and feedback. As such, any mistakes are obviously theirs.

Special thanks to Ashgate for their support and the superb job that they have done, and with particular thanks to Kirstin Howgate. As fellow writers and editors know only too well, none of this is possible without the support provided by our families and in particular we would like to thank Gill Marsden, Miriam Hogg, Simon Gerrard and Sam Sleight for their inordinate levels of patience, support, encouragement and good humour, without which this would have not been possible.

Foreword: The New Left and the Old Far Right[1]

Nick Cohen

I've got a book out at the moment on the willingness of people who call themselves liberal or left wing to go support or excuse the movements and regimes of the far right, and while I was preparing, I came across a long essay by Berlin that I wish I'd read before I wrote my book.[2] It makes the point far better than I ever could that there is a long, dark and dangerous tradition on the ultra right that stretches back to the most extreme reaction to the Enlightenment and all the notions of democracy, human freedom and, indeed, Jewish emancipation that came with it.[3] It is a marvellous subtle piece of work that Berlin polished and reworked over several decades. It would be vain of me to try to summarise it, but I would like to draw a couple of points from it that will help, I hope, my argument.

Berlin looked at Joseph de Maistre, a thinker who is almost unknown in the Anglo-Saxon world. However, an educated Frenchman or woman with knowledge of intellectual history would, I think, still know that he was one of the great reactionary opponents of the French Revolution, who from 1789 on became ever more implacable in his detestation of the enemies of the old order of monarchy and church. There were plenty of people who hated the French Revolution and many had good reason to do so, and Berlin drew a careful distinction between reactionaries and conservatives on the one hand and de Maistre and the forerunners of fascism on the other.

Reactionaries, stick-in-the-muds, traditionalists, call them what you will, want to turn the clock back. Their basic thought is that the modern world is going to the dogs, a sentiment all of us can share when the mood takes us. Conservatives, as defined in Edmund Burke's attack on the French Revolution are wary of the belief that traditions can be torn up and the world made anew. Once again I would say that all civilised people have their moments of Burkean distrust of novelty at some point in their lives.

---

1 This article is an edited version of the 2007 Isaiah Berlin Memorial Lecture.

2 Nick Cohen (2007), *What's Left? How the Left Lost Its Way*, London: HarperCollins.

3 Isaiah Berlin (1990), 'Joseph de Maistre and the Origins of Fascism', *The New York Review of Books*, Vol. 37, No. 14, 27 September.

The fascist is quite distinct from the reactionary and the conservative. He is dynamic rather than world weary; modern rather than nostalgic. What is fascinating about Berlin's study of de Maistre is that he realised that the origins of the fascist impulse go right back to moment of the birth of the modern world in the late 18th century, and identified two of its original features.

The first is the view that democracy, religious freedom and what we would now call human rights are a sham, a fraud on society perpetuated by a conspiracy which is determined to destroy the old, established order. De Maistre called the conspirators 'la secte'. As Berlin describes it, la Secte consists of:

> Freemasons and Jews, scientists and democrats, Jacobins, liberals, utilitarians, anti-clericals, egalitarians, perfectablians, materialists, idealists, lawyers, journalists, secular reformers and intellectuals of every breed; all those who appeal to abstract principles, who put faith in individual reason or individual conscience; believers in individual liberty or the rational organisation of society; these are the enemy of the settled order and must be rooted out at all costs.

Writing in the 1940s, Berlin barely needed to add that, 'This is a catalogue of which we have heard a great deal since it assembles for the first time, and with precision, the list of the enemies of the great counter-revolutionary movement that culminated in fascism'.

In the 21st century, I suspect that many find Berlin's list odd and think that surely the conspiracy theory of the far right is the Jewish conspiracy theory. In truth the first modern far right conspiracy theory of politics had no Jews in it. Racist laws still confined Jews to ghettos during the Enlightenment. Even the maddest thinkers in Europe could not bring themselves to maintain that persecuted Jews were the secret rulers of the world. The supporters of the far right needed a conspiracy theory none the less to explain away the revolutions of the eighteenth century. When American revolutionaries scandalised them by drafting bills of rights, separating church and state and rejecting the rule of George III, when the French revolutionaries overthrew the king who loved them and the Holy Mother Church that succoured them, the counter-revolutionaries could not accept that millions of American and French men and women had revolted of their own free will. Diabolic conspirators must have duped the masses into rejecting sacred authority, and those conspirators were the freemasons.

Many conservatives at the time would share de Maistre's prejudices. What distinguished him, and what was to distinguish the fascist tradition, was that he wanted to turn against the new and satanic order all the violence and fanaticism which he believed liberal conspirators to have loosed on the world. 'Men can only be saved by being hemmed in by the terror of authority', he wrote:

> They must be reminded at every instant of their lives of the frightening mystery that lies at the heart of their creation; must be purged by perpetual suffering, must be humbled by being made conscious of their stupidity, malice and helplessness

while their rulers must impose rules on them and exterminate their enemies with equal ruthlessness.

All very interesting, you might say, but why drag up the dark thoughts of the ultra right of the 1790s and 1930s? Surely, this is history. Not so. I could produce for you dozens of echoes of far right philosophy from Baathist Syria and Iraq, the Ayatollahs' Iran or Islamist groups. But Article 22 of the Hamas constitution can stand for them all.

> For a long time, the enemies [the Jews] have been planning, skilfully and with precision, for the achievement of what they have attained. They took into consideration the causes affecting the current of events. They strived to amass great and substantive material wealth which they devoted to the realisation of their dream. With their money, they took control of the world media, news agencies, the press, publishing houses, broadcasting stations, and others. With their money they stirred revolutions in various parts of the world with the purpose of achieving their interests and reaping the fruit therein. They were behind the French Revolution, the communist revolution and most of the revolutions we heard and hear about, here and there. With their money they formed secret societies, such as Freemasons, Rotary Clubs, the Lions and others in different parts of the world for the purpose of sabotaging societies and achieving Zionist interests. With their money, they were able to control imperialistic countries and instigate them to colonize many countries in order to enable them to exploit their resources and spread corruption there.[4]

Notice that this might have been written by Adolf Hitler, notice too that the original anti-freemason conspiracy theory from the founding of the modern ultra right has been preserved down the centuries and transferred to the Muslim world. I'm not saying that its various anti-western secular and religious movements are the same as the fascists of the 1930s, but then the fascists of the 1930s weren't the same as the counter-revolutionaries of the 1790s. All, though, are united by recognisable tradition. As for the violence, while de Maistre celebrated the hangman and the Spanish fascists marched into battle with the slogan *viva le meurte* – long live death on their lips – today's Islamists cry that they love death as we love life.

Please notice something else which would shock even a philosopher as worldly as Sir Isaiah. A radical, psychopathic movement of the far right is sweeping the world, but overwhelmingly left-minded and liberal-minded people excuse it, turn their eyes from and fail to confront it, or blame its violence on their own societies or, in a few cases openly support it.

There are so many examples of bad faith that I feel like telling you that if you haven't noticed them yet, then nothing I can say can convince you. I quote

---

4   Hamas Constitution available at http://www.mideastweb.org/hamas.htm, accessed 24 April 2009.

this account from Martin Amis to sceptics as it encapsulated the self-delusion of liberal opinion. He returned to Britain from two years living overseas and found a liberal-left wallowing in self-delusion. When asked by *The Independent* what had shocked him most since he got home he replied:

> The most depressing thing was the sight of middle-class white demonstrators waddling around under placards saying, "We Are All Hezbollah Now". Well, make the most of being Hezbollah while you can. As its leader, famously advised the West: "We don't want anything from you. We just want to eliminate you."[5]

Critics could say that leftists boasting of their conversion to Islamism were a fringe phenomenon, but Amis made it clear that he was talking about the mainstream, not the fringe, when he continued that he then went on *Question Time*, the most popular political discussion programme of the day.

> A woman in the audience, her voice quavering with self-righteousness, presented the following argument. Since it was America that supported Osama bin Laden when he was fighting the Russians, the US armed forces, in response to September 11, "should be dropping bombs on themselves!" And the audience applauded. It is quite an achievement. People of liberal sympathies, stupefied by relativism, have become the apologists for a credal wave that is racist, misogynist, homophobic, imperialist and genocidal. To put it another way, they are up the backside of those that want them dead.

About the same time as Amis was speaking to *The Independent*, Ken Livingstone, the Mayor of London, invited me to a 'Clash of Civilizations' conference. I refused to go, as I knew the form for this type of left wing meeting. The token liberal speaker's sole function is to be ritually denounced by a packed platform and packed audience. However, friends of mine went, and shocked accounts of what they saw are all over the Internet. However, it took a French feminist from the secular republican tradition to speak plainly. Agnès Poirier pulled out because although there were no special facilities for Christians, Hindus and Jews, Livingstone had provided separate prayer rooms for Muslim men and Muslim women. 'Is Ken Livingstone's idea of multiculturalism, one that acknowledges and condones segregation?' she wanted to know.

Yes it was. The conference was packed but in an original way. The white left was in alliance with the Islamist far right. The attacks on the London Underground were, speakers agreed, 'reprisal events'. To oppose radical Islam was to oppose all Muslims and hence mark one self as an 'Islamophobe'. This wasn't a one-off but a long-term strategy. For several years now, Livingstone, left wing journalists

---

5   'Martin Amis: You Ask the Questions', *The Independent*, reader interviews 15 January 2007, http://www.independent.co.uk/news/people/profiles/martin-amis-you-ask-the-questions-432146.html, accessed 24 April 2009.

and the leaders of the Stop the War coalition have been pumping up the Muslim Brotherhood and its south Asian sister organization Jamaat-e-Islami. I'll let Sheikh Yusuf al Qaardawi, the Brotherhood's chief theologian who has been embraced by Livingstone explain its philosophy. On a Muslim who, of his or her own free will, decides to do what everyone in this hall is entitled to do and change their religion, or that they don't believe in any god, Qaardawi said 'He is a traitor to his religion and his people and thus deserves killing'. He has excused female genital mutilation and wife beating as long as the husband does it lightly with his hands, avoiding her face and other sensitive areas. He supports suicide bombers who murder Israeli children and says of gays:

> Muslim jurists hold different opinions concerning the punishment for this abominable practice. Should it be the same as the punishment for fornication, or should both the active and passive participants be put to death? While such punishments may seem cruel, they have been suggested to maintain the purity of the Islamic society and to keep it clean of perverted elements.[6]

Across the Arab world, liberals have risked their lives by taking these ideas on. Iraqi, Jordanian and Tunisian writers organised a petition to the United Nations by 2,500 Arab intellectuals which condemned 'individuals in the Muslim world who pose as clerics and issue death sentences against those they disagree with. These individuals give Islam a bad name and foster hatred among civilizations'. Prominent in their list of the 'sheikhs of death' was one Yusuf al-Qaradawi.

Here's what's odd. If I were to ask you to name the most prominent left wing politician in Britain, you would probably name Ken Livingstone. Yet he is a man who turns his back on liberals, socialist and feminists in the Arab world while offering succour to their enemies. And there is no outcry when he does, no great debates on the BBC or in the liberal press. Turning your back on what we used to call the Left while supporting what we should call the far right is what we expect European leftists to do.

The Stop the War coalition, which organised the largest demonstrations in British history, was led by Trotskyists who proclaimed themselves to be left wing and then formed an alliance with ultra right wing Islamist groups rather than Muslims of liberal background. The protest's chief figure was George Galloway, a degraded man who openly admired the regime of Saddam Hussein, a regime which to use an overused word correctly for once was actually 'fascist'. It didn't do him any harm. Indeed he was elected to Parliament at the last election as the first allegedly far Left wing MP in 50 years.

The point I want to emphasise, indeed the point I can't emphasise to you strongly enough is how bizarre and unprecedented our present situation is. Some

---

6   Sheikh Yusuf al Qaardawi quoted on IslamOnline.net, http://www.islamonline.net/servlet/Satellite?pagename=IslamOnline-English-Ask_Scholar/FatwaE/FatwaE&cid=111 9503547102, accessed 24 April 2009.

conservative critics have given good reviews to *What's Left?* I'm not complaining about that incidentally. If you want to enjoy the dubious pleasure of turning a writer into your slave for life all you have to do is give him, or her, a good review. But because they don't understand the left they have grasped how extraordinary it is for leftish people to go along with ultra-reactionary movements and regimes. The attitude of conservative critics seems to be, well, a few people on the left supported the Soviet Union in the 20th century and many, many more turned a blind eye to its crimes and the victims of its crimes. What's new? What's the difference?

It's only if you come from the old left that you remember that in the 20th century we used to have a hierarchy, or at least we pretended we did. At the top was some form of socialism which we argued about continuously and like the Kingdom of God never came. Next was what we had here in Britain – liberal democracy with its freedoms and a mixed economy and a welfare state. At the bottom were fascist and ultra right wing movements that spouted ethnic or religious totalitarianism usually with large dollops of Adolf Hitler's raging conspiracy theories thrown in.

Now, not just in Britain, but overwhelmingly and everywhere liberals and leftists are far more likely than conservatives to excuse fascistic governments and movements. Not their native far right parties. As long as local racists are white, they have no difficulty in opposing them in a manner that would have been recognisable to the traditional left. But give them a foreign far right movement that is anti-Western and they treat it as at best a distraction and at worst an ally. The reverse side of the debased coinage of modern leftish thinking is a poignant spectacle. Democrats, feminists and socialists in the poor world, who are suffering at the hands of the extreme right, turn for support to the home of democracy, feminism and socialism in the West, only to find that the democrats, socialists and feminists of the rich world won't help them or acknowledge their existence.

If you think the phenomena I am describing are simply the result of the disastrous Bush administration, I would agree with you up to a point. But they were developing long before Bush came to power and show every sign of continuing now he has gone. In any case, a left that still had life in it and a European liberal tradition that meant what it said would have had no difficulty in dealing with Bush in an honourable manner. It would have opposed the second Iraq war, deplored the errors and brutalities of the occupation while supporting those Iraqis who fought al Qaeda and insisted that they wanted something after 35 years of the genocidal Baathist regime. Support was forthcoming from parts of the old and declining labour movements, but the dominant voices on the liberal-left in the media, universities and political parties stayed silent as al Qaeda slaughtered Iraqis without compunction.

'Internationalism', 'solidarity' and 'fraternity' now feel like dead words from a lost age. Even the one foreign cause that does inspire the European left, the Israeli confrontation with the Palestinians, is far less altruistic than it seems. Very few on the left are prepared to support Fatah, which for all its faults is a recognisable national liberation movement that may build a Palestine worth living in, while deploring

Hamas, which wants to impose intolerable burdens on Palestinian women, gays, trade unionist, secularists and Christians. The inability to discriminate between democrat and theocrat is a sign of vacuity. Today's left cannot tell its friends from its enemies because it has no programme for a better world. Blaming its decadence on Bush is as foolish as holding America responsible for every conflict in the world. Deeper historical trends explain the crisis of our times.

The Rise of Consumer Politics

In the 1960s, those who longed for a radical transformation of the status quo, as many people do at some time in their lives, could draw comfort from revolutionary leftist movements that were sweeping the world from Cambodia to Chile, as well as the strength of the student radicals in their own countries. History was on their side. Millions were moved by their slogans. Since the fall of socialism, revolutionary leftism has died everywhere except in Latin America, and even there it is sickly and shallow. The main threat to the status quo comes from radical Islam and the corrupt nationalisms of China and Russia. Far leftists are open in their support for jihadis. The apologias from some liberals are so comprehensive that they must also support radical Islam in their hearts. At some level, these people understand that they have nowhere else to go now that the revolutionary guerrillas and communist regimes of the 20th century are history. A love of violence and hatred of their own societies – well merited or otherwise – leads them to conclude that any killer of Americans is better than none.

Noam Chomsky in his political writings and the cultural theorising of Michel Foucault and the postmodernists anticipated the 21st century left ideology. Read them and you find a leftism without a practical political programme has taken the place of socialism and anti-fascism. All they have is a criticism of the existing order. In this mental universe, no movement that challenges the existing order can be unambiguously condemned. Say what you like about them, but a communist or social democrat in the 1940s had clear ideas about how to transform society. Today, there is no radical alternative that serious people believe they can use, just practical ways of adapting to changes in the economy and environment.

A paradoxical consequence of the death of the socialist idea is that leftism now suits the consumer society very well. Because there is no coherent left wing political programme, anyone can affect a leftish posture, just as anyone can walk into a shop. For example, if I were a socialist, you might agree with a proposal I was making on a cause you endorsed. Maybe I would say that we should do more to improve the treatment of animals on factory farms or increase its aid budget. But because I believed in socialism I would have to add that I also wanted the nationalisation of the commanding heights of the economy, penal taxation, and workers' control. If not you, then other readers might back away saying that after hearing my programme away they could not possibly define themselves as left wing.

Modern leftists do not have to risk alienating potential sympathisers with proposals that might make them uncomfortable. They rarely have proposals for a new ordering of society. They are merely against the West in general or America in particular, both of which, God knows, provide reasons aplenty for opposition. If someone points out that as leftists they have a duty to fight crimes committed by ultra-reactionary movements, the new left ideology instructs them to say that it is 'hypocritical' for westerners to criticise when they carry so much guilt. The correct course is to do and say nothing. The collapse of socialism also explains the general inability of leftists in Europe and North America to work on behalf of feminists, democrats and leftists in the poor world. If you do not have a positive programme yourself, how can you see strangers as comrades who have the right to your support?

These perfidies may be scandalous but they chime with the psychology of modern consumerism. Shoppers don't like altruistic commitments. They have no appetite for boring meetings to raise public consciousness and the lobbying of politicians to change policy. When I go into the homes of the richest people I know, I see Naomi Klein and Michael Moore on their shelves and think, 'Why am I surprised? The left is no threat to the wealthy any longer. Being a leftist is a lifestyle choice. It carries no costs and no obligations'.

Liberal Disillusion

So far I have been talking about the consequences of defeat. But the second half of the 20th century also saw enormous triumphs. European left-wing movements gave the masses better housing, full-time education, employment rights and comprehensive health cover. If you could travel back in time, and tell the reformers of 100-years ago what their country would look like today, they would be astonished and delighted. You would then have to explain to them that the triumph of your shared ideals had the unexpected consequence of turning the liberal intelligentsia against the white working class. The workers let down the intellectuals. They did not lead the charge towards a socialist society as the intelligentsia told them to. They did not use the relative affluence of the welfare state to acquire a taste for avant-garde art and atonal music. On occasion, they voted in large numbers for politicians the middle class left despised – Reagan, Thatcher, Bush and Sarkozy. And all too clearly in the cities of Europe and North America, the utopian plans of the 20th century social reformers did not always create a better society but welfare dependency, family breakdown and crime.

You can see the disappointment of the middle class in the attempts to prevent democratic votes and deny freedom of speech. The centralisation of decision making in the undemocratic bodies of the European Union, the fondness for asking unelected judges to take political decisions and politically correct speech codes all flow from a belief that the working class cannot be trusted to think as the middle classes would like it to think. Beyond a fear that they cannot win majorities in open elections, the liberal middle class across the developed world feels a deeper unease. History no longer seems to be going its way. Market economies undermine the status and comparative wealth of the public sector managers who dominated modern states at the high tide of social democracy in the mid-20th century. Financiers and industrialists have acquired fantastic wealth and political status, while the liberal middle classes lingered in jobs their rulers despised for their failure to be market-orientated. Modern democracy is a system that no longer pleases them. They are less likely than they once would have been to oppose clerical fascist movements and stand up for the best values of their societies.

Multiculturalism and its Discontents

Our progressive intellectual of 1908 would be as astonished by the triumph of human rights as the growth of the welfare state. Women, homosexuals and blacks – groups which had been discriminated against for millennia – have won full legal equality. A measure of the transformation is that it is now impossible for a conservative politician who is against equal rights for homosexuals to become the leader of a mainstream European centre-right party, let alone go on to win an election. Again, there is an ambiguity, however. Although the extraordinary success of campaigns against sexism, racism and homophobia vastly improved the lives of millions of individuals, post-modern liberals did not see them as individuals but as categories. They developed an identity politics based on group definitions that was anti-individualist in its assumptions. They treated women, members of ethnic minorities, gays and others as of blocs with communal interests. Their simplifications weren't always pernicious – a campaign to tighten the law on domestic violence, for example, is a campaign for women not this or that woman. But postmodern multiculturalists have taken the liberal idea of tolerance and pushed it into an extreme relativism which holds that it is wrong for liberals to attack previously disadvantaged groups – 'the other' – even when 'the other' espoused ideas which were anti-liberal. In short, it has become racist to oppose sexists, homophobes and fascists from other cultures.

Such attitudes are a disaster for progressive forces in the poor world, most notably in the Arab world and Europe's immigrant communities. We are now in the extraordinary position where liberals consider it 'left wing' to argue that the emancipation of women is good for white-skinned women in London but not for brown-skinned women in Tehran. Post-modern multi-culturalists have picked up the reactionary anti-universalist philosophies of the counter-Enlightenment and dressed them in modern clothes.

Fear

From the 9/11 atrocities on, the stupidest citizens of the western democracies could be in no doubt that forces were swirling around the globe that would murder them on a vast scale. This is a short and simple point to make, but we are frightened and think it is better to say nothing about the treatment of women, the attacks on freedom of speech, the psychopathic ideologies, medieval hatreds and raging conspiracy theories in case we provoke the killers.

Fear is the most powerful of human motives. Add in the despairing and reactionary turn modern leftish thinking took after the collapse of socialism, the tolerance of the intolerable inculcated by post-modernism and the doubts about democracy in the liberal mainstream, and I hope you can see why so many can't oppose totalitarian movements of the far right or even call them by their real names. However understandable the denial, it remains as pitiful a response to Islamism as climate change denial is to global warming. Both sets of deniers believe that we can carry on as before living our safe, consumerist lives as if nothing has changed.

We cannot in either case, and must face the threats of our time. Reasonable men and women can disagree about how we face them, but we will not be able to see them plainly until we have cleared away the mountains of junk that block our view. The 21st century will not have a left that is worth having until we do.

Introduction

Media, Religion and Conflict

Lee Marsden and Heather Savigny

'The world has changed forever' we were told following the events of September 11, 2001. Not only did politicians make this claim, but this was uncritically repeated throughout the media. Karim suggests that the attacks on the twin towers were most likely intended to maximise media coverage with their attacks (2003) and indeed the media saturation following this event endorses this position. On one level, this may be seen a particular kind of 'media event', although alternatively this could be seen as indicative of the kind of influence the media are able to have on the shaping of world events. Whether the world has changed or not, media coverage of the world has. In contemporary society what we now witness is media coverage and a political discourse which conflates the existence and the threat of conflict with non-Judeo Christian religions; a mediated political discourse involved in the construction of particular kind of religious enemy.

There is nothing new in claiming that security concerns dominate the media agenda, nor indeed that the causes of these security concerns are often linked to particular religious communities in political and media public discourses. However, this simple statement belies a series of assumptions and particular discourses which have implications and potential effects. Where the term security is used publicly this is often taken to imply the existence of a conflict, security measures are necessary to address particular societal conflicts (at both domestic and international level). But this interrelationship, and the way it is publicly presented is neither neutral nor divorced from a particular set of ideological assumptions. Our novel concern in this collection is, through a series of case studies, to reflect upon the way in which conflict and particular religious forms have been linked and explore the way in which they are played out in the contemporary media.

Simultaneously, the way that politicians communicate with the public, and to some extent, other elite actors, is through the media. But the media are not neutral actors in this process. Academic media literature has covered the representation of conflict, and IR literature explores both conflict and religion, but to date, the literature has yet to link the three together. Responding to observed empirical tendencies, we outline the ways in which perceptions of security threats and the escalation of conflict scenarios are increasingly interlinked in the contemporary media (e.g. the conflation of terms such as Muslim and terrorist). The media provide the basis from which we can gain knowledge and understanding of our contemporary environment, yet they are not passive conduits for communication. While direct media effects are highly debated, what the media do achieve is the framing of a contemporary political discourse to which political actors respond and also seek to shape. Most of the information we gain about our politics, our elected representatives, domestic and international institutions and world leaders, comes to us via a media form, be that broadcast media, the press or new media technologies. The particular concern of this book is the political discourse surrounding religion and conflict and the ways in which these are played out in media agendas. The chapters in this volume reflect that this is not simply an Anglo-centric phenomenon, as can be seen by the case studies of the UK, US, Switzerland, Denmark and Turkey. In this introduction we set the scene for the empirical chapters to follow by outlining the political context within which these discourses take place. As we contend that the media are not neutral actors but play a role in constructing these political discourses, we briefly explore the role of the media in contemporary societies. We then examine the re-emergence of religion as an important actor in politics, international relations and the media before considering how this impacts on our understanding, interpretation and contextualisation of conflict.

Political Context

We cannot however, understand the relationship between religion and its construction and presentation as conflictual within the media, without some reference to the broader political context within which this takes place. While religion has been cited as a source of conflict (for example, as oft cited, in respect of the Troubles in Northern Ireland which often negated the broader political context), Western religion is largely unquestioningly presented as a normative 'good', or at least the failure to challenge Western Christianity, may in part be a consequence of the existence of a secular state which provides the context within which we need to understand and analyse religion, conflict and our contemporary media.

The contemporary Western state is underpinned by liberal democratic capitalism, within this is a notion of pluralism which emphasises toleration and the existence of competing views. This particular version of liberalism now dominates the Western political agenda, both nationally and internationally (with very little in the way of a serious alternative). At the end of the Cold War, Fukuyama (1992) proclaimed that we had witnessed the 'end of history', there was no serious challenger to liberal capitalism and democracy. While this thesis was contested, principally by Samuel Huntington's *Clash of Civilizations*, which presented a paradigm urging policy makers to consider the world as divided between nine competing civilizations (Huntington, 1998: 13), this dominant narrative has prevailed in western thought at least. The events of 11 September 2001, however, sent Huntington's book rather than Fukuyama's to the top of the *New York Times* bestsellers list because his division of the world into conflicting civilizations acquired greater resonance with an attack by radical Muslims against iconic symbols of the West, founded on Judeo-Christian principles.

The proclamation of the end of ideology in 1989, was not a new event (although it must be noted that at this time, this claim represented the victory of a particular ideology). The end of ideology had previously been asserted in the late 1950s – then socialism and capitalism were marginally reconciled through conservative acceptance of a welfare state and a degree of agreement from the socialists that state power could impinge on individual freedom (Lipset, 1960). Since 1989, however, the collapse of political structures and regimes which had supported the existence of these competing paradigms on a world stage, has witnessed the ascendancy and now dominance, of neoliberalism, which although has a commitment to truth and progress, takes a particular form which fits with the prevailing ideology and order. The hegemonic Western variant of neoliberalism is not a new phenomenon, and neither is it completely separate from religious ideas. As Gamble notes 'Since the fall of Rome, ideas of the West became strongly associated with Christianity ... and Christianity remains a major shaper of the western ideology, but in the modern era, liberalism became its main expression' (2009: 5). This interlinkage of ideas has been played out on the world stage as competing power struggles have left the US as the superpower, not only militarily but ideologically with its attempts to assert its strength not only through war, but in its desire to promote liberal capitalist democracy, informed by Christian values, across the world. This then is a struggle of power, and competition for power is inherently linked to notions of conflict and the existence of an 'other'. One way in which dominant ideologies reproduce, reinforce and legitimate themselves is through the denigration of an 'other'.

This discourse of 'otherness' is one which has been central to a particular mediated political discourse. During the Cold War era the 'others' were the Soviets. In the contemporary era the Western political discourse has witnessed the construction of religion as the 'other', whereby we see the conflation of particular religion as sources of conflict. Most prominently, in the West, there has been a particular focus upon Islam, and this is often played out in the media which conflates particular religion with the existence of conflict leading to headlines using terms such as 'Islamic terrorist', 'violent Islamic group', 'Islamic terror groups' and 'Islam versus the West' (see Karim, 2003). These discourses link together religion and conflict, conflate media and political agendas, and in turn form part of an overarching narrative and way in which we are encouraged to view the world as riven by religious divisions and conflicts both between and within states (see also Lewis et al., this volume).

This book begins with a reflection upon this type of discourse in the foreword by one of the UK's best known and most controversial journalists, Nick Cohen. Although Cohen's work is a critique of much of what he perceives to be the British left's collusion with right wing Muslim fundamentalism it is situated within the wider debate of how the left should respond to a political discourse dominated by the ideas of Fukuyama and Huntington. Cohen's Isaiah Berlin lecture is at once opinionated, provocative and challenging. The genie of religion has been let out of the bottle and many liberals and academics want to engage with it while others want to put it firmly back in the bottle. Cohen throws down the gauntlet to academics and western liberals to reflect on and consider the relationship between the left and the emerging force of radical religion. Cohen, as a journalist, is part of a media that not only reports on but also shapes the discourse and understanding of the role of religion and religious actors in the world today. When he castigates secular liberals for allying themselves with 'clerical fascists' and invites his audience to distinguish between tolerance and extreme relativism he enters into the debate that lies at the heart of this book. How are we to understand the relationship between media, religion and conflict?

Media

The way in which we find about our politics is through the media, as the media serve as the main channel of communication between the polity and politicians. In this volume we define the 'media' as broadcast and print news media. While we recognise there are a plethora of mechanisms for communication by politicians and the communication of political ideas (such as entertainment programming, films and other forms of popular culture, see for example Street, 1997) we are concerned here with how the news media, both broadcast and print, establish information about the actions of our political elites. The media, however, are not neutral conduits of communication. And communication between elites and their publics is mediated, 'framed' or 'filtered' via the media, who have their own agenda. For some this has meant the media have 'colonised' politics, where politics need to adopt media values, or risk being excluded from the public arena (Meyer and Hinchman, 2002) suggesting that the key political relationship here is an elite level one between the media and politics, rather than between politics (and politicians) and the citizenry.

Yet, according to liberal theories of the media, they are autonomous and independent from the state and function to hold elites to account. Here the media are also assumed to provide a public space where debate and discussion can occur, in order for citizens to make informed judgements about their leaders. Underpinned by a notion of liberal pluralism, legitimation of political systems in part relies upon the existence of informed and participatory citizens able to adjudicate between competing claims and visions of society. In order to evaluate these competing claims, citizens need information. This information is provided through media sources. This liberal view makes an assumption about the neutrality of media sources, either in the case of those which claim to be impartial (such as public service broadcasters, like the BBC) or the 'neutrality' which is assumed to occur as a consequence of the transparent bias which exists between competing viewpoints, as evidenced, for example, by the existence of a partisan press (in the UK) and news broadcasters with an overt political agenda (such as FoxNews, in the US).

Media Effects

Any discussion of the media, however, is underpinned by an assumption that the media have an effect. McQuail suggests those effects are 'significant' (1994: 327), although what is more difficult to establish is the nature of that effect. A wealth of literature has emerged which discusses how these effects may be achieved. There is widespread debate as to whether the media inject us with messages as suggested by the Frankfurt school or that we are unwitting recipients of ideological messages designed to ensure our compliance and 'manufacture [our] consent' (Herman and Chomsky, 1988). This has been countered by the argument that audiences receive their news 'selectively' (Klapper, 1960) that audiences use and interpret the media through their own experiences, rather than as implied by the Frankfurt school, being manipulated by the media. Latterly, difference has been identified in terms of whether the media simply reinforce our existing viewpoints (Blumler and McQuail, 1968). Media studies draw attention also to the differing ways in which audiences may use differing media forms and content, and 'decode' differing messages within media (Hall, 1973). While much of this debate centres around the ways in which the media can effect audiences (or not) Robinson's work on the CNN effect draws attention to the way in which the media are assumed to effect the behaviour of political elites. Here he suggests that electorally sensitive politicians formulate foreign policy as a direct response to news media coverage of events. For example, it was the emotive and critical coverage of the humanitarian crisis in Somalia which was argued to have triggered intervention from the US. This in turn raises the question – if there is no media coverage does this mean no intervention in humanitarian crisis? (Hawkins, 2002). What this does suggest however, is an enormous potential for media influence and effects, not just on audiences but on political elites. As Robinson's argument suggests, because of the likely impact on audiences, politicians must respond (if they want voters to vote for them at the next election). This suggests an incredibly powerful role for the media in shaping the political agenda.

Any casual observation of elite level political behaviour, suggests that politicians believe (and as implied by the CNN effect literature) that the media do indeed have a very significant effect upon public opinion. Both government and opposition parties are surrounded by an array of spin doctors and communications advisors who seek to manage public political communications. Nowhere is this perception of the significance of the media in affecting public attitudes and behaviour more evident than in Blair's studious courting of Murdoch prior to 1997 election in order to secure *The Sun*'s support for Labour. This might suggest that rather than being able to establish any empirical causal effect, it is the perception of effect which becomes significant in structuring political action.

The difficulty of establishing effect, or not, on audiences is long running and wide ranging, but this debate does imply the existence of some effect, however marginal. In this sense, the question becomes not *whether* the media have an effect, but, *what kind of* effect do the media have? Upon whom or what, to what

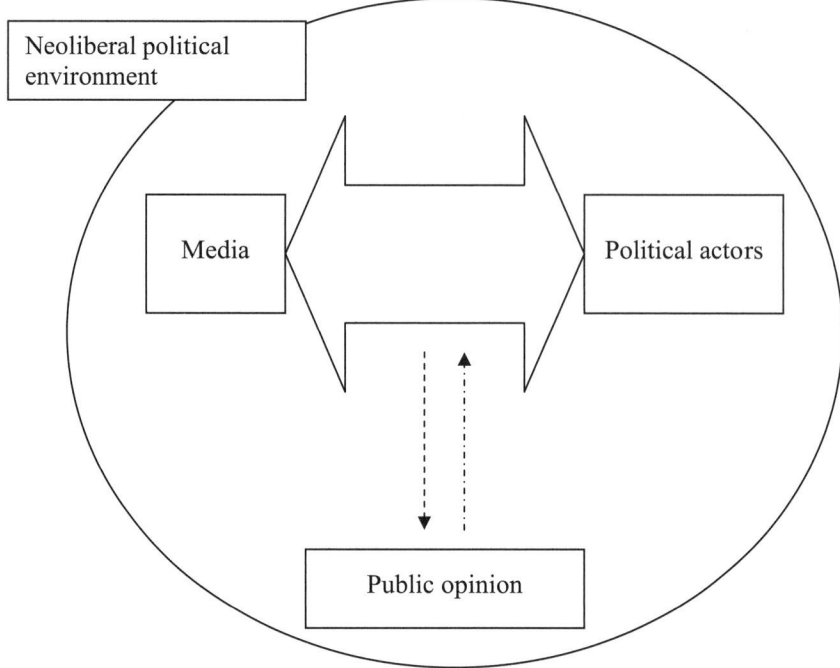

Figure I.1   Interaction between media, politics and the public

degree, and with what consequences or implications? What we argue here is that the relationship is a complex one, and that while it may be difficult to establish causal relationships of effect (from sender to receiver, or producer to consumer), what we do suggest is that the media play a role in structuring the broader context through which we establish information about our political world. In this way, discussion of media 'effects' becomes concerned not only with the way in which news is received by the public, but the way in which it impacts upon the broader political environment not only in shaping the actions and behaviour of politicians, but in playing a role in defining more broadly what is socially and politically acceptable, and what is not. The way in which our news is structured is part of, and contributes to a context within which social and political norms may be both constructed and relayed. In this sense then, we argue, we need to think beyond media effects as simply a relationship between media and their audiences, but one which includes actions and reactions of elite level actors and the interactive relationship between these within a political environment, which is characterised by Neoliberalism (depicted in Figure I.1).

For McCombs and Shaw, the type of effect the media have is influenced through they way in which media content is structured. They argue that the media play an 'agenda setting' function. That is, they may not tell us what to think, but they do define the parameters of what we think about and in this way, may have a considerable effect. The constant imagery of the events of September 11th means the media present this to us as a significant event. An example of the significance attached to this event in terms of its presentation in the media can be seen when in 2006, the *Daily Telegraph*'s headline 'War on America' accompanying an image of the explosion in the Twin Towers front page was voted the most memorable of the last 100 years. This competed with front pages such as 'Mrs Pankhurst arrested at the gates of Buckingham Palace in trying to present a petition to the King' – *Daily Mirror*, 22 May 1914; 'Dunkirk Defence Defies 300,000' – *Daily Sketch*, 3 June 1940; 'The First Footstep [on the moon] – *Evening Standard*, 21 July 1969 and *The Sun*'s infamous 'Gotcha' on 4 May 1982. The significance of this image and the importance attached to it (compared to other political events) may well be as a consequence of its historical closeness. Or it may be as a result of the way in which this image has been linked in (Western) public discourse to a transformation in world politics. But it may also be because of the frequency and saturation of this image, the 'agenda setting' function of the media in displaying this image which means it is regarded as important, rather than for example, events in Somalia or the Sudan, where imagery is less frequent, news coverage considerably less prominent.

In this way, one of the most significant ways in which the media perform an agenda setting function is through the 'framing' (Entman, 1993) of news stories. That is the way in which events are simplified, prioritised and structured as a narrative in the production of news. News 'frames' provide journalists with a structure through which to contextualise and place particular occurrences or events within a context. That is, they provide meaning to an unfolding sequence of events, or they impose meaning and interpretation upon a set of events. This framing may include the intent of the sender but this can also be subconscious (Gamson, 1989). One of the key difficulties for scholars in research is why one particular 'frame' or version of events is chosen over another, and while Norris et al. reflect upon this, they observe that conventional news frames will reflect the common norms and values within society (2003: 11). However, we are arguing that media framing of events does not simply reflect dominant norms and values in society but, given that this is an interactive process, the media also play a role in their construction.

Religion

Over the course of the 20th century, religion became increasingly less important to western social scientists and to the media as a way of understanding and interpreting the world. Academic discussion of religion became the reserved domain of sociologists, anthropologists and theologians trying to make sense of institutions and ways of life that had increasingly less resonance in western Europe and among American liberals. The dominant paradigm was modernisation and/or secularisation theory. The more developed, prosperous and educated citizens of the world became the less they would depend on primitive superstitions and the more rational they would become. Secularisation for many in the field was as certain as Fukuyama's end of history. Certainly there was much statistical evidence in support of such claims within western Europe as church attendances declined dramatically and religion became increasingly relegated to the private sphere. Western Europe and the world of liberal elites across the Atlantic did not of course reflect the rest of the world where religion retained and even increased its influence. While church attendance in the west declined, attendance at mosques, temples, and churches grew exponentially with people flocking to neo-pentecostal churches in Latin America, sub-Saharan Africa and South East Asia, and with radical Islam increasingly resonating with millions of young people throughout the Arab world and wider Muslim world. These developments went largely unreported within western media and academia other than within specialist sections and subfields.

The iconic imagery and the real life event of the attacks on the Twin Towers and the Pentagon meant that media and academy alike were compelled to consider the role of religion in politics, security and international relations. That day marks a turning point not simply in terms of ushering in an era described by George W. Bush as the war on terror but also in moving religion from the inside pages and onto the front pages of newspapers and lead items on news broadcasts. In the intervening period academics have been rushing into print to rediscover religion as the missing dimension in politics and international relations. Secularisation has been seen to be the exclusive preserve of Western Europe with the United States, principally though not exclusively through the Christian Right, and the rest of the world increasingly integrating religion and politics. George Bush's Manichaean world view dividing the world into good (like us) and evil (the other) combined Huntington's civilisation thesis of difference with Fukuyama's efficacy of liberal democratic capitalism, perceived to be a universal desire which could be exported economically, ideationally and militarily. In describing Iran, Iraq and North Korea as an 'axis of evil', initially the war on Afghanistan as 'Operation Infinite Justice', and the war against Iraq as a 'crusade' the Bush administration not only provided the media with great headlines but also helped frame politics and security within a confrontational religious paradigm which encouraged receivers of the message to draw on previous imagery of religious 'otherness' to consolidate notions of identity and perceptions of threat.

Although there were many prior religious images to draw upon the ones which resonated most were those which placed manifestations of Islam in binary opposition to the west. The re-emergence of religion as a force within international politics and security properly dates from 11 February 1979 when the Iranian people overwhelmed the forces of the western-backed Shah ushering in a Shiite Islamic theocratic republic. The subsequent fatwa against Salman Rushdie for his *Satanic Verses*, scenes of book burning and punishments meted out under Sharia law feed into this narrative of difference and otherness and prepare the way in contextualising subsequent events such as 9/11, bombings in Bali, Madrid,

London, Glasgow and Mumbai, race riots in the north of England in 2001 and in Paris 2005, protests against the Danish cartoons and demonstrations against triumphal marches by returning British troops.

Huntington (1993, 1998) saw what most fellow social scientists denied, that religion was not forever confined to the margins of political discourse but that it would determine that discourse. For Huntington the most important objective element defining civilization was 'usually religion' (Huntington, 1998: 42). Conflict with people and groups identified by their religious persuasion would dominate the political agenda into the future. Such a thesis not only sought to be empirically verifiable but also to have a predictive dimension which would assist political decision makers to make informed decisions. The thesis has possibly become self-fulfilling in constructing a security problem that can only be viewed through the confrontational religion paradigm. Just as in the Cold War when every security issue was viewed through a bipolar prism with movements for national independence automatically defined as part of a wider red threat, so the clash thesis successfully posited the Muslim 'other' as part of a wider radical-Islamic terrorist threat. Subsequent debates around religion and the media and religion and conflict inevitably seek to either endorse or disentangle this polarisation.

Conflict

The religious dimension in conflict is hardly a new subject, even a cursory examination of key sacred texts reveal page upon page of bloody conflict. The end of the Thirty Years War and subsequent Treaty of Westphalia (1648) may have presaged the start of the international system, establishing state sovereignty in an anarchic world order and the privatisation of religion but conflict continued and religion refused to be confined to the private sphere. Whereas religion was once the preserve of specialists, in the post 9/11 world religion has become the concern of all and journalists, broadcasters and academics across disciplines. Nowhere is this more significant than in the area of social, political and military conflict. As previously mentioned disdain among secular social scientists and journalists for engagement with religion is deep rooted. This sensitivity to a secular media was particularly noteworthy during Tony Blair's premiership when he steadfastly refused to 'do God' despite being a committed Christian for fear of ridicule. Yet, within two years of leaving office he had set up a faith foundation and was teaching at Yale University on faith and globalisation advocating that all world leaders need to pay attention to religion. Similarly, Madeleine Albright after serving the Clinton administration as Secretary of State has urged the same world leaders to regard religion seriously in diplomacy (Albright, 2007).

Religion has the capacity to serve as both a force for good and for ill in conflict situations. Undoubtedly, many of those involved in conflict situations have used religion to rally troops, call on a common sense of identity, justify their actions, and proclaim a moral superiority over an 'other'. Indeed the very basis of just war theory is set within a Christian tradition. However, increasingly governments, academia and the media are becoming aware of religion's capacity to work towards mediation and conflict resolution through interfaith and peace and reconciliation fora. In Northern Ireland we see this in the bridge building relationship between Clonard Monastery and Fitzroy Presbyterian Church in Belfast among others. Saint'Egidio, an international Catholic non-governmental organisation, is credited with helping to bring civil war in Mozambique to an end in 1992 and the role of Desmond Tutu and the church in South Africa working on peace and reconciliation. Jews for Justice for Palestinians are another religious organisation which have been working for an equitable peace agreement between Israelis and Palestinians. Partners in Humanity seek to highlight through the media areas of partnership and reconciliation between Muslims and the west. Such examples are useful in serving as a reminder of different perceptions of the efficacy of religion in conflict resolution.

Inevitably good news stories receive less media attention than bad news and there is an increased focus on the negative role of religion, or more specifically religious actors, in conflictual situations. Ken Booth sees the emergence of religious based identity politics as essentially problematic for governments faced with sensitive religious audiences. They back away from secularism as 'minorities claiming to be offended or unfairly treated ... risk inciting the growth of intolerance, by appeasing the minority and alienating the majority' (Booth, 2007: 449). The security implications domestically can result in street rioting, discrimination, hostility, suspicion, intolerance and even terrorism. The international implications for Booth are even graver and he posits a potential 'reason/faith security dilemma', in which mutual suspicions fuel mistrust and the perception of the 'other' as a threat, which must be acknowledged and addressed (Booth, 2007: 418).

Clearly, since the end of the Cold War and with the latest phase of globalisation we have become more and more aware of religion as a source of identity for billions of the world's inhabitants. Along side this with countries no longer obliged to bandwagon with one or other of the adversaries of the Cold War, competing actors have been able to vie for power without being constrained by the old superpowers. This has led to an increase in intrastate conflict where religion has often been a designator of otherness. Religious justifications are made for conflict between Israel and the Palestinians, interreligious rivalries in Iraq between Shia and Sunni Muslim, tribal warfare in India between Muslim and Hindu, and Buddhists and Hindus in Sri Lanka, and sections of the US Christian Right claim between Christians and Muslims in Iraq (Marsden, 2008). Terrorist acts are justified by some religious actors in the name of *jihad* or crusade with each one designated in this way feeding the discourse of threat and 'otherness'.

The intertwining of these security and religion issues is played out in the media with newspapers and broadcasters competing with each other to produce the most dramatic pictures or most sensationalist headlines in order to both inform and to sell newspapers and attract advertising revenue. The reality of course is that terrorist incidents do not occur in Europe and North America every day, that most religious minority communities across the world are not plotting the overthrow of the state, and present no security threat. The perception of threat far outweighs the reality of such a threat materialising but such perceptions encouraged by governments and perpetuated by the media dominate political debate and policy making. The highest attention should therefore be paid to how such issues are framed and constructed in the intersection of media, religion and conflict. This book is a contribution to this ongoing discourse.

Plan of the Book

In the foreword, Nick Cohen provides a compelling account of the contemporary political ideological climate which sets the scene for the essays which follow. He provides an historically informed account of the shifting nature of the 'left' in political life, and its failure to develop a coherent political programme and vision for society, beyond critique. In so doing, he reminds us of the importance of the political context within which our media are situated, our ideas and views are formulated, and crucially he reminds us of the crucial significance of political ideas in governing how society operates and functions.

These ideas are presented to us, as noted above, through the media. Here we are suggesting that the relationship between media and politics is both dialectical and interactive and takes place within a neoliberal ideological environment (see Figure 0.1). While the media may play a role in shaping the political agenda, politicians also seek to manipulate the media agenda. Both seek to shape and claim to reflect public opinion. Our primary focus in this volume is to consider this relationship and the way in which it underpins and informs the manner in which religion and conflict is now part of our daily discourse. Reflecting this interaction, the book begins with chapters which privilege the role of the media, exploring media coverage of issues around conflict and religion. The following chapters explore the other side of the relationship, the role of politicians and political actors and the ways in which they use or attempt to manipulate differing media forms to achieve their aims.

In Chapter 1, Justin Lewis, Paul Mason and Kerry Moore explore the way in which media coverage of Islam has been linked to the prevailing terror discourse, but note elites have sought to de-politicise these actions, which in turn serves to discursively delegitimise that motive. Through content analysis Lewis et al. trace the narrative which has linked Islam and terrorism and demonstrate how terrorism has come to be presented as a religious, rather than a political act. They argue that in order to be able to understand and begin to address the problems of terrorism, it needs to be understood in political terms, rather than as simply violent acts. As they highlight, not all practising Muslims are terrorists, nor indeed are all terrorists practising any form of religion. There are also a set of political conditions which need to be recognised and understood. They chart the construction of Islam as an 'other', and argue that the Orientalist assumptions which underpin contemporary media discourse have played a role in constructing the term 'Islamic terrorism' which has informed the overarching narrative.

The theme of conflict is rendered explicit again, in Chapter 2, where Ivor Gaber and Lisa Thomas provide a detailed content analysis of the BBC's coverage of the 2006 Israeli-Hezbollah war. The charge of bias is regularly levelled at the BBC which has sought to establish its reputation upon the notion of impartiality. (The Israeli government's decision to block journalistic access to Gaza in 2008/9 maybe draws attention to the importance that politicians attach to the flow of information and images (which also implies assumptions about the effects of media) – deny access to that information and it is only your view that will be heard, unchallenged). The BBC took allegations of bias in its coverage (which had come from both sides) seriously and commissioned research undertaken by Loughborough University in 2006. This concluded that coverage tended to favour the Israelis. Despite this still complaints have persisted from Israeli supporters, and so Gaber et al. build upon the Loughborough research to establish whether charges of anti-Israeli bias are sustainable. They undertake a content analysis of the war coverage examining the quantity of coverage, alongside more qualitative features such as role of the reporters and whose voices were heard and the language used to describe the war. Again, the broader concern with objectivity and bias implies a particular assumption about the potential effects of media coverage; the assumption that the media do indeed have enormous potential for influence in the shaping of public opinion and political action.

In Chapter 3, Patrik Ettinger and Linards Udris analyse conflict dynamics in considering how political communication in Switzerland has problematised Islam, resulting in a greater polarisation of Swiss society. Based on extensive research as part of a national research programme on religion in Switzerland the authors chart the electoral impact of the right-wing populist Swiss People's party. Using content analysis from media and parliamentary communication the authors demonstrate that a conflict narrative emerges that identifies Islam as a 'threatening other' and seeks to legitimate restrictive counter measures to deal with the perceived threat. The authors identify a homogenisation of Muslims from the heterogeneous minority communities of Albanians, Turks and others. Ettinger and Udris are particularly interested in which actors trigger resonance around such issues and the role the media play in this process.

Reflecting upon news media sources, in Chapter 4, Henrik Bødker evaluates the furore surrounding the publication of the 'Danish' cartoons. He compares the reaction to this by other media, to the way in which the Muslim Danish MP Khader is represented as secular. As Bødker argues, these media events cannot be separated from their mediated social (and political) processes which give rise to them. He charts the development of the cartoon affair and draws attention to the changing nature of the interaction between journalists and the political system, characterised by a re-politicised press. The newspaper in question *Jyllands-Posten*, aligned itself with the government and positioned itself as a champion of free speech, but also picked up on immigration – a significant issue on the political agenda. Here he offers not only an analysis of the way in which this became constructed as a media event, but also draws attention to the changing political and social context within Denmark which facilitated this.

Jeffrey Haynes in Chapter 5 examines the conflict and tensions which exist between Islam and democracy using the example of the rise of the Justice and Development Party in Turkey (AKP). Turkey is frequently seen as a positive example of the compatibility of Islam and democracy and yet Haynes reveals that there are significant problems still to be overcome before Turkey can be regarded as a recognisable liberal democracy. The chapter provides a historical context in which the secular constitution is underpinned by the active participation of the Turkish military, resulting in four military coups since 1960. Although there has been a transition from military rule since 1983 this process has been problematised by the electoral success of what Haynes describes as the post-Islamist AKP. Progress towards democracy has seen progress in the area of human rights as Turkey seeks EU membership. For Haynes, however, this does not go far enough and he identifies the AKP's limited understanding of democracy, whilst resisting ideas of civility and tolerance. The differences of opinion in the EU about Turkish membership divides over the issue of whether the EU is a Christian club and willing to countenance large numbers of Muslims joining or whether it is secular democratic union. Such debates dilutes Turkish enthusiasm for membership. The chapter also focuses on the role of the media, which has shifted from a secularist to an increasingly religious media, from anti-government to pro-government positions based on changes in ownership of key newspapers. Haynes reveals a Turkey in a political impasse, the separation of mosque and state upheld by a military which is at the same time the largest impediment to democracy.

Despite the separation of Church and state at a formal political level, this division is not absolute, and in Chapter 6, John Bradley draws attention to the way in which religion can act politically. His examination focuses on the political role of the Catholic Church, and most notably through its embodiment in the Vatican. Here he details the way in which the Vatican has been able to exert political influence on the world stage. While scholars of media and politics tend to focus upon television, press and new media, more unusually Bradley explores the political aspects of Vatican Radio to propagate a set of particular values. He draws attention to the role of the Church in seeking to foster cooperation between differing faith communities and uses the Lebanese civil war as an example of such intervention.

The theme of using rhetoric to mobilise support for political ends is continued by Michael Higgins, who focuses attention upon one of the most traditional forms of political communication: political speeches. Oratory and rhetoric are methods employed in election campaign to demonstrate leadership and for politicians to outline a vision for society. However, contemporary speeches also take account of modern media demands, including soundbites, repetition and a short 'snappy' message designed for a public (who are implicitly assumed to have a short attention span). In Chapter 7, Higgins provides a lexical analysis of two campaign speeches in the most recent US Presidential campaign (by Palin and Obama). Both these speeches took place in an election campaign that saw the bringing together of political actors who set their campaigns very clearly in a religious context. For Palin, this was made manifest not so much by what she said, but by who she was and who she represented; her role being to appeal directly to the Christian right. Again, the Democratic campaign was concerned to reach out to people 'of faith' and it is within this broader context that Higgins draws attention to the way in which discourses surrounding security were employed to mobilise popular and populist support. In the context of this religious setting within which the campaign was conducted, Higgins focuses on the speeches of the relatively politically inexperienced Palin and her appeals to populism and the 'fear' that populism feeds on, comparing this to Obama's rhetoric, Higgins teases out the way in which both candidates focus upon presenting the public with a perception that they will be 'safe', reinforcing the perception that the current political climate is characterised by insecurity, stemming from the existence of conflict.

In the conclusion we seek to move towards a theorisation of this complex relationship and tease out some of the underlying tensions and issues for debate. What we are seeking to do is to reflect upon the complexity of the relationship between the media, conflict and religion because it is within this nexus that individual and (international) societal well being and security is most problematic. This book serves as a contribution to the greater understanding necessary to challenge dominant narratives, often shared by politicians and the media, and put into perspective how we report, interpret and ultimately create the 'other'.

References

Albright, M. (2007), *The Mighty and The Almighty: Reflections on America, God, and World Affairs*, New York: Harper Perennial.

Blumler, J. and McQuail, D. (1968), *Television in Politics. Its Uses and Influences*, London: Faber.

Booth, K. (2007), *Theory of World Security*, Cambridge: Cambridge University Press.

Davies, N. (2008), *Flat Earth News*, London: Chatto & Windus.

Entman, R.M. (1993), 'Framing: Towards Clarification of a Fractured Paradigm', *Journal of Communication* 43(4), 51-8.

Fukuyama, F. (1992), *The End of History and the Last Man*, London: Penguin Books.

Gamble, A. (2009), 'The Western Ideology', *Government and Opposition* 44(1), 1-19.

Gamson, W.A. (1989), 'News as Framing: Comments on Graber', *American Behavioural Scientist* 33, 157-66.

Hall, S. (1973), 'Encoding and Decoding in the Television Discourse', in S. Hall, D. Hobson, A. Lowe and P. Willis (eds) *Culture, Media, Language: Working Papers in Cultural Studies 1972-79*, London: Hutchinson.

Hawkins, V. (2002), 'The Other Side of the CNN Factor: The Media and Conflict', *Journalism Studies* 3(2), pp 225-40.

Herman, E.S. and Chomsky, N. (1988) *Manufacturing Consent: The Political Economy of the Mass Media*, New York: Pantheon.

Hobson, D., Lowe, A. and Willis, P. (eds) (1980), *Culture, Media, Language: Working Papers in Cultural Studies 1972-79*, London: Hutchinson.

Huntington, S. (1998), *The Clash of Civilizations and the Remaking of World Order*, London: Touchstone Books.

Karim, K.H. (2003), *Islamic Peril: Media and Global Violence*, Montreal: Black Rose Books.

Klapper, J. (1960), *The Effects of Mass Communication*, Glencoe, Ill: Free Press.

Lipset, S.M. (1963), *Political Man*, New York: Doubleday.

Marsden, L. (2008), *For God's Sake: The Christian Right and US Foreign Policy*, London: Zed Books.

McQuail, D. (1994), *Mass Communication Theory: An Introduction. 3rd Edition*, Thousand Oaks, CA: Sage.

Meyer, T. and Hinchman L. (2002), *Media Democracy: How the Media Colonize Politics*, Cambridge: Polity Press.

McCombs, M. and Shaw, D. (1972), 'The Agenda setting Function of Mass Media', *Public Opinion Quarterly* 36(2), 176-87.

Norris, P., Montague, K. and Just, M. (2003), 'Framing terrorism' in P. Norris, K. Montague, and M. Just (eds) *Framing Terrorism. The News Media, the Government and the Public*, New York: Routledge.

Robinson, P. (1999), 'The CNN Effect: Can the News Media Drive Foreign Policy?', *Review of International Studies* 25, 301-309.

Street, J. (1997), *Politics and Popular Culture*, Cambridge: Polity Press.

Slone, M. (2000), 'Responses to Media Coverage of Terrorism', *Journal of Conflict Resolution* 44(4), 508-22.

Chapter 1

'Islamic Terrorism' and the Repression of the Political

Justin Lewis, Paul Mason and Kerry Moore

Introduction

In the ideological struggle between terrorist groups and nation states, there is often a battle between cause and effect. The aim of political violence is to further a cause, while nation states try to limit discussion to the violence itself (Hacker, 1983). So, for example, while Irish Republicans fought for political recognition during the troubles in Northern Ireland, Margaret Thatcher insisted on *de*politicising their actions as purely 'criminal'. As Hayes notes:

> The overall objective was to construct a particular perception of the conflict and, more specifically, manufacture a negative image of its political adversaries. The aim was to portray the British state as essentially benign, acting as a neutral arbiter between irreconcilable communities, and the PIRA as a malevolent criminal conspiracy and primary cause of the violence (2003: 133).

This denial of political motive is, in part, an attempt at delegitimation, allowing a form of condemnation without the need to make a more subtle point about ends and means (Stohl, 2008). Indeed, Miller suggests that 'defining opponents as terrorists represents an active pursuit of legitimacy. Such legitimating strategies are central to the operation of all governments, whether they are dictatorships or liberal democracies' (Miller, 1994: 14).

This repression of the political is facilitated by the way in which, as Dan Berkowitz puts it, such motives get 'lost in the rhetoric of journalism, a journalism that focuses on *what* was done, not *why*' (Berkowitz, 2007: 178). While this denial is understandable – to publicise the political might be seen as rewarding the violence – the recent history of Northern Ireland suggests that repressing the 'political' in political violence sustains the struggle rather than containing it. The 'troubles' are over, in part, not because Irish Republicanism was obliterated but because it was treated overtly as a political movement (Rolston, 2007).

In this chapter we will argue that the repression of the political in discussions of 21st century acts of terrorism has taken a very particular – and more elaborate – form. Traditionally, the repression of political motives rests upon a cross between a syllogism and a self-fulfilling prophecy: terrorist acts are committed by terrorists, who are bad people inclined towards political violence (Stohl, 2008). This mirrors the way in which the causes of crime – despite Tony Blair's famous pledge[1] – are often seen only as a product of the presence of criminals, with no further explanation required. Any discussion of causality thus focuses on individual pathology rather than social conditions (Barton et al., 2006; Hillyard, 2004; Sim et al., 2009).

There is no doubt that elements of this reductive framework remain in place, but in the 'soul searching' that occurred after the terrorist attacks on September 11th, 2001, it was put under considerable strain. The debates about the question 'why do they hate us?' that took place in the US in the aftermath of the attacks forced attention *onto* questions of causality, even if it unleashed an extraordinary public display of denial, in which the political – raising the inevitable spectre of the uglier aspects of US foreign policy – was seen as off-limits (Kellner, 2002; 2004). Thus Chomsky's blunt observation – 'everyone's worried about stopping terrorism. Well, there's a really easy way – stop participating in it' (2005: 54) – was so far outside mainstream discourse that it was not even deemed worthy of discussion. This left commentators and politicians offering decidedly unconvincing tales of 'evildoers' motivated by a hatred of freedom and democracy (Laquer, 2001; Nacos, 2003). Behind these explanations lay a more sinister stock of stereotypes, and it is here that we can begin to see the emergence of more explicit, well-developed narratives about Islam. The coverage of 'Islamic terrorism' has thereby taken a different turn, which *does* deal with the question of motive, but in a way in which *political* motives are more thoroughly sidelined.

While the conflict in Northern Ireland was demarcated along religious lines – Catholics against Protestants – this division was seen as sectarian rather than doctrinal. Although the history of Catholicism is full of intolerance and political violence, the culture and practice of Catholicism was considered irrelevant. More recent coverage of terrorism, we shall suggest, *does* deal with both cause and effect, but in a way that foregrounds religion – specifically Islam – as the explanation for terrorist acts. The phrase 'Islamic terrorism' – a classic example of Stuart Hall's notion of articulation, being both a coupling and expression of an ideological position (Hall, 1986) – does this in an instant, and, in so doing, represses the political motives behind recent acts of political violence.

In what follows, we shall explore how UK print media coverage of British Muslims has developed a narrative in which terrorism is represented as a religious rather than a political act. This is not to say that the religious and the political are somehow mutually exclusive. Our argument is that reducing motive purely to religion means excluding the more secular political context. The stakes are high here, since, as Richard Jackson argues, if the language used to understand or counter terrorism fails to address the 'political' in political violence, it risks exacerbating the problem, as the militarisation of the 'war on terror' appears to have done (Jackson, 2005).

---

1   'Tough on crime, tough on the causes of crime' – Blair, T. (1993).

The Northern Ireland comparison is pertinent. To assume that because terrorist acts are carried out by Islamic groups they can be reduced to the role of Islam is as facile as seeing IRA terrorism reduced to the role of Catholicism. This is not to say that such an argument cannot be made: in both cases the identity of those involved *is* defined partly by their religion, in both cases that religion can be associated with more extreme and intolerant versions, and, historically, with acts of violent repression. But to make such an argument is to ignore the vast majority of people practising both religions, as well as the political conditions that lead people to adopt terrorist tactics. Any serious analysis of the much reported terrorist acts of the last decade – in the US in 2001, Bali in 2002, Madrid in 2004 and London in 2005 – reveals that while Islam may be invoked, the motives are rooted in politics (notably a reaction to post-World War II Western foreign policy in the Middle East, especially support for repressive regimes in the region (O'Duffy, 2008; Stohl, 2008).

This is, emphatically, not a defence of terrorism – the ends do not justify the means – but an attempt to understand what drives it (and hence, the most successful ways to deal with it). Nor does it turn a blind eye to the ways in which Islam is appropriated by political movements and repressive theocratic regimes. But the use of religion in politics is hardly unique to Islam: a doctrinal form of Christianity – specifically the Dutch Reform Church, with its racial inflections on biblical stories – provided the moral underpinning for apartheid in South Africa (Adam and Giliomee, 1979). Indeed, the term first recorded use of the term 'apartheid' came from a Dutch Reform Church pamphlet in 1929 (Giliomee and Mbenga, 2007: 259).[2] More famously, many leading figures in the right of US politics clearly articulate their politics as an overt expression of their Christian beliefs. In short, religion and politics inevitably intermingle. Both are, after all, based on sets of moral presuppositions. But we cannot answer the question: 'why do some people, who happen to be Muslims, commit acts of terrorism?' (any more than we can say why Catholics joined the IRA) without understanding the political grievances that motivate them.

The Narrative of 21st Century Orientalism

Many studies of the portrayal of Muslims and Islam begin with the work of Edward Said. His book *Orientalism* (1979) explores the 'idea that Islam is medieval and dangerous, as well as hostile and threatening' and the succession of stereotypical representations that make this idea 'a kind of *a priori* touchstone to be taken account of by anyone wishing to discuss or say something about Islam' (Said, 1997: 157). As Said suggests, this is hardly a new phenomenon: the history of Western culture is replete with images of an Islamic culture that is sinister,

---

2   We are grateful to our colleague Howard Barrell for his insights on the role or the Dutch Reform Church in South Africa.

malevolent and brutal. Reading *Orientalism*, it is easy to understand how the link between religion and terrorism became 'obvious' in the case of Islam in a way it was not with Irish Catholicism. Catholicism is too deeply embedded in our cultural and political history to see it as a sinister, malevolent force, and yet Islam was already established – through a long history of cultural stereotyping and usually at a distance – as just such a force.

The notion of Islam as a threatening 'other' finds its apotheosis in the coupling with terrorism. If this articulation came to the fore following the terrorist attacks in 2001 in the US and 2005 in the UK (and, to a lesser extent, in Bali in 2002 and Madrid in 2004), it is based on a well-established set of orientalist assumptions. These were most graphically revealed in the aftermath of the Oklahoma City bombing in 1995, when media coverage – backed by 'unofficial sources from the FBI' – quickly leapt to the assumption that the terrorists came from the Middle East (Said, 1998). The fact that the bomber turned out to be a white American Christian was, in many ways, not surprising (Timothy McVeigh was, in fact, much closer to the profile of perpetrators in the recent the history of terrorist incidents in the US than someone from the Middle East), but it was not enough to dismantle orientalist assumptions *about* terrorism.

During the build up to the 2003 war with Iraq (a period that has become associated with official claims based on flimsy evidence) the Oklahoma City bombing was – despite the weight of evidence used to convict McVeigh – audaciously recast with Arabs, once again, in the leading role. As the *Evening Standard* reported:

> Senior aides to US Attorney-General John Ashcroft have been given compelling evidence that former Iraqi soldiers were directly involved in the 1995 bombing that killed 185 people. The methodically assembled dossier from Jayna Davis, a former investigative TV reporter, could destroy the official version that white supremacists Timothy McVeigh and Terry Nichols were solely responsible for what, at the time, was the worst act of terrorism on American soil. Instead, there are serious concerns that a group of Arab men with links to Iraqi intelligence, Palestinian extremists and possibly al Qaeda, used McVeigh and Nichols as front men to blow up the Alfred P Murrah Federal Building in Oklahoma City (*Evening Standard* 21 October, 2002).

Like many such theories, the 'group of Arab men' at the heart of this conspiracy are remarkably (and yet rather vaguely) well-connected. That such a convenient fabrication was taken more seriously than other conspiracy theories – this was, we were told, a 'methodically assembled dossier' sanctioned by US officialdom – demonstrates the strength of orientalist assumptions. Timothy McVeigh may, in evidentiary terms, have been the prime suspect, but cultural stereotyping made a shady 'group of Arab men' seem more in tune with conventional wisdom.

> But cultural stereotypes are, by their very nature, thin descriptions of motivation. The stereotype just *is*: requiring little explanation or understanding. In many

instances this is enough to inform a commonsense understanding – along the lines of "terrorists commit these acts because they are intrinsically bad people" (Hacker, 1983; Stohl, 2008).

However, thirty years on from the Iranian revolution, high profile events and debates surrounding Islam continue to position Muslims in opposition to 'Western' political culture and democratic liberal values. The so called, 'war on terror' has been greatly influenced by the work of neo-orientalists such as Bernard Lewis (1990) and Samuel Huntington (1993; 1996).[3] Especially since the demise of state Communism, Islam has served as a ready substitute 'enemy', in relation to which 'the West' has been defined (Agha, 2000; Mowlana, 2000; Said, 2001; Macdonald, 2003). As a constitutive 'other' of 'the West' (a 'constitutive outside' which seems to threaten the West, but is at the same time necessary to its identity), representations of Islam have been powerfully played out in the realm of cultural politics. Debates about 'free speech' surrounding the 1989 publication of Salman Rushdie's *Satanic Verses* and the Iranian *fatwa* (Poole, 2000), for example and echoed in the dominant media representation of the 2005 'cartoon protests', have clearly associated Muslims in Britain with 'extremist agendas' determined beyond the UK and signified a theocratic, radical and fundamentally anti-democratic Islam in opposition to 'western liberal values' (Poole, 2000). Suspicion of Islam *as a religion* and negative images of *Muslims as a people* are mutually reinforcing images in the news media. Colonial stereotypes which, until recently associated British Asians with passivity (Saeed, 2007) have been supplanted by images of a politicised and potentially extremist Muslim youth.

But if orientalism came to the fore following 11 September 2001, it has since, in the UK at least, moved beyond simple stereotyping. The idea of 'Islamic terrorism', we shall argue, has become a full-blown narrative.

The Rise of Islam as a Problematic Religion

The research we present here is based on our study of the coverage of British Muslims in the UK national press between 2000 and 2008.[4] This work follows other studies indicating that, in recent years, the news media tend to rely on

---

3   Huntington's famous *The Clash of Civilizations: Remaking of World Order* contends that global conflict post-Cold War will be less likely to be determined by economic and ideological rationale than by cultural and religious factors.

4   The authors are grateful to the research team at Cardiff University: Lucie Apampa, Ingeborg Braseth, Jenny Calvert, Stephanie Chlond and Lucy Dominy, Jo Hunt and Steve O'Shea. Also to Channel 4 for commissioning the research and to our colleagues at the production company Quicksilver, especially Ed Watts and Chris Balding. The study was commissioned by Channel 4 for a *Dispatches* documentary entitled, *It Shouldn't Happen to a Muslim* broadcast on 7 July 2008.

orientalist assumptions in their portrayal of British Muslims or Islam in general (Runnymede Trust, 1997; Abbas, 2000, 2001; Abbas et al., 2000; Agha, 2000; Allen and Nielsen, 2002; Poole, 2000, 2002, 2006; Richardson 2004; Allen et al., 2007; Saeed, 2007). Our study, which sought to test and explore the presence of orientalism in media coverage, involved four elements: a simple, quantitative search tracking the volume of stories about British Muslims in the national press between 2000 and 2008 (23,000 in total); a discursive analysis of a sample of 974 of these articles;[5] an analysis of the images used in newspaper articles featuring British Muslims; and a series of case studies of particular stories. In this chapter we want to feature two case studies in the context of our broader quantitative study (see Lewis, Mason and Moore, forthcoming, for a more extensive report on the quantitative data).

As Whitaker (2002) has shown, the attention paid to British Muslims increased dramatically after the terrorist attacks on New York and Washington in 2001. Our findings confirm this and suggest that, following a slight fall in 2002, this increase has been sustained across the decade 2008, peaking in 2006 but remaining high in 2007 and 2008 (see Table 1.1). Indeed, we found almost twice as many articles featuring British Muslims in the four years from 2005 to 2008 as in the four years from 2001 to 2004. What is notable about this increase is that while terrorist attacks – notably in the US in 2001 and the UK in 2005 – are clearly the catalyst for this increase (coverage increasing most markedly in those years, by 520 per cent and 59 per cent respectively), the upward momentum of coverage is, to some extent, independent of these events. In particular, we found more stories about British Muslims in 2006 than in 2005 (i.e. the year *after* the 7 July bombings in London).

Our more in-depth, discursive analysis of a sample of 974 of these articles suggests that around two-third of stories about British Muslims are prompted by one of three main types of news angle (what we have termed 'newshooks' – see Figure 1.1). First, stories about terrorism or the war on terror account for 36 per cent of stories overall. These are, typically, stories about terrorism trials, the 'war on terror' or terrorism more generally, rather than a specific terrorist event. The main 'newshook' on which these kinds of story hang might be a statement or a report about terrorism from politicians or police chiefs.

The second most commonly used news angle involves 'controversial' religious and cultural issues, accounting for 22 per cent of stories overall. Such stories included controversies surrounding Muslim dress codes, such as the debate in October 2006 sparked by Labour Minister Jack Straw, who expressed a preference that Muslim women should not wear the veil while speaking to him in his constituency surgeries, or the row after the Archbishop of Canterbury, Rowan

---

5   To gather this sample we selected roughly one in twenty articles from our corpus of 23,000, excluding those that were not relevant to the study, from the years 2000, 2002, 2004, 2006 and 2008. We chose to exclude 2001 and 2005, preferring to focus on everyday, routine coverage.

Table 1.1   Stories about British Muslims 2000-2008

Year	Frequency of Stories	Percentage increase/decrease
2000	352	
2001	2185	+520 %
2002	1673	-23 %
2003	1917	+14.5 %
2004	2399	+25 %
2005	3812	+59 %
2006	4196	+10 %
2007	3213	-23 %
2008	3466*	+7.9 %

Note: *This figure is based on an extrapolation of the five months of coverage available to us, assuming that coverage from June to December 2008 was commensurate with the coverage from January to May.

Williams, mentioned a possible role for certain forms of Sharia Law in the UK (we will explore the latter in more detail). It is worth briefly dwelling on the nature of these stories, as they become, as we shall see, increasingly significant in the media construction of Muslim identities.

If these reports are 'softer' than terrorism related stories, they often take on a harder edge, most notably in news reports where the negotiation of religious difference and cultural practices between Muslim and non-Muslim communities have suggested more antagonistic cultural encounters. So, for example, a series of reports (following the Bishop of Rochester's comments about Muslim 'no-go areas' in January 2008) appeared to unearth places where, it was reported, Islamic intolerance made Christians – or non-Muslims – feel unwelcome and excluded.

Many of these stories are played out in similar ways, following familiar discourses (Richardson, 2004) and media templates (Kitzinger, 2000). So, for example, the demonstrations against Salman Rushdie's *Satanic Verses* in 1989 provided a framework for a succession of stories in which Muslims who act in vengeful, intolerant and threatening ways become newsworthy. By the time of the 'cartoon controversy' demonstrations in early 2006 – when Muslims protested in response to the publication of an image of the prophet Mohammed in the Danish newspaper *Jyllands-Posten* – this kind of story was made both sharper and more predictable by a familiar repetition of journalistic routines. And by 2008 – after a number of stories about the veil – the image of the hostile, angry Muslim had lost its exclusively masculine inflection. This was encapsulated by a large photograph (above the headline: 'SO YOU THINK THE NO-GO AREAS DON'T EXIST MR BROWN? in the *Express* on 12 January), depicting three veiled women, two of whom looked defiantly into the camera lens. The figure on the right, hand to head obscures her eyes from the gaze of the audience; the figure in the centre, pushing a pram stares straight ahead; and the figure on the left is pictured with her hand raised in an insulting two fingered gesture. While the circumstances in which the photograph was taken are unclear,[6] its powerful signification of Muslim hostility meant it was widely used in the press, and then in anti-Muslim publications such as Melanie Phillips' book *Londonistan* (2007) and British National Party pamphlets.

As Rowan Williams was to point out in a lecture in 2008, these kinds of stories sometimes highlight *cultural* differences between British Muslims and other British people, even if the cultural and the religious are usually conflated. But we also found that a surprisingly high number of news articles dealt explicitly with the role of Islam as a doctrine. Nearly one in five news articles in our sample made direct comparisons between Islam and other religions (usually Christianity), with more than half of these comparisons (55 per cent) in the tabloid newspapers overtly suggesting that Islam was, in some way, a *uniquely problematic* religion (see also Lewis, Mason and Moore, forthcoming).

The third most common newshook – prompting 11 per cent of stories – revolved around notions of Muslim extremism. These stories provide an easy conceptual link between stories about terrorism and stories about Islamic practices and values – both can be seen as coming together under the heading of 'extremism'. The key figures in this kind of coverage are not political but religious – 'radical clerics' or 'fundamentalist preachers' – prompting an intense debate about how Britain should respond (Bawyer, 2006; Phillips, 2006). We also found variations of the couplet 'Muslim extremism' used throughout the coverage: so, for example, in our sample the five most common adjectives juxtaposed with the word 'Muslim' were, in order of frequency, 'radical', 'fanatical', 'fundamentalist', 'extremist' and 'militant' – all words striking a marked contrast to the lesser used 'moderate' (references to 'radical' Muslims outnumbering references to 'moderate' Muslims in our sample, by 17 to one).

The most conspicuous figure in 'Muslim extremism' stories is Muslim cleric, Abu Hamza,[7] who is, in our sample, the single most newsworthy British Muslim. Indeed, at times it appeared that a link with Abu Hamza is enough to elevate an otherwise mundane episode into a news event. So, for example, news about a power cut at the prison which happened to be holding Abu Hamza (Belmarsh) was headlined:

---

6   Taken by an agency photographer, the picture has a staged quality that has led to some speculation about its origins.

7   Abu Hamza was sentenced on 7 February 2006 to seven years imprisonment for eleven offences including incitement to murder and racial hatred.

HELLO, CAN I ORDER 920 HAMZABURGERS TO GO; EXCLUSIVE
TERROR JAIL FEEDS INMATES ON BIG MACS AFTER POWER CUT

The story led with the news that 'more than 900 jail inmates, including hook-
handed Muslim cleric Abu Hamza, will feast on Big Mac burgers today because
the kitchens are out of order' (*Daily Mirror*, 8 December 2007). The focal point of
the story was not prisoners 'feasting' on fast food, but the involvement of 'hook-
handed Muslim cleric Abu Hamza', a villain straight from central casting as a
caricature of orientalist stereotypes. He is invariably depicted hook-hand in shot,
a potent symbol of a more generalised polemics about the threatening presence of
Islam in Europe.

As Richard Jackson suggests (Jackson, 2005), the central role given to figures
like Abu Hamza is part of an explanatory narrative of religious 'conversion',
whereby practitioners of 'extreme' forms of Islam brainwash minds of ordinary
young men and women and turn them into suicide bombers. While this idea makes
little theological sense – suggesting, as it does, that it is a more literal, purer form
of Islam, undiluted by 'Western values', that is allied to terrorism – it also replaces
political motivations with the idea that terrorism is a playing out of religious
doctrine.

These three newshooks – the Muslim as terrorist, as a practitioner of a
'problematic' set of doctrines, and as a religious zealot – are thereby interlinked.
As the question 'why do they hate us' echoes through the decade, the answer
increasingly turns upon the nature of Islam and Islamic practices. Before we develop
this point, it is important to reference a growing body of evidence indicating that
Muslims feel themselves to be misrepresented by these portrayals, and that such
negative associations encourage discrimination and anti-Muslim feelings (Ahmed,
1992; Weller et al., 2001; Ahmad, 2006; Fekete, 2006; Aly, 2007; Armeli et al.,
2007). Despite this, we found that news stories prompted by attacks *on* Muslims

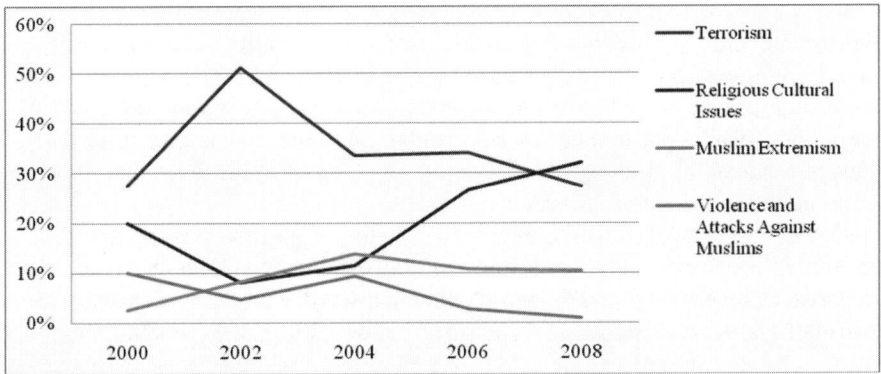

Figure 1.1   Changes in newshooks 2000-2008

Table 1.2   Most prominent discourse used in stories about British Muslims (n=974)

Discourse	Percentage of articles
Muslims linked to the threat of terrorism,	34%
Islam as dangerous, backward or irrational	26%
Islam as part of multiculturalism	17%
A 'clash of civilisations' between Islam and the West	14%
Islam as a threat to a British way of life	9%

are actually becoming less common, peaking in 2004 and declining to just one per cent of stories about British Muslims in 2008.

Figure 1.1 charts the prominence of these newshooks over time. What is striking is the *increase in stories prompted by religious/cultural issues*. Religious/cultural newshooks provided only eight per cent of stories about British Muslims in 2002 but rose steadily in significance to 32 per cent of stories about British Muslims by 2008, thereby overtaking terrorism for the first time as the most likely prompt for a story about British Muslims. It would be a mistake, however, to see these topics as discrete: as we have suggested, the news value of Islam as a religious/cultural issue is given its impetus by a narrative about terrorism, the former becoming a way of explaining the latter.

The character of the coverage becomes clearer when we look more closely at the *kinds of discourses* repeatedly used in these stories. Table 1.2 lists the five most prominent of these discourses, and while one of them suggests an attempt to accommodate Islam within British multiculturalism, the other all come straight from the lexicon of orientalism.

For while each discourse has its distinct features (distinct enough, indeed, for us to distinguish between them in collecting the data), they come together – and can be made sense of – within a broader set of orientalist narratives about Muslim identity. If articles suggesting an incompatibility between Islam and 'British cultural values' are the less menacing aspects of an orientalist discourse, they underpin and explain notions of fanaticism and the 'Islamic terrorist'. The significant rise in the number of stories about Islamic values and practices can thus be seen as the fleshing out of a series of orientalist narratives that find their culmination in the act of terrorism.

We can see *how* these discourses work together if we look at two, fairly typical examples of stories about religious/cultural differences. In both cases, these differences reverberate in a fairly rich but enclosed discursive space, replete with orientalist imagery. In both cases, the 'story' begins with an otherwise unremarkable event, one whose news value *relies entirely* upon orientalist assumptions. Both stories are based on statements – one by a prominent Muslim, one by a prominent

Christian – that might have been interpreted very differently, but whose meaning is at once closed and then amplified.

'Nazi UK' – A Plea for Tolerance Rearticulated as a Problem

The first story began innocuously enough, with an interview with Dr Muhammad Abdul Bari, head of the Muslim Council of Britain (MCB), in the *Daily Telegraph* on 10 November 2007. The MCB were widely used by the media to speak on behalf of British Muslims, and while often portrayed as a 'moderate' mainstream body (although this did not mean sympathetic coverage, as the *Sunday Express*, in an unsubtle attempt at delegitimation put it: 'the unelected so-called Muslim Council of Britain'[8] – *Sunday Express*, 18 November). In the interview, Bari addressed what he saw as a rise in anti-Muslim feeling, fuelled by negative media coverage, and was quoted saying:

> Every society has to be really careful so the situation doesn't lead us to a time when people's minds can be poisoned as they were in the 1930s. If your community is perceived in a very negative manner, and poll after poll says that we are alienated, then Muslims begin to feel very vulnerable.

But his attempt to draw attention to what he saw as Islamophobia found little echo in the dominant discursive space. On the contrary, it was swiftly reappropriated by orientalist discourses.

In the week that followed, 21 articles and letters to the editor were printed by the UK press, all basing their story on a particular interpretation of one line of the *Telegraph* interview. Admittedly, Bari's reference to 'a time when people's minds can be poisoned as they were in the 1930s' was decidedly vague. But its most likely referent was the rise of fascist politics and the subsequent scapegoating of minorities in Britain in the 1930s. Indeed, (then) London mayor Ken Livingstone had already made this more precise analogy, comparing contemporary Islamophobia to the anti-semitism of the pro-fascist sections of the British press in the 1930s. In an article in the *Morning Star* a year earlier (4 November 2006) – one featured on the British Muslim Initiative (BMI) website – he suggested that in 'the 1930s anti-semitism was fed by the drip, drip, drip of attacks on the Jewish community by newspapers like the Nazi-supporting *Daily Mail*'. The fact that Livingstone's analysis was promoted by the BMI website suggests that Bari's comments would have been informed by a similar comparison, clearly locating them in British history.

This was not, however, how the press chose to interpret Bari's statement, which, despite the absence of any words to that effect, was understood as a direct

---

8   The words –'unelected' and 'so-called' could, of course, be applied to most groups, including august British institutions.

invocation not of *British* anti-semitism but Nazi Germany. This interpretation, despite the lack of evidence to support it, was quickly solidified in a series of headlines, such as:

> COMPARISONS TO NAZI GERMANY INACCURATELY REFLECT MUSLIM STATUS IN BRITAIN (*Daily Telegraph*, 12 November).

> MUSLIM IN FEAR OF A 'NAZI UK' (*The People*, 11 November).

While this interpretation has a certain syllogistic logic ('there is Islamophobia in the UK, Islamophobia is like 1930s anti-semitism, the most extreme example of 1930s anti-semitism was in Nazi Germany, therefore the UK is like Nazi Germany), any attempt to find the reference points for Bari's comments would have suggested it was a leap of bad faith. This is not to say that this interpretation has no plausibility (the history of British anti-semitism having being subsumed by stories of Nazi Germany in popular memory) but it is easy to see how such a referential relocation might be convenient for some sections of the British press. It deflects attention from their *own* history of anti-semitism (or, more collectively, 'our' history) and comfortably onto that of a well-known enemy.

Having made this leap of faith, Bari's comments were pushed onto more controversial territory. Since the interview was printed in the *Telegraph* the day before Remembrance Sunday, it only took a little journalistic imagination to then see this as an 'insult' to the British soldiers who had fought against Nazi Germany. As a letter to *The Sun* put it: 'How dare the head of the Muslim Council compare Britain to Nazi Germany after 305,800 of our soldiers died fighting the Nazis' (*The Sun*, 15 November). It was thus a short step to:

> FURY AS MUSLIM BRANDS BRITAIN 'NAZI' (*Sunday Express*, 11 November).

From this point on, orientalist oppositions between British values and British Muslims gave the story momentum, and the ensuing 'outrage' at such an 'insult' was such that, within a few days, Bari's point about anti-Muslim attitudes was entirely lost in a sea of invective. The *Sunday Express*, a week later, went so far as to ask: 'SURELY the comments made by Dr Bari, the head of the Muslim Council of Britain, must constitute some sort of offence for which he could be arrested?' (*Sunday Express*, 18 November).

The 'backlash' against Bari's comment (or, more accurately, a bad faith interpretation of his comment) drew upon various orientalist discourses. Jon Gaunt in *The Sun*, for example, quickly moved from discrediting the comparison to what it saw as incompatibilities between British and Muslim culture:

> Come to think of it, I don't think there were stupid Jewish girls using public money to bring court cases about their rights to dress like Daleks in the

classroom, or not show their hair if they wanted to be hairdressers (*The Sun*, 13 November).

Meanwhile *The Express*, with a rather bizarre metaphor, invoked the 'clash of civilisations':

> The loudmouth leaders of British Islam are the equivalent of the self-centered stiletto wearers who have damaged St Paul's. They are abrasive rather than soothing presences, leaving dents and craters in our civilization (*The Express*, 13 November).

The next step in this orientalist narrative was to take it to its inevitable conclusion, overtly discrediting Bari's comments by linking the people he spoke for with terrorism:

> It was British Muslims who committed mass murder on July 7, 2005. It is Muslim extremists whom MI5 is keeping under surveillance by the thousand because of the danger they pose to the rest of us (*The Express*, 13 November 2007).

> I don't recall Jews carrying out suicide bombings or calling for their own form of law in Germany (*The Sun*, 13 November 2007).

> In Nazi Germany, Dr Bari may recall, it was Jewish children who were rounded up to be killed. Not the Jewish children who were trained to do the killing (*Daily Mail*, 14 November).

If it seems strange that an appeal against Islamophobia should end up as yet another story linking Muslims with terrorism, it is indicative of the centrality of orientalism's discursive repertoire – and the peripheral status of attempts to critique it. Perhaps the ultimate insult, from Dr Bari's perspective, was *The Sun* headline:

> ONLY PEOPLE STOKING ANTI-MUSLIM FEELING ARE IDIOTS LIKE BARI (*The Sun*, 13 November).

The irony here is so glaring that it seems almost heavy-handed to point it out. What was, after all, a plea for more even-handed media coverage became a catalyst for recasting British Muslims as a problem, thereby unleashing just the kind of treatment that Dr Bari was trying to draw attention to.

Sharia Law and Disorder

On 7 February 2008, Dr Rowan Williams, the Archbishop of Canterbury delivered a lecture at the Royal Courts of Justice, London. The lecture was a careful, scholarly discussion of the relationship between religion and the law, and the difficult questions that arise when minority communities find that their religious convictions are neither recognised nor protected by a secular state. Williams begins the lecture by acknowledging that:

> the idea of *Sharia* calls up all the darkest images of Islam ... It has reached the extent that many Muslim intellectuals do not dare even to refer to the concept for fear of frightening people or arousing suspicion of all their work by the mere mention of the word.

He then proceeds to reject the more reactionary and repressive aspects of Sharia Law, which he describes as 'wholly unacceptable', stressing the need to make 'sure that we do not collude with unexamined systems that have oppressive effects or allow shared public liberties to be decisively taken away by a supplementary jurisdiction'.

The bulk of the lecture is then devoted to ways in which the secular state can pay 'a higher level of attention to religious identity and communal rights in the practice of the law' to create what he call a form of 'plural jurisdiction'. This is an issue, he argues, that 'is relevant not only to Islamic law but also to areas of Orthodox Jewish practice'. Williams is at pains, throughout, to *enhance* the rights of citizenship, and to rule out legal or quasi-legal practices that limit those rights. The following passage is fairly typical:

> If any kind of plural jurisdiction is recognised, it would presumably have to be under the rubric that no 'supplementary' jurisdiction could have the power to deny access to the rights granted to other citizens or to punish its members for claiming those rights. This is in effect to mirror what a minority might themselves be requesting – that the situation should not arise where membership of one group restricted the freedom to live also as a member of an overlapping group, that (in this case) citizenship in a secular society should not necessitate the abandoning of religious discipline, any more than religious discipline should deprive one of access to liberties secured by the law of the land, to the common benefits of secular citizenship.

By this measure, *all* of the more repressive aspects associated with Sharia Law are thereby ruled out. He thus rejects:

> any model that ends up 'franchising' a non-state jurisdiction so as to reinforce its most problematic features and further disadvantage its weakest members.

So, for example, he is dismissive of a number of such practices – such as forced marriage – as having 'more to do with custom and culture rather than directly binding enactments by religious authority'. As a consequence:

> The secular lawyer needs to know where the potential conflict is real, legally and religiously serious, and where it is grounded in either nuisance or ignorance. There can be no blank cheques given to unexamined scruples.

In essence, the speech is well within the bounds of a fairly mainstream multiculturalism, arguing for a legal structure that is sensitive to serious religious convictions, but, crucially, *without* compromising the freedoms enshrined in a liberal democratic state.

Despite the scholarly language and tone of Williams' address, in the week that followed (between 7 February and 14 February) it succeeded in generating over 250 articles in the UK press. Like the coverage of Dr Bari's statements about Islamophobia, the news value of the speech was based entirely on a highly skewed interpretation that ignored its general gist and disregarded most of its content. Williams' suggestion that 'the idea of *Sharia* calls up all the darkest images of Islam' turned out to be prophetic with more fervour than he could have imagined, driving an orientalist sledgehammer through all his careful reasoning.

The overpowering strength of orientalism operates, in this sense, rather like a crude alarm system – triggered by certain words and incapable of appreciating subtlety or context. Thus, once alerted by the phrase 'Sharia Law', all hell broke loose in a fearful clamour of recrimination. In a particularly zealous effort to cut to the chase, the only word from the speech to be widely quoted was the final word in the following passage:

> If what we want socially is a pattern of relations in which a plurality of diverse and overlapping affiliations work for a common good, and in which groups of serious and profound conviction are not systematically faced with the stark alternatives of cultural loyalty or state loyalty, it seems unavoidable.

Quite *what* is 'unavoidable' is unclear from this passage alone, but the context makes it clear that he is *not* referring to Sharia Law, but to a kind of 'interactive pluralism' a careful balancing act in which 'the common benefits of secular citizenship' do 'not necessitate the abandoning of religious discipline' as long as both can be seen to 'work for a common good'. Many newspapers leapt, instead, to the assertion that:

ARCHBISHOP SAYS UK MUST ACCEPT ISLAMIC SHARIA LAW (*The Sun*, 8 February).

ARCHBISHOP OF CANTERBURY WARNS SHARIA LAW IS INEVITABLE
(*The Independent*, 8 February).

The Express went so far as to put the Archbishop's seeming insistence that
'MUSLIM LAWS MUST COME TO BRITAIN' (*The Express*, 8 February) in
speech marks (although the phrase was very much theirs, not the Archbishop's),
while the *Daily Mail* stated that the speech 'raised the prospect of Islamic courts
with full legal power' (*Daily Mail*, 8 February). It was as if a line had been drawn
through six thousand word of text leaving just four. A reasonable summary might
thus have been: 'blah blah…Sharia Law…blah blah blah… seems unavoidable'.
In his speech, Williams dismisses what he calls 'committed Islamic primitivists',
in the press coverage, he appears to bow down before them.

Not all the coverage of the Archbishop's speech was negative or hyperbolic,
and some reporters do appear to have either read the speech or a more faithful
synopsis of it. Broadsheet newspapers, in particular, were more likely to offer
a less histrionic assessment: the *Daily Telegraph* suggesting Williams' views
were 'not that outlandish' (*Daily Telegraph*, 8 February) and *The Guardian*
(8 February) noting that the Archbishop was attempting to encourage social
cohesion in Britain (the newspaper also pointed readers to the full text of the
speech on its website).

Most press reports, however, regularly and consistently focused upon the
violence, barbarism and irrationality in precisely the forms of Sharia Law that
Williams dismisses as unacceptable. In over half the stories published – 52 per
cent – we found that Williams was, through the speech, associated with the most
violent, brutal aspects of 'Islamic Law'. Only six per cent of reports, by contrast,
expressed support for Williams, and only five per cent discussed (as William
did) any of the complexities and nuances of Sharia Law.

When we looked at the specific associations used to signify Sharia Law in the
coverage of the speech, we found a rich seam of a very physical, orientalist excess.
The three most frequent examples used of the practice of Sharia Law were stoning
(26 per cent), limbs/limb removal (16 per cent) and beheading/execution (11 per
cent). Indeed, we found that only 4 per cent of adjectives used in association with
Sharia Law did *not* carry these negative connotations. The emphasis on brutality
was underpinned visually in these news reports by pictures of stoning, flogging
and beheading in Iran and Afghanistan. It was this kind of brutality, some reports
declared, that made the Archbishop's speech 'a dangerous moment in our national
story' (*The Express*, 8 February). Both *The Sun* and *The Express* began phone-ins
on the topic: 'Should the Archbishop be sacked for his comments on Sharia law?'
asked *The Sun*, while *The Express* noted that 'Thousands of *Daily Express* readers
posted comments on our website www.express.co.uk and 95 per cent of callers to
our phone vote line said Sharia law should be banned'.

Like Dr Bari, Williams found himself the butt of a wave of criticism as an
apologist for Muslim extremism. His status as head of the Church of England,
however, required a very different set of stereotypes – as a bearded, woolly-minded

liberal with a leftist past. The *Daily Mail* described Williams as A BATTY OLD BOOBY, BUT DANGEROUS WITH IT (*Daily Mail*, 8 February), *The Star* called him 'a prize chump' (*The Star*, 8 February) and *The Sun* summed up the speech with the front page headline WHAT A BURKHA (*The Sun*, 8 February). In our analysis of adjectives used to describe Williams, he was referred to as 'liberal' and 'dangerous' in equal measure (12 per cent of adjectives used in both cases). In only 6 per cent of all the adjectives used was Williams referred to as 'moderate', while the power of the visual stereotype was such nearly the most common adjective used to describe his was 'bearded' (24 per cent of adjectives used).[9]

If there was a common theme that ran through most of the coverage, it was to assert that:

> Nobody in his right mind...would want to see in this country a kind of inhumanity that sometimes appears to be associated with the practice of the law in some Islamic states, the extreme punishments, the attitudes to women as well.

And yet, as hard as it would be for many newspaper readers to imagine, this passage comes not from an outraged editorial, but from Rowan Williams' speech.

As we saw in the coverage of Dr Bari's statements about Islamophobia, the contemporary orientalist narrative quickly moves from the portrayal of a threatening Islam to the risk of full-blown terrorism. Many reports, especially in the tabloid press, explicitly presented the prospect of Sharia Law as a 'victory for terrorists', linking Sharia Law with the Taliban and al Qaeda. *The Sun,* for example, suggested that Williams' speech, 'handed al Qaeda a victory last night' (*The Sun*, 8 February). To anyone reading Rowan Williams' speech, the idea that it could be read as 'a victory for al Qaeda' is not so much unfair as bizarre. To convert a discourse on a sensitive, cautious form of multiculturalism into a threat to national security requires – to repeat an appropriate metaphor – a leap of faith. The fact that such a thing is not only possible but so plausibly insistent demonstrates, once again, the dominance of the orientalist narrative in contemporary culture.

Conclusion

Our analysis of the coverage of British Muslims in the UK national press could simply be read – with some honourable exceptions – as a rather depressing commentary on the robust influence of orientalism in contemporary culture. For all the diatribes about a country shackled by the forces of multiculturalism and

---

9   References to his beard might be seen to invoke a kind of symbolic stereotypical connection between the woolly-minded liberal and that other bearded figure, the Islamic extremist.

'political correctness', there are few signs of our national press – (especially, though by no means exclusively, the more popular tabloids) – exhibiting any restraint in a remorseless display of stereotyping. The backlash against tolerance, sensitivity or multiculturalism, meanwhile, appears to be in rude health.

In terms of the crude currency of positives and negatives, the history of orientalism suggests that this is nothing new – although the sheer *scale* of coverage indicates that the presence of orientalist discourses is more voluminous than they have ever been (with the bulk of the coverage taking place not immediately after the terrorist attacks in 2001 but in the last four years). What we have tried to show, however, is that the *character* of the coverage has shifted. If the idea of the 'Islamic terrorist' emerged from a shady corner of our cultural heritage as a distant and inexplicably sinister figure, they have increasingly been understood as the product of a well-defined set of religious practices.

The consequence of this move is that the set of political questions that underpin the more well-known recent acts of terrorism are not merely suppressed but denied. Moreover, the implication of seeing terrorism as a religious act is as old-fashioned – and brutal – as Islam is sometimes portrayed as being. For if the problem is religion, the solution must be some form of crusade – a mass conversion to more benign systems of belief. It is not surprising, in this context, that we have seen a 'war on terror' carried out against Islamic States (even if one of them was, ironically, of a more secular kind, with its own set of rationales – see Lewis, 2005).

Once Islam stands in for the political, we have the image of a peaceful, western, liberal democratic politics posited against a potentially violent, unyielding, religion that cannot and will not engage. Islam is therefore at once 'political' (and as such, perhaps illegitimate as a religion – Christianity being benign and non-political by contrast) and *outside of the political* – a force that has nothing to do with 'our' politics, and which we cannot allow to penetrate and potentially subvert our genuinely political space of rational liberal pluralism.

We thus have a slippage between the representation of the idea of 'political Islam' and that of 'mainstream Islamic cultural practices' in our case studies. Representing cultural practices which are 'incompatible with mainstream British values' has a rhetorical power because it reproduces the notion of a clash of civilisations, serving as an index to this political antagonism. Islam thereby serves as a 'constitutive outside' – although it threatens 'our identity', it is also necessary to it – the means through which 'our identity' is also rendered meaningful. It is in this sense that it becomes persuasive to see Islam as having become a 'replacement enemy' to the West in the post-Cold War period.

What remains to be unravelled are the complex articulations between politics and religion – articulations that applied as much to apartheid South Africa as to Islamic theocracies. And in the case of 'Islamic terrorism', this requires a recognition of the political grievances and conditions – some real, some imagined – that inform it. This is, of course, difficult territory in a country like Britain, whose history is closely bound up with inglorious attempts to control the Middle East and who continue to play a key role in the militarisation of the region. The British state has, in other words, played its part in creating a set of political conditions that give terrorism its meaning. These are, for many, uncomfortable ideas, even if they do nothing to justify terrorist acts – which have their own crude, brutal and indiscriminate notions of blame. But they do create the possibility of pushing the politics in political violence *away* from violence and onto a political terrain.

References

Abbas, T. (2000), 'Images of Islam', *Index on Censorship* 29(5): 64-8.

Abbas, T. (2001), 'Media Capital and the Representation of South Asian Muslims in the British Press: An Ideological Analysis', *Journal of Muslim Minority Affairs* 21(2).

Abbas, T. (ed.) (2005), *Muslim Britain: Communities under Pressure*, London: Zed Books.

Abbas, T., Hall, A. and Shaheen, N. (2000), *The Demonisation of Muslims in the British Press: Islamophobes, Fundamentalists and Political Cartoons*, London:Runnymede Trust.

Adam, H. and Giliomee, H. (1979), *The Rise and Crisis of Afrikaner Power*, Cape Town: David Philip.

Agha, O. (2000), 'Islamic Fundamentalism and Its Image in the Western Media: Alternative Views', in K. Hafez (ed.), *Islam and the West in the Mass Media: Fragmented Images in a Globalizing World*, Cresskill, NJ: Hampton Press.

Ahmad, F. (2006), 'British Muslim perceptions and opinions on news coverage of September 11', *Journal of Ethnic and Migration Studies* 32(6): 961-82.

Ahmed, A.F. (1992), *Post Modernism and Islam: Predicament and Promise*, New York: Routledge.

Allen, C. and Aziz, A. et al. (2007), *The Search for Common Ground. Muslims, Non-Muslims and the UK Media: A Report Commissioned by the Mayor of London*, London: Greater London Authority.

Allen, C. and Nielsen, J. (2002), *Summary Report on Islamophobia in the EU After 11 September 2001*, Vienna: European Monitoring Centre on Racism and Xenophobia.

Aly, A. (2007), 'Australian Muslim responses to the discourse on terrorism in the Australian popular media', *Australian Journal of Social Issues* 42(1): 27-40.

Armeli, S.R., Marandi, S.M., Ahmed, S., Seyfeddin, K. and Merali, A. (2007), *The British Media and Muslim Representation: The Ideology of Demonisation*, Islamic Human Rights Commission.

Barton, A., Corteen, K., Scott, D. and White, D. (eds) (2006), *Expanding the Criminological Imagination: Critical Readings in Criminology*, Cullompton: Willan Publishing.

Bawyer, B. (2006), *While Europe Slept: How Radical Islam Is Destroying the West from Within*, New York: Broadway Books.

Chomsky, N. (2003), *Power and Terror: Post-9/11 Talks and Interviews*, New York: Seven Stories Press.

Fekete, L. (2006), *Integration, Islamophobia and Civil Rights in Europe*, London: Institute of Race Relations.

Giliomee, H. and Mbenga, B. (2007), *New History of South Africa*, Cape Town: Tafelberg.

Gross, B., Moore, K. and Threadgold, T. (2007), *Broadcast News Coverage of Asylum April to October 2006: Caught Between Human Rights and Public Safety*, Cardiff: Cardiff School of Journalism, Media and Cultural Studies.

Grossberg, L. and Hall, S. (1986), 'On Postmodernism and Articulation: An Interview with Stuart Hall', *Journal of Communication Inquiry*, 10(2): 45-60.

Hacker, F.J. (1983), 'Dialectic interrelationships of personal and political factors in terrorism', in L.Z. Freedman and Y. Alexander (eds) *Perspectives on Terrorism*, pp. 19-31. Wilmington, DE: Scholarly Resources, Inc.

Hayes. M. (2003), 'Political Violence, Irish Republicanism and the British Media: Semantics, Symbiosis and the State', in P. Mason (ed.) *Criminal Visions: Media Representations of Crime and Justice*, Cullompton: Willan Publishing.

Hillyard, P., Pantazis, C., Tombs, S. and Gordon, D. (eds) (2004), *Beyond Criminology: Taking Harm Seriously*, London: Pluto.

Huntington, S. (1993), 'The Clash of Civilizations?', *Foreign Affairs*, Summer Issue.

Huntington, S. (1996), *The Clash of Civilizations and Remaking of World Order*, New York: Simon & Schuster.

Jackson, R. (2005), *Writing the War on Terrorism: Language, Politics and Counter-Terrorism*, Manchester: Manchester University Press.

Kellner, D. (2002), 'September 11, Terrorism and Blowback', *Cultural Studies, Critical Methodologies*, 2(1): 27-39.

Kellner, D. (2004), '9/11, Spectacles of Terror, and Media Manipulation', *Critical Discourse Studies*, 1(1): 41-64.

Kitzinger, J. (2000), 'Media Templates: Patterns of Association and the (Re)construction of Meaning over Time', *Media, Culture and Society*, 22(1): 61-84.

Laqueur, W. (2001), *The New Terrorism*, London: Phoenix Press.

Lewis, B. (1990), 'The Roots of Muslim Rage', *The Atlantic*, September Issue.

Lewis, J. (2005), 'The Power of Myths: The War On Terror And Military Might', in H. Nossek, P. Sonwalker and A. Sreberny (eds) *Media and Political Violence*, Cresskill, NJ: Hampton Press.

Macdonald, M. (2003), *Exploring Media Discourse*, London: Hodder Arnold.

Miller, D. (1994), *Don't Mention the War: Northern Ireland, Propaganda and the Media*, London: Pluto.

Mowlana, H. (2000), 'The Renewal of the Global Media Debate: Implications for the Relationship between the West and the Islamic World', in K. Hafez (ed.) *Islam and the West in the Mass Media: Fragmented Images in a Globalizing World*, Cresskill, NJ: Hampton Press.

Nacos, B. (2003), 'Terrorism as Breaking News: Attack on America', *Political Science Quarterly* Spring (118): 23-53.

O'Duffy, B. (2008), 'Radical Atmosphere: Explaining Jihadist Radicalization in the UK', *Political Science and Politics* 41(1): 37-42.

Phillips, D. (2006), 'Parallel Lives? Challenging Discourses of British Muslim Self-Segregation', *Environment and Planning D: Society and Space* 24(1): 25-40.

Phillips, M. (2007), *Londonistan*, London: Gibson Square.

Poole, E. (2000), 'Framing Islam: An Analysis of Newspaper Coverage of Islam in the British Press', in K. Hafez (ed.) *Islam and the West in the Mass Media: Fragmented Images in a Globalizing World*, Cresskill, NJ: Hampton Press.

Poole, E. (2002), *Reporting Islam: Media Representations of British Muslims*, London: I.B.Tauris.

Poole, E. (2006), 'The Effects of September 11 and the War in Iraq on British Newspaper Coverage', in E. Poole and J.E. Richardson (eds), *Muslims and the News Media*, London and New York: I.B.Tauris.

Richardson, J.E. (2004), *(Mis)Representing Islam: The Racism and Rhetoric of British Broadsheet Newspapers*, Amsterdam: John Benjamins.

Rolston, B. (2007), 'Demobilization and Reintegration of Ex-Combatants: the Irish Case in International Perspective', *Social and Legal Studies* 16(2): 259-80.

Runnymede Trust (1997), *Islamophobia: A Challenge for Us All*, London: Runnymede Trust.

Saeed, A. (2007), 'Media, Racism and Islamophobia: The Representation of Islam and Muslims in the Media', *Sociology Compass* 1/2: 443-62.

Said, E. (1979), *Orientalism*, New York: Vintage.

Said, E. (1997), *Covering Islam: How the Media and the Experts Determine How We See the Rest of the World*, London: Vintage.

Said, E. (2001), 'The Clash of Ignorance', *The Nation*, 22 October.

Sim, J. Tombs, S. and Whyte, D. (eds) (2009), *State, Power, Crime: Critical Readings in Criminology*, London: Sage.

Stohl, M. (2008), 'Old Myth, New Fantasies and the Enduring Realities of Terrorism', *Critical Studies on Terrorism* 1(1): 5-16.

Weller, P., Feldman, A. and Purdam, K. (2001), *Religious Discrimination in England and Wales*, Home Office Research Study 220: Research, Development and Statistics Directorate, London: Home Office.

Whitaker, B. (2002), 'Islam and the British Press After September 11', *Islam and the Media*, London: Central London Mosque.

Chapter 2

Is the BBC Biased? The Corporation and the Coverage of the 2006 Israeli–Hezbollah War

Ivor Gaber and Lisa Thomas

Introduction

Since the establishment of the state of Israel in 1948, media coverage of the Arab–Israeli conflict has been a matter of extreme interest and sensitivity, not just for those directly or indirectly involved, but also to international broadcasters and media academics. Never was this more the case than during the 2008/9 Israeli invasion of Gaza when the Israeli Government's decision to block international journalists from entering the Gaza war zone provoked widespread concern and condemnation. With the world's major news organisations forced to position their television correspondents and crews on a hillside in Israel several miles from the battlefront, and restricted to using pictures shot by local, and sometimes unknown, camera crews inside Gaza, frustration and anger ran high. Nic Robertson, CNN's senior international correspondent, was quoted on the CNN website as saying:

> It's really frustrating, you can't be there, see there and feel it ... and you see these pictures from the hospital, but what's happening behind the hospital? What's Hamas doing? ... The questions we would ask that go beyond the immediacy of the civilian casualties that you want to know about, but the other stuff that really informs you (CNN, 2009).

The United Nations Relief and Works Agency for Palestine Refugees in Gaza, said the absence of journalists prevented the truth from getting out, and the Israeli Foreign Press Association criticised the restrictions, saying: 'The unprecedented denial of access to Gaza for the world's media amounts to a severe violation of press freedom and puts the state of Israel in the company of a handful of regimes around the world which regularly keep journalists from doing their jobs' (ibid). It's worth noting that despite the ban the Israelis were only partially successful in their attempts to restrict the flow of television coverage from Gaza to the outside world. This was because coverage from Palestinian journalists and camera crews based inside Gaza (notably those working for Al-Jazeera), continued to flow via satellite and the internet from Gaza to the outside world.

The official Israeli position was that they had introduced the ban because it was too dangerous to allow foreign correspondents to enter Gaza and that to offer them protection would divert Israeli forces from their main mission of quelling Hamas. However, on occasion, the Israeli guard did drop and they revealed the real rationale behind their decision. Daniel Seaman, the Director of the Israeli Government Press Office, commenting on the international television coverage of the 2006 Israel-Hezbollah war, was quoted by CNN as saying: 'There was too much exposure, it had an effect on our ability to achieve strategic goals, so that's one of the lessons we learned from the war in Lebanon' (Ibid).

As this chapter reveals, the Israelis were probably right to have concerns, not about the veracity of the international media's coverage of the Lebanese war, but about the impression that it would have given to the viewers and governments that saw it. For the coverage, as far as the two main UK terrestrial channels (BBC1 and ITV) were concerned, was dominated by images that the Israelis would have regarded as 'unhelpful'. There were pictures of Israeli troops and aircraft entering southern Lebanon and attacking what they believed to be Hezbollah fighters based, as they were, among the civilian population. There was a great deal of coverage of the damage done by Israeli armed forces to villages and villagers in Southern Lebanon – much of this coverage was highly emotional with a particular emphasis on the sufferings of children and elderly people. There was no coverage of Hezbollah fighters or weaponry that would have provided some sort of context, if not justification, for the Israeli attacks. But by contrast there was coverage of Israeli civilians inside relatively sophisticated bunkers, safe from enemy action. There were interviews with Israeli civilians, including those who were opposed to the war, but no coverage of any Lebanese who might have been critical of Hezbollah – thus it was hardly surprising that the pro-Israeli lobbyists, such as BBCWatch, claimed BBC coverage was biased against Israel.

A corpus of academic literature exists that attempts to demonstrate media bias for or against one side or the other in the Israel/Palestine conflict. For example, in their study of the *New York Times* reporting of the first intifada, Zelizer et al. (2002) found a clear bias towards Israel in the newspaper's coverage; but Kalb and Saivetz (2007), in their study on global media coverage of the 2006 Israeli–Hezbollah war, found that Israel was 'victimised by its own openness', whilst Hezbollah, as 'a closed sect', managed to 'retain almost total control of the daily message of journalism and propaganda' (Kalb and Saivetz: 43). Conversely, Philo and Berry's (2004) extensive content studies of BBC and ITV news coverage of the Al-Aqsa Palestinian Intifada found that Israeli voices were heard twice as many times as Palestinian, and that there were major disparities in the language used to discuss both sides. Overall, they concluded that the two main terrestrial channels demonstrated significant bias toward Israel.

The BBC, in particular, has been subjected to intense scrutiny in its coverage of the conflict, with both sides systematically accusing the Corporation of being more favourable to the other. Paul Adams, a former BBC Middle East correspondent, has noted 'for every Jew who thinks the BBC is violently anti-Semitic, there is an

Arab who fervently believes that we are pro-Israel' (BBC, 2000). The pro-Israel campaign group, BBC Watch, claims that in its analyses it has found a 'disquieting policy of discrimination in the way that Israel is treated by the BBC' (BBC Watch, 2004). Pro-Arab media campaigners, such as Arab Media Watch, argue that the BBC is innately biased towards Israel; and the broad thrust of most recent academic research suggests that the claims of pro-Israeli bias are more substantiated than those arguing that there is an anti-Israel bias in mainstream media coverage (see, for example, Philo and Berry, 2004; Loughborough University, 2006).

Unsurprisingly, the BBC regularly receives a large volume of complaints from both sides, including a significant number from outside the UK. For example, between 3 October and 25 November 2005, the BBC received around 700 emails and 80 letters, most of which were from pro-Israel supporters who 'thought the BBC was anti-Israel' (Independent Panel, 2006: 24). The BBC notes that there is evidence of 'pressure group activity', revealed through 'the number of identical letters or parts of letters ... often with the same complaint, on the same date and/or from the same state' (2006: 23).

In 2005, the BBC Board of Governors responded to these persistent complaints by appointing an independent panel to evaluate the claims. The panel commissioned both quantitative and qualitative research, including content analyses and audience studies.[1] Researchers at Loughborough University conducted a content analysis on BBC news and current affairs programmes over a six-month period. They concluded that the majority of news reports failed to provide sufficient historical context, or to mention the ongoing land annexations taking place in East Jerusalem and the West Bank. There were also 'significant differences across BBC news programmes and services in the allocation of talk time and appearances of actors' and overall the coverage tended to be 'in favour of Israelis' (Loughborough University, 2006: 87). Furthermore, there was an imbalance in the reportage of fatalities, with Israeli deaths generating more coverage than Palestinian ones. However, despite the evidence that there is an imbalance in representation, the audience reception study carried out by Opinion Leader Research found that the majority of participants interviewed perceived the BBC as 'impartial in its coverage of the conflict' (2006: 45).

The Independent Panel's report concluded that, whilst 'there was little to suggest deliberate or systematic bias', overall, the 'BBC output does not consistently give a full and fair account of the conflict. In some ways the picture is incomplete and, in that sense, misleading' (2006: 3-4). The Panel identified several areas where the BBC could improve on its editorial practices. Key recommendations included

---

1   The BBC commissioned two analytical research projects: a content analysis carried out by Loughborough University (2006), and an audience study conducted by Opinion Leader Research (2006). Several organisations were also invited to submit reports, including the Anglo-Israel Association, Arab Media Watch, BICOM (British Israel Communications and Research Centre) and CAABU (Council for Arab-British Understanding). The Independent Panel's Report was published in April 2006.

more historical, and other, background and context, greater attempts to avoid being 'picture-driven' and the appointment of a Middle East editor to provide an editorial 'Guiding Hand' (2006: 4).

In the light of these findings and recommendations, and the fact that most of the bias accusations against the BBC's Middle East coverage continue to come from supporters of Israel, this research sought to investigate whether their claims of anti-Israel bias during the BBC's coverage of the 2006 Israeli–Hezbollah war could be sustained. In addition, ITV News coverage (produced by ITN) was examined both because of intrinsic interest and as a control group. The research was essentially a content study of what was actually transmitted; it did not seek to interpret what the broadcasters *might* have been seeking to broadcast, merely what they actually *did* broadcast.

Methodology

All weekday reports relating to the Israeli–Hezbollah war that were broadcast between 12 July and 14 August 2006 on the 'flagship' bulletins of the two major terrestrial broadcasters, namely *BBC News* at 10.00pm and *ITV News* at 10.30pm were analysed in detail. During this period, the BBC devoted 269 minutes (110 items) and ITV 246 minutes (118 items) to the conflict. For reasons of strict comparability, the weekend bulletins were not included in this study due to the variations in their length and timing. Consequently, and it is important to note, this analysis does not cover the controversial bombing of Qana in southern Lebanon by the Israelis, which took place on 30 July and which led to the deaths of more than 50 people, of whom half were reported to be children, and provoked worldwide condemnation.

Quantitative and qualitative content analyses were employed to discern the ways in which all the parties involved were represented, in terms of both parity and style. A coding frame was devised that sought to categorise the coverage by a number of criteria, and the data were then analysed in terms of that frame. Using ITV News coverage as a comparative measure, all news content was examined in terms of:

- The balance of the coverage in terms of 'point of view' (POV);
- The amount and balance of the contextual material transmitted;
- The issue of asymmetry and how it did, or did not, feature in the coverage;
- Whose 'voices' were being heard;
- 'Reporter Involvement';
- The issue of picture-led and over-sensationalised coverage;
- Use of language; and
- The role of the BBC's Middle East editor.

Content analysis studies of news often use the concept of news framing, which involves analysing the diverse ways in which a particular story can be recounted, or framed. As Entman notes 'To frame is to select some aspects of a perceived reality and make them more salient in a communicating text, in such a way as to promote a particular problem definition, causal interpretation, moral evaluation, and/or treatment recommendation' (1993: 52).

During the Israeli–Hezbollah war, a number of news frames could have been invoked, including:

- The war seen as the Israeli military response to the kidnapping of its soldiers;
- An attempt by Israel to eliminate the Hezbollah threat to its northern borders;
- A continuing part of the story of the Palestinians' struggle for a homeland;
- As part of Israel's ongoing conflict with its neighbours (and the Palestinians);
- As part of the wider US/Israel proxy war with Syria and Iran;
- As part of the wider 'war on terror' (including its implications for Iraq);
- In terms of the chaos it brought to civilians, in southern Lebanon, northern Israel and the foreigners caught up in the hostilities; or
- In terms of wider issues such as the ability of the UN to respond to international crisis post-Iraq.

However, news frames have certain inadequacies as means of analysis. First, they are not exclusive – a news frame about the war as a response to Hezbollah's kidnapping of Israeli soldiers could also contain framing related to the wider issues of Israel's conflicts with Syria and Iran and the 'war on terror'. The other shortcoming is that it offers little in terms of 'perspective'. In other words, a news frame can appear to be, and can indeed be, neutral. For example, a story about efforts to achieve a ceasefire at the UN might tell us very little as to from whose perspective the story was being framed.

In an attempt to overcome these limitations, this research sought to merge news framing analysis with a concept borrowed from film studies known as 'authorship', which involves an attempt to analyse film by decoding from the words and the pictures, the 'dominant voice'. It seeks to assess the extent to which audiences are being presented with the narrative from the distinctive point of view of one particular character, of the director, the writer or someone else. For example, the report that led ITV's coverage on 12 July contains a distinct Lebanese POV. Apart from the pictures – which showed the reporter standing on a pile of rubble, presumably the result of Israeli bombing raids, the script (with the striking POV phrases italicised) read:

> The flames were rising above Beirut again. Flames of war signalling another attack by the Israelis. The target was an oil depot at the international airport. The second strike there in barely twelve hours. It's not clear what caused this

blaze but it's believed to have been shells fired from an Israeli warship out at sea. Witnesses describe the shells coming in low and flat and hitting the oil terminal. *It promises to be a long night here. This is how the day began.* Israeli jets shattered the early morning calm as they swooped on the airport bombing the main airways. It was the start of a dramatic new phase in this latest Middle East crisis. A mile away there was panic as an Israeli helicopter launched a missile attack on a TV station controlled by Hezbollah. Yesterday it had broadcast the announcement that two Israeli soldiers had been kidnapped in southern Lebanon. It was in the south that Israel vented the worst of its fury.

(It is important to stress that the notion of POV, in this analysis at least, does not carry any implications of bias or imbalance; it is, as far as can be achieved, an objective measure). Identifying an unambiguous POV in the BBC and ITV coverage was, for the most part, a relatively straightforward task. Using a 'blind trial' methodology a POV was, without disagreement, assigned to around 80 per cent of the material analysed. Around 20 per cent of the material defied obvious characterisation and were defined as 'No Discernible POV' (NDP); reports that summed up the day's events were, for example one such category of NDP stories and were thus not included in the overall POV totals.

On another issue, attempts were made to distinguish a distinctive Lebanese POV from a Hezbollah one, but this proved virtually meaningless, since all of those interviewed in Lebanon (with the exception of Government spokespeople) either explicitly or implicitly identified themselves with Hezbollah, although pointing out that they were not 'terrorists'. However, a separate 'Evacuees POV' was constructed, since the reporting of the evacuation of (mainly British) citizens caught up in the fighting was very much from the perspective of individuals trying to escape a bad situation. In addition, a number of distinctive international POVs were identified, which proved important for making assumptions about the overall balance of the coverage.

Results and Discussion

Reporting Locations

The specific locations from where the news reports were broadcast were categorised as follows (Table 2.1):

- reports from the Israeli 'battlefield';
- from the Lebanese 'battlefield';
- from Israel away from the frontline;
- from Lebanon away from the frontline;
- from other international locations; and
- from non-specific (mainly studio) locations.

Table 2.1   BBC and ITV reporting locations

	BBC		ITV	
	N	%	n	%
Israel (battle)	22	20	21	18
Israel (non-battle)	7	6	9	8
Total Israel	29	26	30	25
Lebanon (battle)	29	26	36	31
Lebanon (non-battle)	11	10	15	13
Total Lebanon	40	36	51	43
International*	19	17	28	24
Non-specific**	22	20	9	8

Note: * New York/Washington/Rome/London/St Petersburg etc.

** General strategy/analysis/nature of the crisis

Table 2.2   Summary of direct speech

	BBC			ITV		
	n	seconds	%	n	seconds	%
Israel	41	745	34.1	37	926	36.7
Other pro-Israel	19	391	17.9	26	407	16.1
Total pro-Israel	60	1136	52	63	1333	52.8
Lebanon/Hezbollah	42	653	29.9	43	825	32.7
UN and other pro-Lebanon/Hezbollah	19	192	8.8	9	229	9.1
Total pro-Leb/Hez.	61	845	38.7	52	1054	41.8
'Neutral' Official	12	583	2.7		403	16.0
'Neutral' Unofficial	12	202	0.9	15	365	14.5

The analysis revealed that of the BBC's 110 items, 22 came from the Israeli battlefield (which includes both the frontline on the Israel/Lebanon border and the sites of rocket attacks) and 29 from the Lebanese battlefield. However, considering that southern Lebanon was the main 'theatre of war', such an imbalance, in terms of 'newsworthiness', could be justified. For ITV, the proportions were 21 and 36, demonstrating a greater preponderance towards Lebanon. However, in terms of the non-battlefield locations, the BBC balance was seven from Israel and 11 from Lebanon – which possibly reflected the fact that, for the majority of the time, the BBC went back to a Lebanese location to sum up the day's events.

Accessed Voices

Perhaps more important than the locations of reports is the issue of who is 'allowed to speak' (Table 2.2). Throughout the war, the BBC ran a total of 36 minutes and 23 seconds of direct speech from participants; ITV ran 41 minutes and 59 seconds.

On BBC News, Israeli voices took up 34.1 per cent of all direct speech and Lebanese/Hezbollah voices took up 29.9 per cent. On ITV, the figures were 36.7 per cent Israeli voices and 32.7 per cent Lebanese/Hezbollah voices. If we add in the various 'allies' of the two protagonists, i.e. US and UK government voices on the Israeli side, and other Arab and Iranian voices on the Lebanese side, and even if, (perhaps a shade contentiously) we add in the UN voices as being more 'pro-Lebanese' than 'pro-Israeli' (given its support for calls for an immediate ceasefire), the overall BBC balance remains with the Israelis, with the total percentage of time given to 'pro-Israel' direct speech on the BBC as 52 per cent and 'Pro-Lebanon' 38.7 per cent. The comparative ITV figures, with the UN added in, are 52.8 per cent pro-Israel and 41.8 per cent pro-Lebanese. In other words, there was a distinct pro- Israel bias on the part of both broadcasters in terms of whose voices were being heard.

Breaking down these figures further, it is instructive to note that, of the Israeli direct voices, civilians accounted for 14 per cent (in terms of time) as against 27 per cent coming from official Israeli sources. For the Lebanese, these figures were exactly reversed, with civilian voices making up 28 per cent of all direct voices whilst official Lebanese and Hezbollah spokespeople accounted for 14 per cent. Of this civilian group, the largest single category on the BBC was made up of those Lebanese directly affected by the violence, accounting for 14 per cent of all direct voices. In comparison, Israeli civilians directly affected by the conflict accounted for just two per cent of the voices heard. Figures for ITV were 11 per cent for Lebanese civilians directly affected against two per cent for Israelis.

There are a number of possible explanations for this disparity; one being that, because Hezbollah fighters deliberately kept themselves away from the camera, the broadcasters had little option but to interview civilians in the areas under attack. Second, Israel is a more stable society in which access to official military and political spokespeople is relatively easy to organise. In Lebanon, such access was problematic, as Lebanese political and military leaders were not always seen to speak on behalf of the protagonists (Hezbollah) in the south of the country. In other words, broadcasters would not have seen a statement from a Lebanese minister as a direct counterweight to a statement from an Israeli government spokesperson. Third, the dominant news frame was the impact the Israeli attacks on Hezbollah were having on the Lebanese civilians caught up in the fighting, which largely explains why their voices dominated much of the coverage. Finally, the impact of Israeli attacks on Lebanese civilians was far more severe than the impact of Hezbollah rocket attacks on Israeli civilians. Thus, although more Lebanese 'victims' were interviewed than their Israeli counterparts, this apparent anti-Israel bias disappears when the proportion of civilian casualties on the two

Table 2.3   News frames (minutes within all reports)

	BBC	ITV	BBC %	ITV %
Israeli military/political strategy	54.1	33.1	20.5	13.5
Direct impact on Lebanon/attacks/civilians	61.9	66.5	23.5	27.1
Direct impact on Israel/attacks/civilians	24.4	31.3	9.3	12.8
Diplomacy/international politics	53.6	50.3	20.3	20.5
Indirect impact on Lebanon	3.3	6.8	1.3	2.8
Lebanon refugees	11.6	6.8	4.4	2.8
Indirect impact on Israel	0	2.9	0	1.2
UK politics	8.9	9.3	3.4	3.8
UK evacuees	12.6	15.9	4.8	6.5
Context: nature of crisis/combatants	16.4	6.4	6.2	2.6
Context: historical	0	2.5	0	1
Context: other	8.8	0	3.4	0
Hezbollah strategy	7	9.3	2.6	3.8
Humanitarian general (both sides)	1.1	4.2	0.4	1.7
Total Israel			**29.8**	**27.5**
Total Lebanon/Hezbollah			**31.8**	**36.5**
Total diplomacy/politics			**23.7**	**24.3**
Total context			**10**	**5.3**
Total other			**4.8**	**6.5**

sides is taken into account i.e. that casualties on the Lebanese/Hezbollah side were ten times greater than on the Israeli side.

News Frames

One of the most contentious aspects of the coverage of any war is the way in which the news reports themselves are framed (Table 2.3).

In terms of news frames, the analysis reveals that 23.5 per cent of the BBC's coverage and 27.1 per cent of ITV's was focused on the direct impact of the war on Lebanon and its population. Coverage of the direct impact of the war on Israel and its civilians consisted of 9.3 per cent of the BBC's content and 12.8 per cent of ITV's. Again, this might appear to represent a disparity in coverage favouring the Lebanese side but, given the disparity in casualties there was in fact a pro-Israeli bias in coverage by both the BBC and ITV. The other main story frames used during the war were as follows: 20.5 per cent of BBC coverage and 13.5

Table 2.4   Coverage measured in terms of identifiable point of view (POV/minutes)

POV	BBC (217 min)	ITV (222 min)	BBC %	ITV %
Israeli	80.8	61.6	37.2	31.8
US	16.9	16.8	7.8	8.7
UK	9.6	7.5	4.4	3.9
Total pro-Israel	107.3	85.9	49.4	44.4
Lebanon	82.4	83.9	37.9	43.3
Evacuees	16.6	16.2	7.6	8.3
UN	4.3	5.6	6.2	2.9
Syria	1.2	1.6	0.6	0.8
Iran	1.2	0	0.5	0
Al Qaeda	2.6	0	1.2	0
EU	9.5	0	0.4	0
Dissident UK	0.6	0	0.3	0
Anti-US	0	0.7	0	0.4
Total pro-Lebanon	118.4	108.0	48.7	55.7

per cent of ITV coverage was in terms of Israel's military and/or political goals; diplomacy and international politics accounted for 20.3 per cent and 20.5 per cent respectively; and the plight of evacuees from Lebanon (mainly British) accounted for 9.2 per cent of the BBC's coverage and 9.3 per cent of ITV's. The only other category of any significance, and certainly of significance in terms of this study, is that of 'Context' (where most of the other news frames listed above could be found) accounting for 9.6 per cent of the BBC's coverage and 3.6 per cent on ITV.

Point of View

The analysis found that an identifiable 'point of view' could be assigned to 80.7 per cent of the BBC's coverage and 78.8 per cent of ITV's. The POV, as mentioned before, is not a simple aggregation of story location or story content, although obviously these are elements. The assignment of a POV to a package or report involved reviewing the coverage and making an evaluation as to whose POV the story, or segment, would be seen to be reflecting. Much of this coding was straightforward; a report from Jerusalem on Israel's strategic goals in Lebanon, for example, was simple enough, but a report on the current state of international diplomacy involved more nuanced judgements as to how much of each report was reflecting the Israeli or Lebanese perspectives, or neither.

In order to achieve as high a degree of accuracy as possible this analysis was initially undertaken as a double-blind operation – i.e. the researchers independently assigned POV values to the coverage and then compared evaluations that mostly coincided, with any differences being resolved through discussion and re-examination.

In terms of the balance of the overall coverage, it can be seen from Table 4 that 37.2 per cent of the BBC's coverage that had an identifiable POV (by time) reflected an Israeli POV against 31.8 per cent for ITV. The Lebanese/Hezbollah POV was reflected in 37.9 per cent of the BBC's coverage and 43.3 per cent of ITV's. The striking aspect of these figures is the BBC's achievement in attaining near-equality between Israeli and Lebanese POVs, particularly when compared with the inequality of the coverage on ITV. However, when we add in a broader measure of Israeli POV – i.e. including US and UK Government POVs – we see that 49.4 per cent of the BBC's coverage reflected this POV against 44.4 per cent on ITV. Adding in the broader pro-Lebanese POVs, which included Lebanese and Hezbollah sources plus international supporters and the UN, takes the BBC's total to 48.7 per cent and ITV's to 55.7 per cent. In other words, despite the problematic nature of this aggregation, it can be seen that the BBC, more or less, achieved equality of coverage in terms of its POVs reportage, whilst the figures for ITV News demonstrate a bias, in terms of POV, against Israel.

Context

One of the key roles a national news organisation should be performing is delivering to an audience, not just an account of the day's events, but also putting those events in context. A general lack of contextual material, in terms of reporting of the Israel–Palestine conflict, was one of the key criticisms made by the independent report commissioned by the BBC Governors, and recognised by the BBC News management, in as much as they indicated that one of the roles of the new Middle East editor was to provide greater context for audiences. To what extent did the BBC (and ITV) succeed in achieving this greater context? Overall, in the almost nine hours of coverage devoted to the war by both broadcasters, only 34 minutes of material could be defined as context. There was just over 25 minutes of contextual material on the BBC, which amounted to 9.6 per cent of the total time they devoted to the war. ITV carried just less than nine minutes of contextual material, which accounted for 2.6 per cent of their overall coverage. Only 6.2 per cent of the BBC's coverage was devoted to the background to the immediate crisis and the nature of the combatants, whilst other historical material accounted for a further 2.4 per cent. ITV devoted 1.6 per cent of their coverage to the immediate background to the crisis and the combatants, with just one per cent of time devoted to the historical background.

However, the contextual material that was presented was, generally, of a high standard. A total of 44 contextual references was identified – 31 within the BBC's coverage and 13 within ITV's coverage. One aspect of 'context', which was less evident, was that relating to the reasons behind Israel's offensive against Hezbollah. Clearly there was the issue of the kidnapping of the two Israeli soldiers, but behind that 'causus belli' lay Israel's concerns that Hezbollah (and Lebanon) were in breach of the UN resolution 1559 which called for the disarming of Hezbollah and for southern Lebanon to be vacated by Israeli and Hezbollah forces. Overall, this resolution was only referred to twice by the BBC – once on 20 July and again on 26 July. In comparison, ITV News made four references to the resolution.

Another aspect of context that, for Israel and her allies, was highly relevant was the role of Syria and Iran in the conflict. Syria and Iran were referred to in a number of contexts – as allies of Hezbollah, as possible arms suppliers, and as countries that had an interest in the dismemberment of Lebanon. Overall, 15 references were made to Iran or Syria on the BBC and six such references on ITV, all of which occurred within interviews or as direct quotes. In other words, the BBC did make greater efforts to provide a regional context for the dispute than did ITV. The BBC also made greater efforts to put the conflict into the wider context of the so-called 'war on terror'. Overall, the BBC made eight references to the 'war on terror', and ITV just one.

Context is always a difficult issue to identify. One measure was to examine the location and content of the live 'two-ways' – these are the moments in the bulletin when the presenter, whether in London or the Middle East, turns to his colleagues on location and asks them to sum up the day's events. These summaries are particularly significant when carried out by one of the BBC's senior correspondents – their on-screen appearance, talking live to the camera, provided an authoritative summary of both current developments and their context. These editorial devices become even more significant when they take place at the end of the bulletin's daily coverage of the war – as they can be seen to represent the BBC putting its editorial stamp on the day's events. A review of the BBC's use of this editorial device found that there was a summarising two- or three-way from the region on 19 of the 24 days of coverage. Of these 19, 10 came from Lebanon and seven from Israel, one was a three-way involving correspondents in both Lebanon and Israel and one was from the border. Jeremy Bowen, the BBC's Middle East Editor, presented seven of the 10 from Lebanon. He summed up the view from Israel just once, and this was immediately followed by a summing up from John Simpson in Lebanon. Thus, there is a slight preponderance of Lebanese locations for the live reports from the region on the BBC. However, given that the main 'theatre of war' was in Lebanon, this was hardly surprising. Whether it was 'significant' is a harder question to answer, and one that would require audience research about perception and context although the 'significance' of the location imbalance of the BBC's Middle East Editor is dealt with later.

Asymmetrical War

The issue of asymmetry is particularly problematic. In terms of television news, it can be interpreted in two ways. One is the argument that most modern wars involve asymmetry: that is, a national army doing battle with irregular insurgents. Almost inevitably this means that, because the insurgents tend to shelter among the civilian population, casualties on their side will be greater. This asymmetry is compounded by the fact that national armies generally have access to more sophisticated weaponry and air power. The question thus arises as to what extent should the news-provider keep reminding the audience of this asymmetry, particularly in the context of casualty figures that will, invariably, show more fatalities on the side of the insurgency than on the side of the national army? No examples of this were found when either broadcaster reported their tallies of the casualties – this might have been difficult to do in editorial terms but was a point that perhaps should have been made in order to enable viewers to better understand why there were such disproportionate casualty figures. Clearly, and parallels are poor but nonetheless worth making, there is little doubt that similar, and perhaps even greater, asymmetry in casualty figures could have been found between Russian forces fighting in Chechnya and those of the Chechen rebels and civilians, or in any other recent asymmetrical conflict. However, there were occasions when reporters did seek to contextualise the asymmetry of the fighting, mainly by reminding viewers that Hezbollah based themselves in the civilian areas of southern Lebanon, although this contextualisation only occurred on the BBC in the latter stages of the war.

Inevitably, both the BBC's and ITV's coverage focused on the damage being done to Lebanon and its population, the vast majority of whom were not Hezbollah fighters. On 20 July, for example, the BBC's Jim Muir, over pictures of children in hospital, reported:

> Israel's high-tech war machine is killing and injuring 10 times more of them [civilians] than the toll of Israelis from Hezbollah's random rocketing. So far the doctors here say they've received 285 patients all of them civilians not a single military casualty or anybody from Hezbollah. It is estimated that at least one third of the casualties here are children. In many border villages people have died because attacks on the roads make it impossible to take them to hospital.

Such reporting is undoubtedly factually accurate, but to what extent is it misleading, in the absence of references to this being the inevitable consequence of the fact that this war involved a national military machine doing battle with an insurgent group based in civilian areas? Whilst clearly it is not possible to make these references in every report, some acknowledgement in this direction could have been made more frequently than was the case – and this applies equally to the BBC and ITV. However, there were occasions when this issue of asymmetry was addressed. For example, Israeli Labour politician Ehud Barak told the BBC on 27 July:

We had no choice but to respond. Once you respond there are casualties on the other side. We are using very highly accurate weapons. There is no carpet bombing. Everyone who was hit, a few mistakes, Hezbollah deliberately live within population. We cannot stop protecting our citizens that's the primary contract of a government with its citizens.

One other point needs to be made, and that is that in a war such as this – between a modern state and an insurgent movement based in a relatively poor region – there is bound to be asymmetry not just in fire power and targets, but also in terms of the state's ability to provide its citizens with means of civil defence and medical care. Israeli casualties were lower in part because most had access to underground shelters and good hospital facilities. There were other reasons as well, including Hezbollah's weaker fire power and their lack of any airpower; hence relatively little damage done to the Israeli infrastructure compared to southern Lebanon and, as a result, Israeli emergency vehicles could move around with relative ease despite the hostilities. In addition, because parts of southern Lebanon became virtually inaccessible to the media, when journalists did finally reach the more remote villages, there was a sense of their 'discovering' a story about Lebanese civilians cut off from the world and this gave a highly dramatised flavour to some of their reports. This never applied to Israeli victims. In addition, there was a tendency, understandable but not necessarily journalistically defensible, to focus on the women, children and elderly people as the 'victims' (particularly noticeable on ITV).

Civilian Voices and Images

There was also a disparity in the portrayal of how Lebanese and Israeli civilians were affected, not only in the proportion of civilian voices used, but in terms of the framing of the overall coverage. This was particularly true of ITV. On the whole, the focus of stories from the 'Lebanese' POV (in terms of content and pictures) was one of innocent civilians caught up in a conflict between a state power and irregular forces – a focus emphasised by the concentration on women, children and the elderly. And while the threat to Israeli civilians was often mentioned, stories concerning them were more likely to emphasise how they had escaped the violence, or focused on their 'defiance' in the face of the threat from Hezbollah. Compared to pictures and descriptions of desperate, distraught or isolated Lebanese civilians, images of Israelis in northern Israel were usually reassuring – getting on with life inside the bunkers. The main reference to displaced Israelis came in a story on the BBC on 27 July, featuring a woman and her family who were forced to move in with strangers but, who nonetheless had found a happy and secure environment.

While reporters and presenters often emphasised that civilians on both sides were paying a heavy price following the outbreak of hostilities, the key message that came across was that the Lebanese civilians were paying the heaviest price. Moreover, the focus, on ITV in particular, was on children as the victims of the violence – hospital scenes tended to focus more on injured children than injured adults, which added to the dramatisation of the conflict. This disparity was reflected in the differences between Lebanese and Israeli civilian voices used by both the BBC and ITV. While Israeli civilians were mostly defiant, strong or resistant, the voices of the Lebanese were usually bewildered or helpless, and the prevailing discourse supported the Lebanese claim that the conflict was a 'war on civilians'.

Reporter Involvement

The issue as to whether the broadcasters deliberately attempted to re-weight coverage to 'compensate' for the greater military strength of the Israelis is a difficult one to assess. There were no obvious examples of this taking place. Nevertheless, it is impossible to measure the extent to which, sub-consciously at least, reporters in the field were affected by the huge imbalance in resources between the two sides. Increasingly, broadcasters are placing more and more emphasis on what is known as 'reporter involvement' or 'RI'. This involves more than just ensuring that reporters incorporate 'pieces-to-camera' into their packages. In order to give the audience a sense of involvement, and to boost the notion of 'our reporter on-the-spot', correspondents are now actively encouraged to get involved with the story. Reporters in war zones such as southern Lebanon, coming across civilians in need, would be less than human if they did not offer some sort of assistance, even if that extended to no more than providing them with water. As admirable as this might be in humanitarian terms, it can lead to coverage that is picture led and imbalanced. For example, Fergal Keane on the BBC reported on 31 July:

> For the first time we saw the very worst the war had done ... In the ruins of this house we found old people trapped by the fighting. She was desperate for water. There were no rescue workers in this part of town so it fell to journalists to carry them out to the ambulance.

Reporters can hardly be condemned for acting in a humanitarian way, or that they, or their editors, subsequently run the pictures of them so doing. However, this footage does give the audience an asymmetry of impact. Such incidents happened only in Lebanon, most likely because the scale of devastation there was so much greater, and the ability of the local infrastructure to respond was so much the less. Efficient Israeli paramedics and hospital staff ensured that no reporters there came across victims requiring immediate assistance. This might also partly explain why the BBC and ITV only carried 19 and 20 seconds respectively of the voices of Israeli victims.

Picture-led and over-dramatised coverage

The asymmetry of assisting elderly people or children in distress leads to a discussion of measuring the extent to which the broadcasters' coverage was 'picture led'. It is a problematic area: first, because television news is, by definition, picture driven; and, second, because stories, such as the conflict in the Middle East, are complex and broadcast journalists would argue strong pictures help to dramatise, and therefore make comprehensible, the narrative. Others might argue that strong visuals distract from the main narrative and should ideally be eschewed.

In order to investigate this issue further, the reports were analysed to see whether there were instances of one channel running a story, because it had exclusive access to good pictures, whilst the story was completely ignored by the other channel. There were two such examples. On 26 July John Simpson, the BBC's World Affairs editor, gained exclusive access to an Israeli army helicopter over Northern Israel and filed this report:

> The Israeli air force agreed to fly us over the border area to see the effect of Hezbollah rockets for ourselves. We flew over a factory in Haifa where a direct hit killed eight people last week. The third biggest city in Israel and it's almost at a standstill. This is quite extraordinary. You don't get any sense of how empty it is until you fly over it […] just below us two Hezbollah rockets had just landed. Unguided missiles fired in the general direction of civilian targets. They hit at random. Only because the area is so deserted that more people haven't been killed.

The report is interesting, in that this is an example of picture-led coverage that illuminated a wider issue. Presumably, the streets of Haifa had been deserted since the Hezbollah offensive had begun. However, it is one thing to show shots of a deserted city at street-level, but quite another to have aerial access which so much more dramatically illustrated the extent to which Hezbollah's attacks on civilian areas in northern Israel had brought this part of the country to a halt. There was no particular story over Haifa that day – the eight people had been killed the previous week – but the availability of such dramatic pictures could justifiably be used because they illuminated the current situation, literally on the ground. Therefore, in this instance, whilst the BBC was, undoubtedly 'picture led' it could be justified in editorial terms.

The other example came on 31 July when ITV gained exclusive access to mobile phone coverage of a supermarket being bombed. The commentary made clear the provenance of the material and ITV used the supermarket bombing footage again on 14 August, at the end of the war. The BBC had no such coverage and made no reference to the attack. The mobile phone coverage was dramatic but it is arguable as to whether it threw any particularly new light on events. Nonetheless, it would be difficult to suggest that, in a competitive news environment, dramatic film footage has no place – although this does not absolve editors from taking into consideration imbalances in coverage that this might lead to.

Use of Language

The choice of words and labels, in particular when reporting the Middle East conflict, is crucial; those selected can 'obscure the proper considerations of causes and possible solutions' of ongoing events (Philo and Berry, 2004: 173). Therefore, to *capture* the language is essential to both sides in the conflict (and their allies), as idiosyncratic language can significantly influence the ways in which viewers interpret the conflict. Among the most controversial terms are 'terror', 'terrorist', and 'terrorism'. The BBC's editorial guidelines state: 'The word "terrorist" itself can be a barrier rather than an aid to understanding. We should try to avoid the term without attribution. We should let other people characterise while we report the facts as we know them' (BBC, 2006: 12).

In this study, a variation of one of these three terms was used on 43 occasions. BBC News made 32 references to terror, terrorism or terrorist(s). On ten of these occasions it was used by Israeli (or by American) spokespeople directly against Hezbollah. On one occasion it was used by a Lebanese spokesperson against the Israeli army, twice it was used in a neutral context ('We are not terrorists'), and ten times in the context of the 'war on terror'. On ITV News it was used 11 times, nine times by Israelis or Americans against Hezbollah, once neutrally and once in the context of the 'war on terror'. This brief analysis does not move forward the complex debate about the use of the term, but it does indicate that the BBC's coverage – through its references to the 'war on terror' – paid more attention to the frame that suggested that the war could be seen as part of a wider global conflict than did ITV. It remains debatable as to which side would see this particular aspect of contextualisation as a positive.

Role of the Middle East Editor

The BBC appointed a Middle East editor – Jeremy Bowen – shortly before the war broke out. The editor's specific role, according to BBC News management, was 'to go beyond striking pictures to place stories within a broader, often historical, context and amplify the issue of dual narratives' (BBC, 2006: 4). Out of the 24 days of BBC coverage analysed, Jeremy Bowen reported on 14 of them. In general, his language was measured and his analysis perceptive and unbiased. However, it is worth noting that on 13 of these 14 occasions he reported from Lebanon and of these 13 bulletins he appears in either recorded packages or live spots, summing up the situation ('upsums' in the trade) a total of 21 times – 13 packages and eight 'upsums'. In all the recorded packages, Bowen does a 'piece-to-camera' – and in seven of these 13 pieces he is seen on or near rubble caused by Israeli bombing. By contrast, he reports from Israel only once, on 7 August. This consists of a package about current diplomacy and a live two-way, but not on, or near, any devastation, but from Jerusalem.

On one level, it can be argued that this tells us little – there were plenty of other BBC correspondents reporting from Israel and surely, the damage caused by the Israeli bombing raids was central to the coverage of the war? However, the BBC's Middle East editor is not just another correspondent covering the war; he was appointed by the BBC specifically to give greater context to its reporting out of the region. As such, his reports – particularly his two-way interviews between himself and the newscaster at the end of the daily war reports – had a particular role. And although his analysis of the situation does not raise any questions about his impartiality, the fact that he so often used scenes of rubble for his 'pieces to camera' and two-ways must inevitably have affected how viewers saw the conflict. Hence, there is an argument that Bowen should have, at some stage, reported from northern Israel close to the scenes of damage caused by Hezbollah rocket attacks.

This study also looked at whether the BBC achieved the right balance between Bowen as 'reporter' and Bowen as 'editor'. Bowen filed 14 packages during the war, but, given the sheer logistical difficulties involved in recording and then editing location packages from war zones, one is bound to question how much time, and metaphorical space, did Bowen allow himself to enable him to present a dispassionate summing up of the day's events which he did after these packages had been transmitted. Another question must be the extent to which he was able to distance himself from the intense suffering of the people of Lebanon that he was witnessing, close at hand, on a daily basis.

Conclusion

One of the key criticisms of the broadcasters, and this comes from both sides in the conflict, relates to the claimed lack of context. It is a valid criticism but it could probably equally have been made by those monitoring coverage of the war in Bosnia, or Afghanistan or wherever. For it is in the nature of television news, in a highly competitive environment, to shy away from providing anything but the most up-to-date 'it happened today' coverage; and never more so than when it comes to international news, which is generally believed to be of less interest to domestic audiences.

However, this analysis has revealed some valid criticisms of the broadcasters' coverage. First, both the BBC and ITV demonstrated a slant towards the Israeli side in terms of the percentage of time given to the direct speech of Israel and her supporters compared with Lebanon/Hezbollah and their supporters. The proportionate coverage of casualties also favoured Israel in that, on the BBC, 20 per cent of the coverage was devoted to the impact of the fighting on Israeli civilians and 28 per cent to the impact on Lebanese civilians (on ITV the respective figures were 18 per cent and 26 per cent) but, in terms of actual casualties, the Lebanese suffered ten times as many deaths as did the Israelis.

However, balancing this, the question has to be posed – was enough recognition given to understanding and communicating the Israeli (and wider Jewish) existential fear that resulted directly from the experience, and now memory, of the Holocaust? The weight this has in the Israeli national psyche can never be overestimated. Similarly, it is important to recognise that the Palestinians have their own 'primary mover' – the 'catastrophe' (the Nakba) – the view that 1948 involved Palestinians' (or their parents' or grandparents') forcible expulsion from their homeland. Neither of these two 'narratives' received significant attention on the BBC and ITV news bulletins during the course of the war.

Second, the issue of asymmetry (as problematic as it undoubtedly is) was not always handled well. Whilst the temptation to use dramatic pictures is understandable, consistent efforts ought to be made to explain why there is, and always will be, disproportionate casualties when insurgents engage with a state military machine. And there needs to be constant recognition that it is just as terrifying to live under the daily threat of inaccurate rocket attacks as it is to live under the threat of more accurate aerial bombardment. The 'lack of voice' of Israelis directly affected by the attacks – identified in this study – was noticeable on both channels. Victims who look 'helpless', for example children and elderly people bombed out of their homes, make 'better television' than victims who, as a result of good civil defence and inaccurate rocket attacks, look to be 'getting by'.

Third, there is the role of the BBC's Middle East editor and his on-screen appearances. For whilst what he said was, as far as we can ascertain, free of any bias, the visual imagery he presented could have given rise to allegations of imbalance. Primarily, and most obviously, he based himself in Lebanon virtually throughout the period of the war. This must inevitably have influenced how he was seeing the situation, in terms of sources and sheer human empathy. The power of visual imagery over words is a well-recognised phenomenon and hence the words of Bowen's balanced summing up could be overwhelmed by the simple fact of where he was standing. Moreover, the fact that such a high proportion of the pieces-to- camera he recorded took place at, or near, rubble caused by Israeli bombing sent strong messages to his audience about what was at the heart of this conflict.

Nonetheless, despite these important shortcomings, the conclusion has to be that, given the complexities of the issue, the pressures of time and space and the sheer difficulties of reporting from hostile environments, both BBC and ITV News acquitted themselves well in their reporting of the 2006 Israeli–Hezbollah war. However, whatever lessons the international broadcasters might, or might not, have learnt from this experience it is clear that the Israeli authorities learnt as well. Their attempts to control the international media's television reportage of the 2008/9 Gaza War, resulted in international coverage which might have been comparable, in terms of volume, with the coverage of the war in Lebanon, but in terms of intelligibility and insight, was, for the broadcasters at least, less than satisfactory.

References

BBC (2000), 'Journalists Caught in the Middle', http://news.bbc.co.uk/2/hi/programmes/from_our_own_correspondent/1021166.stm, accessed December 2008.

BBC (2006), 'Governors' Statement and BBC Management's Response to the Independent Panel Report on Coverage of the Israeli-Palestinian Conflict', http://www.bbcgovernorsarchive.co.uk/docs/reviews/israelipalestiniangovernors_statement.df, accessed December 2008.

BBC Watch (2004), 'Report: The BBC and the Middle East: The Documentary Campaign 2000-2004 (July)', http://www.bbcwatch.com/reports.html, accessed November 2008.

CNN International.com (2009), 'Israel explains Gaza media restrictions', 14 January, http://edition.cnn.com/2009/WORLD/meast/01/14/israel.gaza.media.restrictions/index.html, accessed January 2009.

Entman, R. (1993), 'Framing: Toward Clarification of a Fractured Paradigm', *Journal of Communication* 43(4): 51-8.

Independent Panel (2006), 'Report of the Independent Panel for the BBC Governors on Impartiality of BBC Coverage of the Israeli–Palestinian Conflict', http://www.bbcgovernorsarchive.co.uk/docs/reviews/panel_report_final.pdf, accessed November 2008.

Kalb, M. and C. Saivetz (2007), 'The Israeli–Hezbollah War of 2006: The Media as a Weapon in Asymmetrical Conflict', *The International Journal of Press/Politics* 12(3): 43-66.

Loughborough University (2006), 'The BBC's Reporting of the Israeli-Palestinian Conflict August 1 2005 – January 31 2006', Communications Research Centre, http://www.bbcgovernorsarchive.co.uk/docs/reviews/loughborough_final.pdf, accessed November 2008.

Opinion Leader Research (2006), 'BBC Governors' Impartiality Review on Coverage of the Israeli-Palestinian Conflict', http://www.bbcgovernorsarchive.co.uk/docs/rev_israelipalestinian.html, accessed December 2008

Philo, G. and M. Berry (2004), *Bad News from Israel*, London: Pluto Press.

Zelizer, B., D. Park and D. Gudelunas (2002), 'How Bias Shapes the News: Challenging the *New York Times*' Status as a Newspaper of Record on the Middle East', *Journalism* 3(3): 283-307.

Chapter 3

Islam as a Threat? Problematisation of Muslims in the Mass Media and Effects on the Political System

Patrik Ettinger and Linards Udris

Introduction

'Switzerland instead of Sharia' ('Schweiz statt Sharia') was one of the most noteworthy slogans in the political campaign for the general elections in Switzerland in 2007. Starkly contrasting an allegedly fundamentalist, Sharia-oriented Muslim minority with a nativist understanding of the 'Swiss people', the populist radical right Swiss People's Party (SVP) prominently used the issue of Muslim immigration to and integration in Switzerland in the fight for parliamentary seats. In this process, both the media and political opponents reacted and heavily attacked the SVP by pointing out the allegedly Islamophobic content of the SVP campaign, thus raising the salience of this issue even more. In this contested election campaign, then, one could observe both a problematisation of Muslims and a problematisation of the SVP. On a political level, both seemed to be successful. The SVP carried again more seats in October 2007 than any other party in parliament, underscoring its upward trend since the 1990s, but it also experienced a massive defeat when, two months later, parliament did not re-elect the SVP's ideological leader, Christoph Blocher, as a minister for the seven-member all-party coalition government.

What was at work here? A look into Switzerland's recent history suggests that the elections of 2007 are part of a growing (political) polarisation in Switzerland, with the SVP becoming both the most successful and most criticised (even 'ostracised') political camp (Imhof and Udris, 2009; Mazzoleni, 2003). But, most fundamentally, it also indicates a broader struggle about what should (or should not) constitute the identity of Switzerland (Imhof, 2006b) or, in brief, what the boundaries of Swiss society should be.

Whenever foreigners and ethnic minorities are made a problem, this regularly tells us a lot about the state of the 'majority' of a given society, for example the extent of an 'identity' or 'orientation crisis'. In the Swiss case then, are the boundaries of the 'majority' becoming more rigid, enhancing the political salience of ethnicity? Or can we observe a strong influence of actors that counter the politicisation of ethnicity, for example by stressing other boundaries and forms of social conflict (e.g. economical)? To what extent do Muslims become the threatening 'Other' and who makes them a problem?

To tackle these questions, our contribution systematically analyses public communication – the principal medium where modern societies observe and regulate themselves (Habermas, 2006; Peters, 1993; Imhof, 2008). Thus, public communication detects and defines the relevant problems a society (and the political system, respectively) has to solve. Public communication as an intermediary structure between the citizens and the state consists of several levels and arenas (Habermas, 2006), but it is overall heavily shaped by the mass media. This is why we chose to examine mass mediated public communication.

Also, public communication (and thus the mass media) defines and shapes the relevant 'semantics of difference' – quite stable structures of identity and culturally accepted and therefore understandable forms to distinguish the 'other' from those who belong to the 'we'. Rooted in the central differentiations of the modern nation-state generally (Alexander, 2006: 53ff.) and shaped in periods of orientation crisis specifically, these symbolic structures and semantics of difference create path-dependencies for identity debates. Especially when segmentary semantics of difference (focusing on commonly shared understanding of ethnicity and excluding the 'other') converge with stratificatory semantics of difference (e.g. scandalizing foreigners for abusing the welfare state) or temporal semantics of difference (e.g. glorifying a past with an allegedly ethnically homogenous 'community'), this overall means a high salience of the politicisation of ethnicity. It is exactly under these circumstances that boundaries towards foreigners and ethnic minorities are drawn in a rigid manner.

When we analyse public communication and the problematisation of Muslims in public communication, we focus on two main aspects:

Firstly, we will take the case of Switzerland to empirically test whether Islam now forms the 'Other' and replaces other types of 'threats' (e.g. asylum seekers, the European Union etc.). For this, we can rely on data that we gathered in Swiss public communication for the years 1980 to 2007. We chose to go back to 1980 both because, with the revolution in Iran 1979, this is the first time (after World War II) that Islam received broad attention, and because we need to include a somewhat stable period before a major 'identity crisis' set in end of the Cold War.

Secondly, based on data from content analyses conducted in an ongoing research project,[1] we will reflect on the *quality* of public communication about Islam. Insights from sociological conflict theory show that social conflicts do have an integrative function for societies (e.g. reintegrating both conflicting camps) – provided that conflicts are 'cultivated' (Dubiel, 1998). This presupposes that the conflicting camps recognise each other, come to regard the conflict as divisible and

---

1   The research project 'Politicization of ethnicity and religious difference as a problem in political discourse' is part of the National Research Programme NRP 58 'Religions in Switzerland', supported by the *Swiss National Science Foundation*. For this programme, see www.nfp58.ch.

procedural and that the conflict is led within an institutional framework and on the basis of basic values accepted by both camps. On the other hand, identity conflicts and conflicts about basic values, respectively, can easily come to be regarded as 'fundamental conflicts' and conflicts of 'either-or' (Hirschman, 1994; Imhof, 2009) which highly aggravate a (peaceful) conflict solution. In order to capture this, we will analyse whether there is a differentiation between 'global' and 'domestic' Islam or a new threat perception, and whether there is differentiation in the debates over fundamental values. In addition to that, we will briefly focus on the effects these constructed threat perceptions have on the political system.

Problematisation of Foreigners and Ethnic Minorities: Methodological Approach and Overview

Every society has its 'outsiders' or the 'Other', as the definition of an 'in-group' or the 'civil sphere' making up a society is – empirically speaking – often made *ex negativo* (Alexander, 2006). Especially in times of (orientation) crisis, insecurities result in more virulent identity debates and a more striking problematising of the 'Other' (Imhof, 2009). The obvious questions following from this are: who are these 'outsiders'? What are the characteristics that make them the 'Other'? To what extent are they made the 'Other'? And which actors manage to define what the relevant boundaries regarding 'in' and 'out' groups are? In the continuum of conceptions of 'society' versus 'community', the former stand for less rigid distinctions, the latter for a rigid understanding of who should belong to a 'community'.

The 'Other', i.e. those not belonging to a 'community', does not have to be, as a lot of studies on ethnicity suggest, solely ethnic groups within a country, such as immigrants. As the ideology of the (populist) radical right shows (Mudde, 2007: 65), the actor which holds a Manichean worldview and most fervently makes the case for 'identity politics' (Betz and Johnson, 2004: 318; for a cleavage-oriented approach also Kriesi et al., 2006: 928f.),[2] the 'Other' can also include actors or organizations in foreign countries (e.g. the EU) or the political 'elite' or 'deviants' (e.g. homosexuals, drug dealers) within a given society. Empirically, we observe a scandalisation of foreigners (undermining the values of the 'people'), of international organisations such as the EU (undermining the sovereignty of the country), of deviants such as drug addicts or drug dealers (undermining law and order), and – especially – of the 'political elite' (responsible for not fighting these problems and also undermining the values of the common 'people'). The question

---

2   '… identity politics serves primarily as an ideological justification for selective exclusion. The main argument behind this is that certain groups cannot be integrated into society and therefore represent a fundamental threat to the values, way of life and cultural integrity of the 'indigenous' people'.

of who should be included into the 'we' is, of course, a matter of definition and contest in public communication.

To see whether and to what degree foreigners and ethnic minorities – together with or in contrast to other problematised groups – are (made) a problem in public communication, we conducted a longitudinal analysis of mass mediated public communication from 1980 to the present. As for the elements we are looking at, we capture public communication with 'communication events', defined as series of reports in public communication. Communication events constantly process various articles and reports into a current 'story' (Imhof, 1993: 11f.; Eisenegger, 2005: 136f.).

This way, communication events are defined in a topical, social and temporal dimension. If we analyse public communication systematically and on an inductive basis (i.e. following the actual perspective of the journalists, not making *ex post* classifications) we group articles and news items into communication events. The size of these communication events allows for building a media agenda, reflecting the salience of the communication events. Examples of communication events prominent on the media agenda in Switzerland in 2008 are – among others – the financial crisis, the war in Iraq, the reform of health insurance in Switzerland or the European soccer championship in Austria/Switzerland.

For the long time range from 1980 to 2007, we captured communication events in three major newspapers in Switzerland. They all have comparably high circulation rates and are regarded as 'leading' media both by politicians and the public for their credibility or agenda-setting power (or both). The sample also takes into account different types of newspapers (for this differentiation see also Lucht and Udris, 2009). The *Neue Zürcher Zeitung* can be regarded a prestigious (high-) quality paper similar to the *New York Times*; *Blick* is a typical tabloid in the German-speaking world (similar to *Bild* in Germany), with slightly more political content than the tabloids in Great Britain. Finally, the *Tages-Anzeiger* is a 'middle-market' or 'forum' paper with a regional bias in Zurich, Switzerland's largest city, financial and media centre. For the largest twenty communication events per year in *Blick*, *Neue Zürcher Zeitung* and *Tages-Anzeiger*,[3] we analysed whether communication events were shaped by a problematisation of foreigners and ethnic minorities (see. Imhof and Udris 2009). The following figure (Figure 3.1) displays the intensity of the selected communication events and thus represents the problematisation

---

3   We use a database created at the Centre for Research on the Public Sphere and Society (fög) at the University of Zurich. In this database, public communication in Switzerland has been systematically measured with 'communication events' for almost one hundred years, from 1910 to the present. Out of all possible communication events, this database contains the twenty largest communication events (sum of column centimeters of the articles) per year and newspaper from 1910 to 1997. For the period from 1998 to the present, the database is even broader, for *all* communication events are included, in a much wider media sample also including TV and radio news.

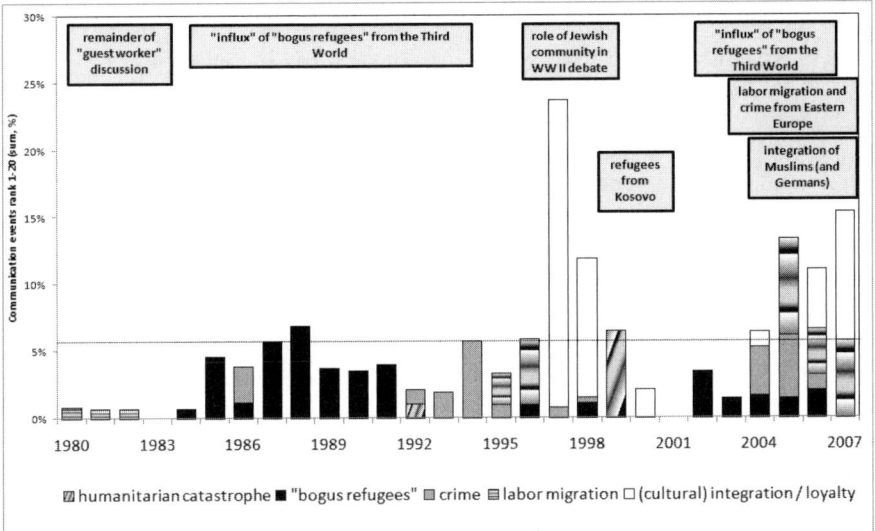

Figure 3.1   Problematisation of foreigners and ethnic minorities in Swiss public communication 1980-2007

Note: Once a communication event has been accordingly coded, the sum of the length of the coded communication events is set in relation to the total of all possible twenty largest communication events, depicted in Figure 3.1. If *Blick* devoted 30 per cent of its coverage (witihn the largest twenty communication events) to foreigners and ethnic minorities in a given year, while the Tages-Amzeiger devoted 15 per cent and *NZZ* one per cent, the depicted percentage would be 15.3 per cent (30+15+1 divided by 3, for the three newspapaers). To put these seemingly low numbers into perspective: given the infinite stream of communication and discussion of all kinds of possible topics in publiccommunication, any number even near 50 per centwould be completely unrealistic. Even the extremly intense coverage on a historic' event such as9/11 and the following, war on terror' (not depicted here) takes up 'only' 25 per cent in the three newspapers in 2001. The analysis of our database shows – roughly – that five per cent and more mean, on top of the media agenda'.

of foreigners and ethnic minorities in Swiss public communication from 1980 to 2007.

Above all, the figure shows a discontinuous but intensifying problematisation of foreigners and ethnic minorities. This problematisation is rooted in a deep scepticism towards (permanent) immigration, although Switzerland historically has been an 'immigration country' for more than a century already. In the years leading to World War I, in the 1960s and since the 1990s, foreigners make up more than ten per cent of the overall population; currently, it is around twenty per cent.

In line with results from the state of the art studies of ethnicity (e.g. Wimmer, 2009: 978-79), the intensity of the problematisation and the time it occurs does not necessarily reflect the 'actual' numbers of foreigners and ethnic minorities; neither does migration of a specific group automatically trigger a problematisation.[4] Over time, certain types of foreigners and ethnic minorities come into focus (and categories are created) while others disappear.

Strikingly, the understanding in the discussions about foreigners and ethnic minorities has mostly been that people coming to Switzerland would stay in the country only on a temporary basis – not only refugees but also immigrant workers. Hence, these kinds of discussion focus on the (allegedly large) numbers of people entering Switzerland, the state of border control, and the question of sheltering and (financially) supporting these people for a short time. These debates then reflect certain path-dependencies in the political approach to integration and asylum policies, which placed only little emphasis on integration. As Skenderovic and D'Amato (2009) and Niederberger (2004) argue, this results both from the fact that integration measures were to be dealt with on the level of states (*Kantone)* and communities (instead of the national level) and from the 'rotation principle' of Swiss immigration policy that supposed foreigners to stay in Switzerland only temporarily and return to their home countries after a certain time.

If we look at the problematisation of foreigners and ethnic minorities (see Figure 3.1), the five following frames stand out which, as problem perspectives, state 'where the problem is' (Entman, 1993). In some cases, they overlap, as in the discussions on 'bogus refugees' and crime. However, they reveal remarkable foci, especially with regard to the understanding of the groups that are made a problem. In a diachronic perspective, it becomes clear that, increasingly so in the twenty-first century, public debate shifts on questions of integration instead of (temporary) migration.

1. The first frame – the 'labour migration' frame – indicates a problematisation of immigrant workers. Since World War II, Switzerland has experienced quite a substantial labour migration. Historically speaking, the 'labour migration' was prominent especially in the 1960s, as 'guest workers' from Southern Europe were believed not only to change the domestic job market but even to 'over-foreignise' and threaten the core of Switzerland's identity (Kamber and Schranz, 2001; Skenderovic, 2007). This frame also stood in tandem with the sudden rise of radical right parties in the 1960s, early in comparison with the rise of the populist radical right in most Western

---

4   Research has convincingly shown that a high number of foreigners in an area does not correlate with a high degree of their problematisation, e.g. the election of extreme right parties or the use of violence towards foreigners (Rydgren, 2007, pp. 250f.). Furthermore, Koopmans and Olzak (2004), for instance, have looked at conceptions of citizenship and pointed at how the media and politicians make certain groups a problem (and not others). In Germany, the large immigration of Russians of German descent in the 1990s ('Aussiedler') caused almost no negative reaction, whereas the significantly lower immigration of asylum seekers was portrayed in extremely negative terms and eventually led to violent attacks (e.g. in Rostock or Hoyerswerda in 1991).

European countries. This scandalisation of 'guest workers' reflected some of the most marked social tensions in Switzerland after World War II (Buomberger, 2004) and a true crisis of identity (Imhof, 2006b). The situation calmed in the mid-1970s after a majority of the political spectrum had designed a different approach to migration policy and after the 'oil shock' had left a lot of foreigners without a job, thus making them leave the country again (Mahnig and Piguet, 2003: 85).

Remainders of this discussion about labour migration are reflected in the discussion on a popular vote on better rights for labour migrants (which was rejected in 1981). Then, for more than a decade, labour migration played a less important role compared to the intense scandalisation of asylum-seekers (see below). More recently, it is mainly through closer collaboration between Switzerland and the European Union (bilateral agreements) since the mid-1990s that the question of labour migration (now from the EU) has been gaining ground. Typically, with every round of EU-expansion ('old' member states, enlargements of 2004 and 2006), popular referenda are held about whether 'EU citizens' should be granted the right to freely move to and work in Switzerland (*Personenfreizügigkeit*). This boosts both the salience of the issue of labour migration and increasingly connects it with the deep skepticism towards the EU that is prevalent in Swiss public communication.

2. In contrast to the labour migration frame, immigrants from the 'Third World' coming to Switzerland since the 1980s are not regarded as (legitimate) 'guest workers'. Institutionally, legal immigration to Switzerland for work becomes mainly restricted to countries of the 'First World', leaving individuals from other countries basically the option to immigrate as asylum seekers (for whatever reason they have to migrate).[5] People applying for asylum are scandalised for coming for economic rather than true humanitarian reasons, thus being 'bogus refugees' which would not qualify as persecuted and legitimate refugees ('bogus refugees' frame). This frame proves to be persistent in public communication.[6] It

---

5   Immigration policies tended towards a so-called 'Three-Circles-Model', designed by the Federal Council in 1991. The rationale was to eventually grant freedom of circulation and residence to citizens from the First Circle (EU and EFTA states), recruit a limited number of working immigrants from the Second Circle (USA, Canada, Australia etc.) and prohibit work migration from all other countries.

6   We need to make clear that there are counter-frames and opposition to the 'bogus refugees' frame in public communication. The graph therefore does not display the 'actual' degree of problematisation or the 'actual' extent of legitimacy this frame is ascribed in public communication. But in view of the mechanisms between public discourse and the possible radicalization by (non-established) political actors (see. e.g. Koopmans, 2004), it is reasonable to suppose strong effects on the overall 'political climate' already if a frame (whatever contested it is) gains high salience and resonance.

starts to take root in the mid-1980s when especially fringe parties from the right and the tabloid paper *Blick* problematise this type of immigration and scandalise asylum policies (a prime example of the interplay between media populism and political populism, see Mazzoleni, 2008). Heavily making use of metaphors such as 'influx' or 'flood of asylum seekers', the media and the radical right perceive and stylise a chaotic situation with Government allegedly being incompetent, helpless and 'out of touch' with the general population. In this populist rhetoric, the fear of asylum seekers and 'bogus refugees' is combined with the fear of government failure and social unrest. It is then that this frame nurtures the 'crime frame' in public communication (see 3 below). After a lower salience in the mid-1990s – which has to do with the shift to problematising the European Union as the 'Other' – the 'bogus refugees' frame since then has again been a significant part in the discussion about foreigners and ethnic minorities. It has slightly changed since the 1980s insofar as the questions of border protection has come to be less and the debate on the limits to financial support for asylum seekers more significant.

3. Communication events shaped by the *'crime frame'* focus on criminal acts that allegedly are the result of immigration of foreigners. Discussions with a pronounced crime frame start in the mid-1980s and are mostly connected with asylum seekers (see also Kamber and Schranz, 2001). In 1994 in particular, asylum seekers from Africa are accused of dealing drugs. Again, the combination of frequent right-wing populist policy proposals and the scandalizing coverage in the tabloid paper *Blick* puts so much pressure on the political system that 'emergency laws' are passed by a popular vote that allow for faster imprisonment of foreign criminals. More recently, the link of immigration and crime can be seen in the context of bilateral agreements with the European Union. Especially the debates on opening the borders with the Schengen/Dublin treaty reveal fear of – mostly Eastern European – criminals (from the Rom minority).

4. In comparison with the scandalisation and criminalisation of allegedly 'bogus refugees', frames focusing on 'humanitarian catastrophes' that stand behind the migration of thousands of asylum seekers are less salient. In any discussion on asylum seekers, one would find some voices pointing at humanitarian catastrophes as reasons for migration (mainly from left-wing political actors). But in the last twenty-five years, this frame was prevalent only in the context of the ethnic wars in Yugoslavia. Both in 1992 and, even more so, in 1999, Swiss public communication focused on the war and the atrocities caused by it. These asylum seekers coming to Switzerland were clearly depicted as victims of wars and thus (legitimate) refugees – also in view of the assumption that these 'war refugees' would return to their home countries once the war would be over. This frame always caused political

opposition as well. Especially right-wing populist actors pressed the claim that, in order to shelter a large number of 'legitimate' war refugees from Yugoslavia, authorities would have to deny asylum to those from other regions of the world (Skenderovic and D'Amato, 2008: 194f.). In this respect, groups of asylum seekers or refugees were negotiated along the question of legitimacy of their motives for asylum.

5. A number of communication events is shaped by the 'cultural integration / loyalty' frame that problematises a certain group for not being integrated into or loyal to the in-group, the 'native' population. It is this frame that most strikingly focuses on groups that, unlike refugees, could be called the 'strangers', a stranger being 'the man who comes today and stays [our emphasis] tomorrow – the potential wanderer, so to speak, who, although he has gone no further, has not quite got over the freedom of coming and going', as Simmel (1971: 143) put it. In some cases, the 'stranger' or 'other' has been living in Switzerland for a long time and obtained Swiss citizenship. Still, these discussions reveal exactly the boundary delimitations as to whether these foreigners and ethnic minorities within the society should be also considered 'within' or 'outside' the 'community', thus whether Switzerland sees itself as a (pluralistic) society or as a 'community' that seems threatened by the 'Other' living on the same territory.

In the period from 1980 to the present, this applies – apart from 'foreigners' in general (mainly immigrant workers in the 21st century) – to the Jewish and the Muslim minority in Switzerland. Jews, making up less than one per cent of the Swiss population, suddenly became the focus of attention in the second half of the 1990s, a result from the controversy about Switzerland's role during World War II (see Udris and Eisenegger, 2007). The pressure from US American Jewish organizations, which asked for financial compensation from banks for their handling of 'dormant assets', caused strong reactions. In this context, the loyalty of the Jewish community towards the Swiss 'nation' was – explicitly or implicitly – called into question, which resulted in a rise of anti-Semitic statements (see Späti, 2005: 419-40; Kreis, 2005: 17-32). However, also given that any overt anti-Semitic attitudes and actions in public are discredited and 'taboo' (as is overt racism and 'neo-Nazism', see Imhof, 2006), the discussion soon shifts towards an empathic portrayal of the Jewish community in Switzerland, and distinctions are made between US American Jewish organisations (portrayed in a negative way) and Jews living in Switzerland (rather positive). The Jewish minority in Switzerland as such is not (made) an issue any longer from the early 2000s on.

On the other hand, as for 'foreigners' in general and Muslims in particular, questions about integration intensify, all of which reflect 'identity politics' and struggles over core values. First of all, this is due to a broadening understanding and thus coupling of asylum and integration policy, as was the case in the long run-up to the popular vote (which took place in September 2006) on both asylum and integration policy. Second, increasingly so, questions of naturalisation become important (Skenderovic and D'Amato, 2009: 86f.) and embedded in the populist ideology and style of the radical right, which attacks the 'political elite' for carelessly 'giving away' Swiss passports to non-integrated foreigners, especially Muslims (Betz, 2007: 46). Value conflicts are also increasingly led in the field of education, where the role of the children of foreigners is more and more problematised. Similar to the question of naturalisation, it is the radical right which most prominently couples the different types of 'Other': the left-wing 'elite' and non-authoritarian and '*laissez-faire*' teachers who are responsible for not doing anything against (allegedly growing) youth violence and the decline of quality in school results, and who are responsible for granting exceptions to children of Muslim origin (such as allowing them not to participate in swimming lessons) , thus allegedly violating the principle of equality. As for the groups linked to these problems, it is above all foreigners from the Balkan countries.

Religion plays a secondary role; if at all, however, it is the Muslim minority which is linked to these issues. Apart from foreigners in general and Balkan immigrants and Muslims in particular, another group has recently become the focus of attention: the Germans. German migration into Switzerland, though in the context of labour migration, is also discussed under the integration perspective, with a significant number of voices warning that the cultural distance between the Swiss and the Germans should not be underestimated. All in all, the peak in 2007 finally reflects the fact that, for the first time in decades, foreigners are (made) the main topic of the elections (Udris, 2007). Looking more closely at the semantics that are used to problematise these groups in this election campaign, it becomes clear that, again, it is 'criminal foreigners' in general, 'foreign young adults or teenagers' (mostly from the Balkans) and 'Muslims' in particular. This is reflected also in billboard campaigns (by the radical right parties) that depict 'criminal foreigners' as a black sheep being kicked out of Switzerland by a white sheep, 'foreign young adults or teenagers' as dark-skinned, violent and threatening 'gangster rappers', and Muslims as women heavily covered with the headscarf, with the slogan going 'Aarau [typical small city in German-speaking Switzerland] instead of Ankara'.

In a nutshell, then, foreigners and ethnic minorities since the 1980s have repeatedly been made a problem. But it is noteworthy that the issue of 'integration', more so than the question of asylum, has gained in importance. This does not only mean that a comprehensive approach to immigration is finally conducted which would strive to grant more 'power' (economic, political, cultural) to foreigners than before. Since 'integration' directly aims at the 'heart' of in-and-out-group distinctions, it also offers discursive opportunities for 'identity politics' and therefore reflects attempts to establish more rigid boundaries towards the 'Other'.

At the moment, it is expected that political actors will keep on exploiting these issues, not only in view of direct-democratic initiatives pending (see below). Especially if the global financial crisis that started to hit Switzerland since the summer of 2008 proves to be long-lasting, there are chances for further politicisation of ethnicity. In times of crisis, one could argue that socio-economic issues and cleavages are expected to gain salience at the expense of socio-cultural issues and cleavages, which would mean the radical right – which is especially strong in socio-cultural issues and 'identity politics' – would fare less well (Rydgren, 2007: 249-50). But this argument underestimates the fact that, during an 'identity crisis', socio-economic issues are regularly linked to the problematisation of foreigners and ethnic minorities. It remains to be seen which ethnic minorities will be most affected in this process. Given the increasing problematisation of Muslims in the last years, Muslims are expected to be most exposed – provided that the political actor most responsible for this problematisation, the SVP, is still perceived as an effective actor, which, increasingly, it is not.

What has led to this problematisation, however? How did a seemingly small (and vastly heterogeneous) 'minority' (a category rather used by the 'majority' than by actors labelled as Muslims) come into focus?

The Problematisation of Muslims

On the following pages, we try to show that the high attention given to international conflicts and terrorist attacks linked to Islamic fundamentalism partially lead to a new threat perception. This creates a window of opportunity for political actors to (also) problematise the Muslim minority in Switzerland. In order to back up our argument, we will first look at the Muslim minority in Switzerland and ask to what extent it offered opportunities for problematisation. In a second step, we will show how the 'window of opportunity' (created by the intense coverage of Muslims in the context of international conflicts and terrorist attacks) was actually used by the radical right for identity politics. The conflict about boundaries between 'us' and 'them' (here: Muslims) was created as a conflict over fundamental values. In a third step, we will look at possible effects on the political system – electoral success, reactions in parliament, and popular referenda and initiatives.

We can clearly see this 'construction' of boundaries at work if we look at the problematisation of the Muslim minority on the one hand and their characteristics on the other hand. In Switzerland, Muslims are a small minority, both in terms of their actual number and in terms of their influence (see also Ettinger and Imhof, 2007). In 1970, the Muslim minority of some 16,000 people was smaller than, for example, the similarly small Jewish community. During the 1980s and 1990s, however, the number of Muslims in Switzerland increased significantly; in 2000, 4.3 per cent of the population were Muslims (see Table 3.1). This increase was both a result of immigration (both through working immigrants and refugees) and of a higher birth rate within the community. Working immigrants came into Switzerland predominantly from Turkey or, at a later stage, the former Yugoslavia,

Table 3.1   Religious affiliation of the Swiss population

	1970	1980	1990	2000
Protestant	46.4%	43.9%	38.5%	33.0%
Roman Catholic	49.4%	47.6%	46.2%	41.8%
...				
Jewish	0.3%	0.3%	0.3%	0.3%
Islamic	0.3%	0.9%	2.2%	4.3%
No affiliation	1.1%	3.8%	7.4%	11.1%

Source: Data of the Swiss census 2000 (see Bovay, 2004).

but also, in the French-speaking part, from North Africa. The largest number of refugees came from the war-ridden regions of the former Yugoslavia.

These working immigrants and refugees saw themselves primarily as members of a specific ethnic group (e.g. as Turks, Albanians, ethnic groups from the former Yugoslavia); accordingly, they organised their cultural lives within ethnic groups and organisations. Religion (or a 'Muslim' identity) played only a secondary role for the self-definition of this 'minority'. This also reflects the fact that these immigrants mainly came from secularised societies. These ethnic groups and organisations also formed the context in which the small group of the more religious members of these minorities began setting up places of worship – mostly in backyards and old factory halls – and requesting burial sites on previously Christian cemeteries. The terrorist attacks in New York 2001 and Madrid 2004 challenged this primarily ethnic self-conception, with Swiss 'majority society' beginning to perceive and problematise an allegedly homogenous (religious) Muslim 'community' as a whole (Behloul and Lathion, 2007), thereby disregarding their ethnic and religious diversity.

How could this minority – heterogeneous, without any powerful interest organisations or lobbyist groups, no involvement in any terrorist action and although growing fast, still small in absolute numbers – become the primary object and target of political campaigns that depicted them as a fundamental threat to Swiss identity and security?

To answer this question, we have to look at the way in which Muslims are portrayed in Swiss public communication. Our basis is a systematic and detailed analysis of 'communication events' from 1998 to 2007 in several leading media in Switzerland.

First, we want to check whether the high attention given to Muslims in Switzerland reflects a 'window of opportunity' created by international war and conflict events and the threat perceptions discursively linked to these events. To answer this (and the following questions), we systematically analyse

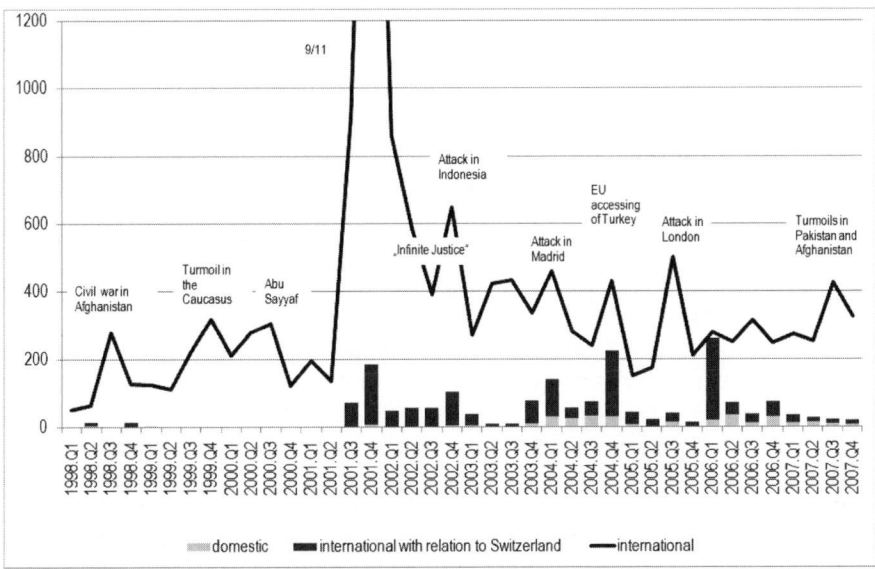

Figure 3.2   International versus domestic communication events on Muslims, Swiss leading media 1998-2007

'communication events' from 1998 to 2007 in several leading media in Switzerland.[7] First, we distinguished three types of communication events: a) communication events that focus on international processes and events without any relation to Switzerland (black lines); b) communication events where international processes and events are discussed in relation to Switzerland (dark-grey columns) and c) communication events where domestic (Swiss) processes and events are discussed without international relations (light grey columns).

The black line clearly reflects the intense coverage of Muslims in international contexts already before 9/11, which then intensifies in reaction to the events in New York and Washington (climaxing in 2,741 reports in the fourth quarter in 2001). As such, this extremely intense coverage of Muslims occurs largely in reaction to wars and terrorist attacks. This includes the civil war in Afghanistan, the turmoil in the Caucasus, the terrorist attacks on 9/11, drawing the largest amount of attention, the so-called 'War on Terror', the attacks in Indonesia, Madrid and London as well as the upheavals in Pakistan. In all these communication events, the coverage and portrayal of Muslims is shaped by the context of violence. The only exception

---

7   *Blick* (tabloid, daily), *SonntagsBlick* (tabloid, weekly), *Tages-Anzeiger* (forum or 'middle-market', daily), *SonntagsZeitung* (mixture of 'middle-market' and 'tabloid', weekly), *Neue Zürcher Zeitung* (quality, daily), *Echo der Zeit* (quality radio news, daily), *Rendez-Vous* (forum radio news, daily), *Tagesschau* (quality TV news, daily), *10 vor 10* (news programme with 'tabloid' elements, daily).

to these highly resonant war and terror communication events is the discussion of Turkey's possible membership in the European Union. In this communication event, media and political actors stress the distance between Muslims and the 'West' insofar as they point to a growing threat of an 'Islamisation' of Turkish society. This assumed process is seen as incompatible with Turkey's integration in Europe because Europe, in the argument of some political actors, is shaped by democratic and Christian values.

This media coverage of Muslims in international contexts and the according threat perceptions also draw the attention to Muslims living in Switzerland, thus mirroring the effect of 'global' Islam in the coverage of 'domestic' Islam (for a similar finding in the UK see Poole 2000). Until 9/11, Muslims in Switzerland were only marginally discussed, for instance in the discussion of burial sites in formerly Christian cemeteries.

It is in the aftermath of 9/11 that the Muslim minority in Switzerland finds some attention in public communication. Here, it is mainly the media as actors that repeatedly contrast reports on terrorist attacks with reports on daily life of Muslims in Switzerland, thus stressing the peacefulness of Muslims in Switzerland (Schranz and Imhof, 2003) and distinguishing between 'global Islam' and 'domestic Islam', a finding similar to the debates in the Netherlands (d'Haennens and Brink, 2006) and the United States (Nacos and Torres-Reyna, 2007: xi). Nonetheless, a wide, encompassing debate and a positive portrayal of 'domestic' Islam is mostly restricted to the quality press. The reason why public communication does not focus more on domestic Islam is the fact that 9/11 first of all triggers a debate on Swiss banking and not on Swiss Muslims. This way, attention in Switzerland first focuses on the attempts of the Bush administration – in the context of the 'war on terror' – to control the financial sources of the al Qaeda network. In this context, discussion intensifies on the role of the Swiss financial sector as a possible 'safe haven' or transit for money stemming from or connected to terrorists. Still sensitized by a decade of intense and controversial debate about the role of the Swiss financial sector during World War II, the Swiss elite perceives this new discussion as (yet another) attack on the financial sector and gives this issue more room than questions of Muslims in Switzerland. As Figure 3.2 clearly illustrates, there are no resonant debates on Swiss Muslims in the 2001-2004 phase.

This, however, changes fundamentally after the attacks in Madrid in March 2004. Increasingly, coverage focuses on the threat Islamic terrorism presents not only to Spain or Europe but to Switzerland and on how to deal with terrorists. It is in this context that the Muslim minority in Switzerland is first made a problem, as the capacity and the willingness of Muslims to integrate are called into question. Actors that contribute to this problematisation are mainly the Swiss People's Party (SVP) and other parties of the radical right and – partially – the Christian Democrats. The problematisation of the Muslim minority in Switzerland is mainly linked to religious symbols (minarets and headscarves). In discussions both in the mass media and in parliament, frames dominate which, on the one hand, problematise the limits of the rule of law and its tolerance towards Islam and, on the other hand, construe Islamic fundamentalism ('Islamismus') as a threat to Swiss identity and security.

We can show this quite accurately by analysing such *domestic* communication events in light of their 'core frames' (for each communication event). When comparing the core frames over time, we can see that before 9/11 – and even more strikingly before Madrid – core frames dominate that depict Muslims living in Switzerland as victims of inadequate integration (policies) and that highlight the question of integration. After Madrid, however, frames depicting Muslims as perpetrators and suggesting an increasing threat to Switzerland through Muslims unwilling or unable to integrate into Swiss society become dominant. In analogy to the threat perception during the Cold War, these frames construct the gloomy figure of the 'Fifth Column'. This triggers a broad discussion of the basis of the democratic rule of law. While members of the SVP in particular claim that the constitutional state is threatened by the Muslim minority, opponents of the SVP counter this claim by arguing that it is exactly this campaign-like problematisation of Muslims with its rigid definition of who belongs to Swiss society (politicization of ethnicity) which threatens the democratic postulate of equality.

Because of this, Switzerland currently faces a fundamental conflict. Since the outcome of this conflict is not clear yet, it is important to look at the quality of this conflictive discussion. From a democratic theory perspective, the quality of a debate can also be measured by the way under which circumstances a political 'problem' is constituted, how political actors react to and how they intensify debates in the mass media, and how the political process as such is affected by the problematisation in the mass media.

The problematisation of Swiss Muslims in public communication does have an impact on the political system and the political process, but to a varying degree. Considering parties and their chances at elections, the effect of this problematisation is obvious because the SVP, the party which most strikingly uses the problematisation of the 'Other' in general and Muslims in particular for political campaigns, receives broad electoral support. This solidified the SVP's position as by far the biggest party in Switzerland in the general elections in October 2007.[8] As recent survey data of more than 2,000 voters show (Lutz 2007: 29-32), the complex 'foreigners, integration, asylum' was mentioned the 'most important' problem by 26 per cent, by far the largest category (social security was mentioned by 16 per cent, climate change and ecology by 15 per cent). Also, the SVP clearly holds the 'issue ownership' (Walgrave and de Swert, 2007) of the problemations

---

8   The 'new' Swiss People's Party alongside the social movement organisation AUNS (Aktion für eine Unabhängige und Neutrale Schweiz [Action for an Independent and Neutral Switzerland]) is gaining increasing importance since the 1990s. Parallel to this, the 'old' SVP transforms itself from an agrarian, conservative party (which, albeit with limited success, had formed part of the government since 1929) into a highly competitive and successful party of the populist radical right in Switzerland (Skenderovic, 2007a: 166f., Mudde, 2007: 57-8; see also Udris and Imhof, 2009).

of foreigners and ethnic minorities – those who hold these groups as the main problem believe that the SVP is the party that is most competent to fix it.

In order to influence the political process (e.g. revision of existing laws), this electoral success would have to be transformed into majorities (parliament, popular votes). This is only partially the case. There are a number of postulates and debates in parliament that problematise the Muslim minority and aim at curtailing their rights; but all these postulates have been rejected by the government and majorities in parliament.

However, in Switzerland's 'direct democracy' political system, political campaigns can also influence the legislative process via referenda and initiatives. One example was the government's proposal to liberalise naturalisation laws, which was rejected by popular vote in 2004 as a result of a campaign (mainly led by the SVP) that had successfully stoked fears of Islam. More recently, the SVP and other radical right actors have launched a popular initiative proposing a ban on the building of minarets in Switzerland (minarets being regarded as symbols of militant Islam), which has so far received the support of over 100,000 citizens (i.e. about two per cent of the electorate, which is the necessary quorum for any initiative). Should a majority of voters accept this initiative – unlikely given the broad alliance against this initiative and given the overall differentiated coverage in the media where views critical of this initiative dominate – Swiss citizens would establish a law that would have a big and direct impact on the Muslim minority in Switzerland.

All in all, this means that the problematisation of Muslims with political campaigns has been successful so far only on the level of electoral success. Parliament so far has 'resisted' the problematisation of Muslims by the SVP through the mass media by not implementing new or toughening existing laws that would curtail rights of the Muslim minority. But will this hold for the future? First of all, several new postulates are currently pending in parliament that problematise Muslims. Second, the 'minaret initiative' will be high on the media and political agenda in the future. But if it is rejected – and there are good reasons to assume this – media attention to Muslims is expected to significantly decrease.

In short, the problematisation of Muslims is – speaking in terms of the policy cycle – in the input phase of the political process. If we choose a metaphor for this dynamic media–policy connection (see Yanovitzky, 2007), it would be that the 'problem' is knocking on the door of the political system increasingly loud but the political system has not opened it yet. Especially if media attention decreases again after the vote on the 'minaret initiative', it becomes rather unlikely that the political system will react with populist ad-hoc solutions. This way, the problematisation of Muslims would eventually lose its salience. Of course, this requires that political actors and the media lead reasoned debates.

Conclusion

This chapter took the alleged problematisation of Muslims in Switzerland as a starting point. In the first part, we embedded this question into the general question of 'boundary work' in a society, asking when and to what extent foreigners and ethnic minorities are made a problem. On the basis of a database including the largest 'communication events' per year, we showed that the affected groups mirror not only institutional frameworks (and immigration policies) (e.g. reaction to labour migration). Also, the problematisation of foreigners and ethnic minorities is a discontinuous process reflecting periods of uncertainty and orientation crisis. In addition to that, the growing conflict intensity in Switzerland since the 1990s and the success of the SVP, the radical right-wing party that successfully brings 'identity politics' to the fore, both lead to a shift towards issues on integration. In this context, it is mainly Muslims – not necessarily other minorities – that become the focus of attention.

Of course, there are no easy answers as to why it is Muslims that are problematised the most. One correspondence with media coverage is the strong link between attention to 'global Islam' and 'domestic Islam'. Overall, the media coverage of Muslims is defined by the intense focus on international wars and conflicts as well as their corresponding frames ('War on terror, 'clash of civilizations'). However, there is not a simple correspondence. Because of political and historical path-dependencies, 9/11 only briefly increases the attention to Muslims in Switzerland and shifts towards the role of Swiss banks as possible safe havens for terrorists instead. But another 'key event', the attacks in Madrid, intensifies the attention. The according frames, which suggest a threat to Europe by Islamic terror, create a window of opportunity which is actually used by certain political actors. Mainly the SVP uses it for the problematisation of Muslim minorities in Switzerland, for the discussion of a clash of values ('Religion vs. Democracy', 'Freedom of opinion vs. Respect for religious beliefs') and for the spread of threat scenarios ('Threat of Islamic Terror').

We can only outline the reasons for this development. One important reason is certainly the fact that, with the Swiss People's Party, an established and influential political actor has chosen the problematisation of Muslims as a central tool for its political campaigns. The SVP benefits from novel 'media logics', which become more marked with the commercialisation of the media system (for this point see Mazzoleni, 2008; Mudde, 2004). In the competition over circulation and viewing rates and under pressure from competitors, these commercialised media willingly offer a platform, even where the editorial department does not share the party's political ideas.

However, this only partially explains the political success of the problematisation of Muslims in Switzerland's political communication. A more thorough explanation would, in our view, have to take into account the growing loss of orientation within Swiss society. The end of the Cold War and its clearly defined fronts, the debate around accession to the EU dividing Swiss society, plus an increasing social disparity in the wake of neoliberal politics have plunged Swiss society into a veritable crisis of orientation. This creates a window of opportunity for those populist actors which promise clear cut boundaries of belonging and simple solutions to its own people by means of a generalising problematisation of the 'other' (here, in the guise of Muslims).

But populist actors do not always have a long life span, and their reputation is fragile. After the electoral breakthrough, attention now seems to shift onto the electoral persistence and thus the internal workings of the party itself (Mudde, 2007: 301-302). After the SVP's charismatic leader, Christoph Blocher, was denied re-election into the Federal Govenment by Parliament in late 2007, the SVP has been increasingly labelled as an incoherent party with major internal struggles. This has already led to a breakaway and the founding of a new party which aims more at the centre of the political spectrum. If the SVP is losing its credibility as an effective party, then its political campaigns will lose their attractiveness. In the end, this would enhance the chance for a more differentiated debate about the situation of the Muslim minority in Switzerland.

References

Alexander, J.C. (2006), *The Civil Sphere*, Oxford: Oxford University Press.

Behloul, S.M. and Lathion, S. (2007), 'Muslime und Islam in der Schweiz: viele Gesichter einer Weltreligion', [Muslims and Islam in Switzerland: many facets of a world religion] in M. Baumann and J. Stolz (eds), (2007) *Eine Schweiz – viele Religionen* [One Switzerland – many religions], Bielefeld: Transcript.

Betz, H. (2007), 'Against the "Green Totalitarianism": Anti-Islamic Nativism in Contemporary Radical Right-Wing Populism in Western Europe' in C. Schori Liang (ed.), *Europe for the Europeans: The Foreign and Security Policy of the Populist Radical Right*, Aldershot: Ashgate.

Betz, H. and Johnson, C. (2004), 'Against the Current – Stemming the Tide: The Nostalgic Ideology of the Contemporary Radical Populist Right', *Journal of Political Ideologies*, 9 (3): 311-27.

Bovay, C. (2004), *Religionslandschaft in der Schweiz* [Religious landscape in Switzerland], Neuchâtel: Federal Office for Statistics.

Buomberger, T. (2004), *Kampf gegen unerwünschte Fremde. Von James Schwarzenbach zu Christoph Blocher* [Fight against the unwanted Other. From James Schwarzenbach to Christoph Blocher], Zurich: Orell Füssli.

D'Amato, G. and Skenderovic, D. (2009), 'From Outsider to Playmakers: Radical Right-Wing Populist Parties and Swiss Migration Policy', in M.A. Niggli (ed.), *Right-wing Extremism in Switzerland: National and International Perspectives*, Baden-Baden: Nomos (Studien zur Schweizer Politik, 2).

D'Haenens, L. and Bink, S. (2006), 'Islam in the Dutch press: with special attention to the Algemeen Dagblad', *Media, Culture and Society*, 29 (1): 135-49.

Dubiel, H. (1998), 'Cultivated Conflicts', *Political Theory*, 26 (2): 209-20.

Eisenegger, M. (2005), *Reputation in der Mediengesellschaft: Konstitution – Issues Monitoring Issues Management* [Reputation in the media society: Constitution – Issues Monitoring – Issues Management], Wiesbaden: VS Verlag.

Entman, R. (1999), 'Framing: Toward Clarification of a Fractured Paradigm', *Journal of Communication*, 43 (4): 51-8.

Ettinger, P. and Imhof, K. (2007), Religionen in der medienvermittelten Öffentlichkeit der Schweiz' [Religions in mass mediated public communication], in M. Baumann and J. Stolz (eds) *Eine Schweiz – viele Religionen* [One Switzerland – Many Religions], Bielefeld: Transcript.

Habermas, J. (2006), 'Political Communication in Media Society: Does Democracy Still Enjoy an Epistemic Dimension? The Impact of Normative Theory on Empirical Research', *Communication Theory*, 16 (4): 411-26.

Hirschman, A. (1994), 'Social Conflicts as Pillars of Democratic Market Society', *Political Theory*, 22 (2): 203-18.

Imhof, K. (1993), 'Vermessene Öffentlichkeit – vermessene Forschung?', [Measured public sphere – impudent research?] in K. Imhof and H. Kleger and G. Romano (eds) *Zwischen Konflikt und Konkordanz: Analyse von Medienereignissen in der Schweiz der Vor- und Zwischenkriegszeit* [Between Conflict and Concordance. Analysis of media events in Switzerland in the era before the war and between the wars], Zurich: Seismo.

Imhof, K. (2006a), Mediengesellschaft und Medialisierung' [Media Society and Mediatisation], *Medien & Kommunikationswissenschaft M & K*, 54 (2), 191-215.

Imhof, K. (2006b), 'Sonderfall Schweiz' [Switzerland – a special case], *Swiss Journal of Sociology*, 32 (2): 197-223.

Imhof, K. (2008), 'Theorie der Öffentlichkeit als Theorie der Moderne' in C. Winter, et al. (eds) *Theorien der Kommunikations- und Medienwissenschaft. Grundlegende Diskussionen, Forschungsfelder und Theorieentwicklungen* [Theories of communication and mass media research. Fundamental discussions, research fields and theory work], Wiesbaden: VS Verlag für Sozialwissenschaften, pp. 65-89.

Imhof, K. (2009), *Öffentlichkeit und Krise: Theorie des sozialen Wandels* [Public Sphere and Crisis: Theory of Social Change], Frankfurt: Suhrkamp.

Imhof, K. and Udris, L. (2009), 'Conflict, the Media and the Far Right: Theoretical Foundations and Empirical Evidence from the Case of Switzerland', in F. Virchow (ed.) *Media and the Far Right in Contemporary Europe – Theoretical Considerations and Case Studies (Working Title)*, London: Taylor & Francis.

Kamber, E. and Schranz, M. (2001), 'Die Wahrnehmung des Fremden in deutsch-schweizerischen Medien' [The perception of the Other in German-speaking media], in H.-J. Hoffmann-Nowotny (ed.) *Das Fremde in der Schweiz: Ergebnisse soziologischer Forschung* [The Other in Switzerland: Results From Sociological Research], Zurich: Seismo.

Koopmans, R. and Olzak, S. (2004), 'Discursive Opportunities and the Evolution of Right-wing Violence in Germany', *American Journal of Sociology*, 110 (1): 198-230.

Kreis, G. (2005), 'Israelkritik und Antisemitismus – Versuch einer Reflexion jenseits von Religion und Nationalität' [Criticism of Israel and Anti-Semitism – Attempt to reflect beyond religion and nationality], *Tel Aviver Jahrbuch für deutsche Geschichte* [Tel Aviv: Yearbook for German History], XXXIII.

Kriesi, H. et al. (2006), 'Globalization and the Transformation of the National Political Space: Six European Countries Compared', *European Journal of Political Research*, 45 (6): 921-56.

Lucht, J. and Udris, L. (2009), 'Transformation of media structures and media content. A diachronic analysis of five European countries', *International Communication Association (ICA), Keywords in Communication* [Online]. Chicago, May 21-25, Available at: www.icahdq.org.

Lutz, G. (2007), *Eidgenössische Wahlen 2007. Wahlteilnahem und Wahlentscheid* [General elections 2007, Election participation and decision], Lausanne: Selects – FORS.

Mahnig, H. and Piguet, E. (2003), 'Die Immigrationspolitik der Schweiz von 1948 bis 1998: Entwicklung und Auswirkungen' [Immigration policies of Switzerland from 1948 to 1998: development and effects], in H. Wicker et al. (eds) *Migration und die Schweiz. Ergebnisse des Nationalen Forschungsprogramms 'Migration und interkulturelle Beziehungen'* [Migration and Switzerland. Results from the National Research Programme 'Migration and Intercultural Relations'], Zurich: Seismo (Sozialer Zusammenhalt und kultureller Pluralismus).

Mazzoleni, G. (2008), 'Populism and the Media', in D. Albertazzi and D. McDonnell (eds), *Twenty-First Century Populism. The Spectre of Western European Democracy*, Basingstoke: Palgrave.

Mazzoleni, O. (2003), *Nationalisme et populisme en Suisse: la radicalisation de la 'nouvelle' UDC* [Nationalism and Populism in Switzerland: the Radicalization of the 'New' Swiss People's Party], Lausanne: Presses polytechniques et universitaires romandes (Collection le savoir suisse; 9).

Mudde, C. (2004), 'The Populist Zeitgeist', *Government and Opposition*, 39 (3): 541-63.

Mudde, C. (2007), *Populist Radical Right Parties in Europe*, Cambridge: Cambridge University Press.

Nacos, B. and Torres-Reyna, O. (2007), *Fueling our Fears. Stereotyping, Media Coverage, and Public Opinion of Muslim Americans*, Lanham: Rowman & Littlefield.

Niederberger, J. (2004), *Ausgrenzen, Assimilieren, Integrieren. Die Entwicklung einer schweizerischen Integrationspolitik* [Exclude, Assimilate, Integrate. The Development of a Swiss Immigration Policy], Zurich: Seismo.

Poole, E. (2000), 'Framing Islam: an Analysis of Newspaper Coverage of Islam in the British Press', in K. Hafez (ed.), *Islam and the West in the Mass Media. Fragmented Images in a Globalizing World*, Cresskill, NJ: Hampton Press.

Rydgren, J. (2007), 'The Sociology of the Radical Right', *Annual Review of Sociology*, 33: 241-62.

Schranz, M. and Imhof, K. (2003), 'Muslime in der öffentlichen Kommunikation' [Muslims in public communication], in Schweizerische Akademie der Geistes- und Sozialwissenschaften (eds), *Muslime in der Schweiz* [Muslims in Switzerland], Bern: Schweizerische Akademie der Geistes- und Sozialwissenschaften.

Simmel, G. (1971), 'The Stranger', in G. Simmel (ed.) [1908], *On Individuality and Social Forms*, Translated from German by Donald N. Levine, Chicago: Chicago University Press.

Skenderovic, D. (2007), 'Immigration and the Radical Right in Switzerland: Ideology, Discourses and Opportunities', *Patterns of Prejudice*, 41 (2): 155-76.

Skenderovic, D. (2009), *The Radical Right in Switzerland: Continuity and Change, 1945-2000*, Oxford and New York: Berghahn Books.

Späti, C. (2005), 'Kontinuität und Wandel des Antisemitismus und dessen Beurteilung in der Schweiz nach *1945*' [Continuity and Change of Anti-Semitism and Its Assessment in Switzerland after 1945], *Schweizerische Zeitschrift für Geschichte [Swiss Journal of History]*, 55 (4): 419-40.

Udris, L. (2007), 'Medienwahlkampf 2007: Alles drehte sich um die SVP' [Election campaign 2007 in the media: everybody was focused on the SVP], Medienheft, [Online] 28 (December 2007), http://www.medienheft.ch/politik/bibliothek/p07_UdrisLinards.html, accessed March 23, 2009.

Udris, L. and Eisenegger, M. (2007), 'Jewish and Muslim Actors in the Media: Presentation of a Method for Capturing Typifications of Inclusion and Exclusion', *Relation: Zeitschrift für vergleichende Kommunikationsforschung* (New Series), 2: 121-37.

Walgrave, S. and Swert, K. (2007), 'Where Does Issue Ownership Come From? From the Party or from the Media? Issue-party Identifications in Belgium, 1991-2005', *The Harvard International Journal of Press/Politics*, 12 (1): 37-67.

Wimmer, A. (2008), 'The Making and Unmaking of Ethnic Boundaries: A Multilevel Process Theory', *American Journal of Sociology*, 113 (4): 970-1022.

Yanovitzky, I. (2007), 'The Dynamics of the Media–Policy Connection', in D.A. Graber (ed.) *Media Power in Politics. 5th Edition*, Washington, DC: CQ Press, pp. 278-90.

Chapter 4

Muslims in Print, or Media Events as Nodes of Cultural Conflict[1]

Henrik Bødker

The international reactions to the Muhammad cartoons published by the Danish national daily *Jyllandsposten* on 30 September 2005, sparked off what some called Denmark's worst foreign affairs crisis since World War II. In terms of Danish politics and public debates, this was seen by some as a welcome end to a hitherto too lenient and relativistic attitude to values and practices seen to undermine Danish and Western traditions of secularism and freedom of speech. Others saw the event as an opportunity for Denmark to face up to an increasingly multicultural and global reality where notions of equality, tolerance, nationality and security were in need of re-interpretation. Yet, although the domestic and inter- or transnational developments in this affair cannot be fully separated, the following focuses primarily on the affair as it played into processes within the Danish newspaper market with special reference to the two major competing national dailies *Jyllandsposten* and *Politiken*. These processes are, for reasons that will be presented shortly, seen in relation to the Danish MP Naser Khader, who is of Syrian-Palestinian descent. The cartoons of Muhammad and the public figure of Khader are therefore the title's 'Muslims in print'.

The cartoon affair pushed religion to a more central role in the public realm in Denmark. The role of religion in the public spaces had, however, been steadily climbing the public agenda with the growing visibility of voters and politicians whose demarcations between politics and religion were different from that of most ethnic Danes. Khader had a background, which to most ethnic Danes was characterised by such a difference. His public presence and political conduct was, however, seemingly devoid of religious content. This is why some perceived him as a model immigrant and this is also why his 'intervention' in the cartoon affair is an important part of the ensuing analysis. Denmark's secular political climate in large part explains why the public presence that religion gained as part of the cartoon affair called forth well-established notions of notions of modernity and

1   I wish to thank Professor Will Straw, McGill University, Montreal, for thoughtful and constructive feedback on an earlier draft of this chapter. This chapter, as well as Bødker (2007), grow out of the Danish research programme: "Newspapers and Journalism in Transition: The Printed Press as a Political and Cultural Resource", funded by the Danish Research Council for Culture and Communication, 2007-10.

its cultural and/or ethnic others within or outside Denmark. The fact that newer academic conceptions of modernity in Denmark have tried to incorporate religion (see Shantz, 2008) is yet to filter into the public debate.

It is, in this connection, important to underline the obvious but perhaps not always acknowledged premise that all such cross-cultural conflicts are to some degree mediated. Analysing cross-cultural conflicts is thus inherently linked to attempts to understand their mediation. One often cannot separate what we know about cultures 'directly' from what we know through media representations and clashes are thus to be understood as mediated cross-cultural conflicts and it is from this perspective that the Danish cartoon affair will be approached in this chapter. Such a starting point draws our attention to ways in which various forms of conflicts are underlying the construction of major media events. The following discussion of the cartoon affair seeks, on the one hand, to foreground aspects of the affair linked to conflicts within/between media and its publics and, on the other, to sketch out a more general perception of media events as important and perhaps necessary nodes of social and cultural conflicts.

Linking journalism to this perspective on media events it is important to note that predominant journalistic news criteria are interwoven with notions of conflict. Thinking in terms of conflicts (and oppositions) is thus an inherent part of the journalistic practices. There are a number of more or less obvious reasons for this: one of the most obvious is that news is often related to what sticks out, i.e. that which is extra-ordinary and/or norm breaking, a practice that is intricately linked to community-linked aspects of media (maintaining boundaries) as well as aspects of identification (something which I will come back to).

Another explanation for the conflictual character of journalism is the practice of staging opposing views and statements in order to 'balance' reporting. Such a staging, however, does not necessarily correspond to the actual weight and character of such opposing views. This is linked to the widespread practice of framing events as conflicts. Since no events can be completely isolated from their social and thus mediated contexts, it is often, at least in the final journalistic product, difficult to draw any clear lines between events and their framing. Larger mediated cross-cultural conflicts, or events, can, therefore, not be separated from their mediation. Or, put differently, they only exist as events through their mediation – and this was especially true in the cartoon affair. It therefore makes little sense to explain 'how the Danish cartoon affair became a 'mediatized public crisis' (Powers, 2008: 341). What I object to is separating the affair from its mediation and mediation is linked to audiences as well as a range of other 'participants'. I wholly agree with the editors of a recent anthology on the cartoon affair that 'we know too little about how the media today function in such transnational contexts' although their claim that an 'investigation of the ways in which such an event is mediated' seems to suggest that the event predates its mediation (Eide, Kunelius and Phillips (eds), 2008: 11). The mediated event is obviously linked to a range of concerns that predate the event; this is, as will become clear, precisely why it turns into an event in the first place.

A final note on the mediated character of such events concerns their presence across a range of media. Again, this may seem obvious but studies of such events often focus mainly on their presence in major and serious printed newspapers. This might be a remnant of hierarchies in the landscape of news in terms of both agenda setting and importance with relation to audiences. It might also be linked to methodological convenience of the printed press leaving behind well-contained and discrete objects of study that, in addition, are easy to obtain. Following an event across the entire media matrix is virtually impossible but it is very important to stress, certainly with regard to the cartoon affair, that a majority of the public arguably constructed meanings within spaces interspersed with a whole range of media. The cartoon affair was thus present as an event through TV news, TV interviews with the Prime Minister, TV debates between him and the leader of the main opposition party, the Social Democrats, various current affairs programmes on both TV and radio, various websites and, of course, a whole range of printed media from magazines to both serious and tabloid newspapers. A view through selected articles from established newspapers thus only reveals aspects of an event. Some of the main fault lines may, however, be visible in such articles.

The notion of media events as nodes of social and cultural conflict partly grows out of my work on the Khader, whom I will return to below, and partly from more general attempts to conceptualise media events. There are no set definitions of what it takes to turn more low-key stories across media/newspapers (common stories) into what may be termed events. And it might be noted here that the recent anthology *Transnational Media Events* (Eide, Kurnelius and Phillips, 2008) makes no explicit attempts at a definition either. However, Elmelund-Præstekjær and Wien (2008) list four main necessary criteria, based on case-studies, for a story to be deemed a media event:

1. The event must be appropriate for public debate, i.e. there must exist a range of legitimate positions as well as people willing to air and debate these.
2. The issues at stake must be, and this is linked to the first point, something that can be interpreted within a number of contexts or frames.
3. The event must also, at least in their study of a limited number of events, contain some deviation from, a break of, norms.
4. And finally, the event must be able to condense a complex problem into a striking image and/or draw upon a number of existing stereotypes (Elmelund-Præstekjær and Wien, 2008: 24-25).[2]

The cartoon affair was not part of this study but it seems to fit in rather well with all four criteria: the main legitimate positions we see on either side of the question of whether the cartoons should have been published or not, a question that was

---

2   This and all further quotes from Danish sources have been translated/paraphrased by the author.

framed within a context of free speech on the one hand and cultural/religious sensitivity on the other (the first two criteria). A break of norms was also part of the cartoon affair but not in the most obvious sense that the cartoons somehow broke with a tradition in which cultural issues linked to Islam had been dealt with less explicitly – and/or graphically. 'The drawings cannot', say Seidenfaden and Larsen (2006: 7), 'be seen as an isolated phenomenon in Denmark in the year of 2005. It is rather the case that the publishing of the cartoons appear as part of the normal arena of debate in Denmark, where Islam criticism takes up a lot of space'. The break of norms was, however, more clearly linked to the international reaction to the cartoons and Denmark, a reaction that ran counter to the perception that most Danes had of the image of their country in the wider world. Finally, and most importantly, the event managed to condense (the fourth criteria) a whole range of interlocked issues linked to religion, culture, immigration, violence, terrorism and security into a few images and whether these should have be made public or not.

These four interlinked criteria underlie the point that media events are to be understood as events, which – through some kind of trigger event – brings to the surface a range of important existing and divergent positions that are, or become, issues of the event. Such a view is close to the assumptions and result of my earlier work on celebrity politicians, exemplified by Khader and it is this that brings me to term media events as important nodes of social and cultural conflicts. Khader was, I argued, an important public figure precisely because his life trajectory traversed a number of social and cultural fault lines. While Khader to many was a prime example of successful integration and pragmatic politics, he is seen by some immigrants as someone who has totally abandoned his religious and ethnic background in order to access Danish society (a highly exposed house slave basking in the spotlight!). By relating to Khader one thus relates to politics. The construction of life narratives therefore cannot be separated from constructing politics, which brought me to the notion of Khader as a 'node' in a complex web of interlinked social and cultural conflicts and that this is an important element in understanding in many celebrity politicians.[3] A very good and wider known example of this is obviously Barack Obama. In the sense that celebrity politicians may be seen as ongoing media events in which the narrative takes the form of an ongoing construction of a life trajectory it is hardly surprising to find similar views in the literature on media events. In a Danish anthology on political journalism, it says:

> The media storm [hype or event] does not rage because newspapers of their own free volition can make it happen but because a range of very different and differently motivated interests are present at the same time and within a relative short period are willing to invest these interests in creating a narrative. The narrative is not created by the newspapers but by the common – or collective

---

3   This is based on a paper given at 'The Future of Newspapers' conference in Cardiff in September 2007 and published in Danish (Bødker, 2007).

– result of the fact that [a range of agents] manage to take actions and issue statements that can be interpreted as a way of maintaining the forward momentum of the narrative (Pedersen, 2000: 240).

This is much in line with the criteria above in the sense that it is stressed here that media events become events because of a range of people outside the media have strong and diverging interest in the issues at stake. This is important to stress because many views on media events tend to be too media-centric. In his very helpful discussion of the cartoon affair as a 'mediatised' cross-cultural conflict Powers rightly argues for the performative nature of such processes but wrongly – at least when it comes to the cartoon affair in a Danish context – that this was almost wholly 'reliant on and escalated by a series of performative acts by media institutions to maintain its emotional resonance' (Powers, 2008: 348). Obviously, the media have vested interests in such events but it needs to be stressed that such/most events are created and, not least, maintained through an interaction between various media and outside agents willing to contribute.

Within a Danish context there was a whole range of people – politicians, academics, commentators and religious leaders – outside the media institutions themselves more than willing to contribute to maintaining the momentum of the event. The Danish politician Khader was only one of these. It should also be noted here that the cartoon affair as a major media event was not really sparked off by the publication of the cartoons in *Jyllandsposten* but by a tour by a number of Danish Muslims in December 2005 to a range of countries in the Middle East where they 'presented a 43-page dossier that included the 12 original cartoons, in addition to three cartoon-like images that had net been published in any mainstream newspaper, several examples of anti-Muslim hate mail and a controversial interview with a Dutch member of parliament Ayaan Hirshi Ali' (Powers, 2008: 344). This indeed shows the inadequacy of simply treating the affair within a framework that stresses mainstream and transnational media. The affair grew into a major media event in Denmark in late January 2006 – almost three months after the first publication of the cartoons – mainly because of mediated international reactions that followed in the wake of the tour by the Danish Muslims. Powers writes that:

> understanding mediatized public crises *as* social dramas provides an additional level of analytic depth, pointing to the importance of examining social dramas not as singular events but as the unfolding of a series of occurrences that are typically narrated by media through the deployment of deeply cultural and ideological stories and conventions (Powers, 2008: 346).

I wholly agree with this, although Powers somehow only seems to demarcate the social drama as it is 'narrated by media'. The important point here is not whether we refer to such processes as events, rituals, spectacles, dramas or something else but whether we wish to focus on the interaction within media and other agents or whether we wish to restrict the analysis to the available texts. The notion of performance must here, I will argue, be linked more clearly to a conceptualisation of such processes as inter- or transmedia narratives seen in relation to the constellation of audiences.

Elmelund-Præstekjær and Wien (2008) talk about trigger events and maturation. It is to this development that various media and/or journalists contribute by interpreting either their own or the action of others and thus enter into either an explicit or implicit dialogue. A great deal of the media content making up the cartoon affair was thus also covering the coverage. In addition to being highly linked to various social and cultural fault lines pre-existing the event, such events are themselves also to be seen as processes through which positions are redrawn. They are, in other words, processes that allow agents both outside and within media to work through their positions. And some of this may be linked by processes in which journalists engage in what may seem a wholly inter-journalistic dialogue of competition and positioning. A good example of this occurred when Khader formed his own party in May 2007. This example also – at least indirectly – illustrates how Khader's role in the cartoon affair positioned him as a politician.

A highly economical journalistic move or trope when trying to understand people taking up new public positions is by comparison with existing or former political figures. And the possibility of constituting a historical break, the ability to embody various political, perhaps contradictory but seemingly idealistic values, the straddling of socio-economic and cultural boundaries, the relatively young age, and the ability to embrace a new medium pushed for a comparison of Khader with John. F. Kennedy.

'Khader is our Kennedy' wrote David Trads on the morning just prior to the public announcement of the new party in 2007 and continued:

> Naser Khader is something as rare as a real politician – he holds opinions, he has long-term goals, he manages to air pointed beliefs after which he makes compromises, but he never fails his fine democratic ideals. ... Khader is the closest we in Denmark are to a new Kennedy – with a smiling dedication, strong values, real feelings and first and foremost a colossal drive in relation to solving the fundamental political battle of the coming decades, namely to win the fight over the soul of young Muslims so they land in our democratic camp.[4]

Trads is well-known within Danish political journalism. He had held the position as editor of *Information* and had repositioned the fairly new free-sheet *Nyhedsavisen*. The comment setting up the Kennedy comparison appeared in Trads' blog on the homepage of this paper. Trads and/or his comparison thus became oft-used reference points, either implicitly or explicitly, in many of the articles that followed the development of Khader and/or his new party The New Alliance.

The point is not, it must be stressed, whether the comparison with Kennedy can be sustained on historical grounds. The public and journalistic myths of Kennedy

---

4   Avisen.dk, 7 May 2007.

live their own lives at a distance from the work of historians. This was clear later when Trads, confronted with his early characterisation of Khader, said that he saw the role of Khader as one 'healing the gap between Muslims and Christians just as Kennedy did between Blacks and Whites in the US in the 1950s'.[5] Most historians will arguably agree that the issue of civil rights for African Americans was forced upon the Kennedy administration by the press within a cold war context, and that the important legislative changes were initiated by Lyndon Johnson rather than Kennedy. It was, however, not such issues that were at stake when later articles used the Khader/Kennedy comparison as a way of evaluating Trads' ability to judge political developments. The ongoing coverage thus also became a process of positioning both journalists and newspapers.

A few days after Trads' blog an article in the major regional paper *Nordjyske Stiftstidende* opened with: 'It has been easy to be party leader during The New Alliance's first twenty-four hours. Naser Khader has been carried forth by headlines such as "King Khader" and has also been called a new Kennedy'.[6] The reference point that Trads' blog entry had set up thus made much of the coverage of Khader almost inseparable from covering the coverage of Khader. Many of the articles that I looked at therefore, by implication, somehow deal with the relations between politicians and journalists as exemplified by the 'case' of Khader. This meant that journalistic competences were constructed just as much as those of politicians.

Shultz (2006) is precisely focused on understanding identical or related practices in her aim to study 'the media's relations to each other, the media's relational practices and how these affect the daily construction of news' (p. 17). Shultz also writes that the competition between media and journalists 'often is something that cannot be related to the readers' (p. 169). The long cross-media narrative that makes up the construction of Khader as a public persona is full of examples of cross-references that may serve no other purpose than positioning journalists vis-à-vis each other and as such seem insignificant to readers. But although there is a measure of inter-journalistic strife based on various notions of professionalism somehow removed from matters of readership it might also be pointed out that the competition between newspapers (and journalists) are highly related to readership in the sense that it constitutes a constant effort to hold on to an audience by convincing them that their newspaper delivers the news and interpretations that they subscribe to. A part of being competitive is also a continuing concern with profiles and positions.

Shultz's focus on competition takes a slightly different direction in that she argues for the often-overlooked news criteria of 'exclusivity' (Shultz, 2006: 18) as a means of differentiation. Linking this to media events Elmelund-Præstekjær and Wien (2008) point to the apparent paradox that this news criteria seems to mitigate against media partaking in common stories and consequently argue that

---

5   Nordjyske.dk, 18 January 2008.
6   Martin Stein, *Nordjyske Stiftstidende*, 9 May 2007.

the criteria of exclusivity is being negotiated through framing (p. 21). Based on '232 selected articles from seven different newspapers from 15 January to 15 March' (Hervik, 2008: 60), referring to an earlier study, presents 'three broad frames employed for making sense of the case'. These three frames, where the first one is dominant, are:

- 'Freedom of speech as a Danish freedom';
- Freedom of speech; a Western universal human right threatened by Islam';
- 'Demonisation of Muslims and political spin is the issue; not freedom of speech' (Hervik, 2008: 60).

In terms of newspapers, *Jyllandsposten* was 'highly visible as' a 'champion' of the dominant frame whereas the last of the frames above was mainly 'sponsored by' *Politiken*, and I will return to this in more detail below.

The Danish newspaper market originally grew out of what was called the four-party system, which meant that each of the four major political parties – the conservative, the liberal, the centre-liberal and the social democratic party – each had their own both local and national dailies. Remnants of this system still exist in the sense that the two major dailies, *Jyllandsposten* and *Politiken*, have a lineage that connects them to the conservative and centre-liberal parties respectively. While most of the dailies have moved closer to an omnibus position ideological differences have never disappeared. In relation to a more general development of the political landscape, *Jyllandsposten* has since moved closer to a neo-liberal position while *Politiken* has started to lean more towards the social democrats (as the main newspaper growing out of the labour movement closed in the late 1980s). None of the newspapers have, however, any formal links to any political parties.

This has happened as the Danish political landscape has become more dichotomised with a Government (since 2001) consisting of the Liberal and Conservative parties (who need the Danish Folk party, a nationalist party, for parliamentary support) and the opposition headed by the Social Democrats. During the period in which this Government has been in power questions of immigration and culture have been relatively high on the agenda. This is largely due to the Danish Folk Party, which has been very good at setting the agenda as well as making their mark on the legislative process by being the preferred parliamentary foundation of the Government. This political development is an important background for understanding the unfolding of the cartoon affairs as a media event in Denmark.

Newer descriptions of the printed press underline, however, that there has been a more general process through which journalism has become more independent vis-a-vis the political system. The political agenda is thus increasingly set through a dialogue, or interaction, between the institution(s) of journalism and the political system. Hjarvard (2006) thus argues that the publishing of the cartoons must be seen not as an isolated event but rather as a continuation of developments within Danish printed journalism just as Seidenfaden and Larsen (2008) argued that the event had to be seen in relation to the political development. These developments were highly interlinked in the sense that the growing re-politicisation of the established newspapers was partly in response to a more polarised political landscape, and partly a more general response to the more neutral free newspapers. Hervik (2008) argues similarly, also with reference to Hjarvard, that the Danish government's success in framing the affair as an issue of free speech is to be seen in connection to this re-politicisation.

In the cartoon affair this meant that *Jyllandsposten* managed to set an agenda focused on free speech while at the same time positioning itself politically through a focus on questions related to immigration, an issue, which has been intricately linked to the polarisation of the political landscape to start with. *Jyllandsposten* here clearly aligned itself with the sitting government, which had stood firm in the formative parts of the affair in its refusal to meet with, or apologise to, offended Muslims. *Jyllandsposten*'s main competitor had throughout the affair, like the opposition in Parliament, tried to argue that what was at stake in the cartoon affair was not solely about free speech but also about aspects linked to multiculturalism, recognition, respect and tolerance (cf the three frames above). This was a position much more difficult to communicate in the sense that it said 'we are not against free speech but ...' which could be, and was, perceived as wavering. On an overall level this can be seen as the continuation of a strategic framing in which the 'freedom of expression' frame (Eide, Kunelius and Phillips (eds), 2008: 11) or what Powers (2008: 354) calls the 'clash frame', aimed at foreclosing positions differing from this.

Seen in relation to the notion of media events as nodes of conflict it might be argued that media events constitute welcomed opportunities for both media and other agents to carve out their positions in a more clear-cut manner. With regard to the cartoon affair such a view fits well with the findings of Kunelius and Nossek (2008) who, based on a 'survey of the coverage in 14 countries', conclude that the 'most dominant finding [was] ... that the news media largely acts as a domestication device' and that the 'national media events – through which the broader global event becomes meaningful – are dependent on local actors and their willingness to take part in the potentially global dramas' (Kunelius and Nossek, 2008: 258). And, linked to the role of media they add that '[w]ithout such willingness, the media seems to play a rather passive role'. This was indeed the case when *Jyllandsposten*, as the cartoon controversy was winding down in 2006, awarded its newly instigated Freedom of Speech Prize to Khader. Khader had made himself part of the cartoon affair, or media event, when he (re-)launched the organisation Democratic Muslims, which had the two-fold aim of arguing against fundamentalist Muslims and, through that process, aimed at presenting a more nuanced view of 'modern' Muslims accepting the democratic tenets of western liberal democracies. As such, Khader himself, having a Danish degree in political science, embodied a mediating stance between secular democracy and Islamic religion and culture.

Khader's 'intervention' in the cartoon affair was thus based on his ascription of religion to the private sphere while arguing that the loudest Muslim public voices in the controversy – both domestic and foreign – were not speaking for a majority of Muslims. The entry of Khader into the public debate was seen by many as a welcome addition in the sense that it seemed to fill in a position that had been left absent. However, although this initially may have seemed a mediating position, it was – in a sense – co-opted by *Jyllandsposten*. This, of course, cannot have come as a big surprise to Khader, who then, and later, was very good at analysing the marketplace for ideas in search of positions to mine for publicity. Looking back, Khader's intervention into the cartoon affair may be seen as part of a larger strategy leading up to the formation of his new party in the late Spring of 2007.

Back in 2005/6 Khader did not directly endorse the publication of the cartoons as such but argued that being part of a more secular democracy was based on an acceptance of certain values. In an interview in *Jyllandsposten*, he said 'I don't think that we in Denmark should be cultural imperialists. But I will ask Danes to be value-imperialists. And in practice this means that we must fight for everything that concerns freedom of religion, personal freedom, equality in terms of gender – and freedom of speech'. In the same interview he also said, much in line with the reading of media events proposed here, that the affair 'in reality meant that I became more clear with regard to my position'.[7] As a reason for awarding this prize to Khader, the spokesperson for *Jyllandsposten* said at the ceremony to Khader: 'Especially your undaunted exposure of and challenge to both the domestic and international Islamism has caught our attention and admiration. The formation of Democratic Muslims is just one of the steps towards this'.[8]

This can be seen as *Jyllandsposten*'s attempt to have the final word in a long dialogue within the Danish national media with regard to the cartoon affair. By instigating the prize and awarding it to Khader, *Jyllandsposten* arguably wished to cement its recurrent frame of the affair described above as well as underlining its position that they were not against Muslims as long as they – like Khader – had relegated their religion to a 'safe' private sphere. Khader's public position as a model immigrant served this purpose very well. That a well-established national daily newspaper through this wished to cement its position on free speech was a smart move within a market where every serious competitor somehow shared this value but simultaneously had to differentiate themselves. This was precisely what made *Jyllandsposten*'s move ingenious in a newspaper market where former modes of differentiation were waning. The affair, it seems, gave some of the main dailies – each with their own specific party-political history – an opportunity to (re-)position themselves in a new political landscape where old ideological boundaries increasingly were felt to be insufficient.

Much of the contemporary centre of Danish politics is made of a (neo-)liberal consensus based on individual rights, opportunities and obligations as well as notions of freedom. In this sense the major centre of Danish politics is beginning at least structurally, to resemble that of the where there is no fundamental ideological

---

7   *Jyllands-Posten*, 3 October 2006, section 1, p. 4.
8   *Jyllands-Posten*, 3 October 2006, section, 1, p. 5.

barrier separating the two major parties but rather questions of emphasis and focus. In Denmark, like elsewhere, this has meant that more traditional political issues have become less important while issues linked to culture and identity have become more central – linked to the development of the EU and globalisation in general. Seen in this light, the cartoon affair became an event through which the two Danish newspapers could reconstruct and reinforce their respective value-related positions on the newspaper market. Seen in relation to the papers' ideological genealogies, the attempt of positioning made by *Jyllandsposten* could just as well have been taken by *Politiken*. In this context, however, this would have aligned them with the sitting government, which was not in accordance with the newspaper's position. This goes to show that new forms of positioning may be more contingent – yet not less political for that. Going back to the notion of media events as important nodes of conflict such a view will, however, have to be linked to questions of how newspapers are interspersed in a larger media landscape with a whole range of audience constellations.

What is being (re-) aligned through media events are thus not only, as the discussion above may have suggested, newspapers, politicians and other public figures but rather a larger and more complex set of processes interlinking media, politicians and audiences around shifting kernels of values. In order to understand such an event fully, if that is at all possible, one would have to think of it as processes through which a set of important motifs circulate through different spaces of politics, culture and media. The question is not whether such an event is mediated (or constructed) but rather how.

Seen from this perspective, the main argument here is that the cartoon affair became such a forceful media event because, as was pointed out above in relation to the four criteria, it resonated somehow with issues felt as deeply important by a whole range of people. The event thus became an event because of this and part of it was a myriad of discussions over kitchen tables, at work and in pubs, discussions, which in a deep and fundamental sense were mediated in the sense that they took place against the backdrop of, or 'within', a whole range of interlinked media images. Whether these discussions, which in some degree or other were related to the positions being carved out in the newspaper market and the media landscape in general, were focused on the 'right' issues in a 'good' and 'nuanced' way is not to be decided here. The point is that the publishing of the cartoons turned into a media event because enough people felt that it was important and because the discussion needed to be taken. And because, as the first criteria listed above states, there existed a range of legitimate positions within which the discussions could take form and through that both sharpen and reshape such positions.

It is these less traceable instances of talk that parts of a growing body on the concept of cultural citizenship are trying to grasp. Although this term is hardly used with any consistency, and regardless of whether this in fact is a good analytical concept, it is safe to say that one of the concerns behind this work is that a focus on political activities emerging directly from more traditional perceptions of citizenship does not catch a range of important processes. Dahlgren (2006) writes:

'the character of civic talk is dynamic, open-ended and reflexive: self-creation takes place in part via civic participation. If we wish to be conceptually precise, we could say that "messy conversation" is part of the larger terrain of civil society' (p. 279). This coupling of reflexivity and self-creation through the concept of 'messy conversation' runs counter to the dichotomy of 'ritualising' and 'rationalising' put forth by Kunelius and Nossek (2008) in order to distinguish 'strong social functions' from practices of 'self-reflection and criticism' in relation to journalism and media. Such a distinction is only helpful insofar as one primarily seeks evidence in discrete media texts and not in the meanings negotiated between them or – not least – the many instances of 'messy conversation' taking place in relation to such media texts. The media are meaningful well beyond the individual text and judging from the debate spurned by the media and their internal relations in the cartoon affair there is no inherent juxtaposition between ritualising and rationalising. Such processes are, as this chapter has pointed in the direction of, wholly intertwined.

Media events cannot therefore be understood by simply focusing on the dominant frame (often defined numerically) of main newspapers. Although much of Hervik's (2008) analysis is focused on the dominant frame, he also shows that this is countered by other frames. And these exist, I will add, on various media platforms. Such contrasting frames might not be as wide-reaching but they are nonetheless there. Studying this at a level where such intervening frames disappear and where quotes from *The New York Times* and *Los Angeles Times* get to represent 'mainstream Western media' (Powers, 2008: 350) is hardly a true picture of the event. Seen in the light of the argument (exemplified by the Seidenfaden and Larsen quote above and stressed by others) that the cartoons ought to be seen as a continuation of the public debate on Muslims and immigration in Denmark it can rather be argued that this event precisely made the more general media presence of Islam an issue of discussion. This was, of course, the official goal of *Jyllandsposten* and as such they succeeded – although the force of the event was in no way anticipated. Surely, for some it cemented a right to be vocally critical of Islamism but for many others it called attention to a need to be more tolerant and nuanced in relation to culture and religion within a more globalised setting. And for many (or most?) it left a sharp sense of how difficult it is to reconcile conflicting interests and values and the question as to what this may mean for public debates in the future. That the affair left a climate of debate more open to insults legitimised by notions of free speech is thus only part of the story.

This is indeed a point often overlooked when the affair is analysed. The framing discussed above can thus only be argued to 'divert attention from troublesome issues' (Hervik, 2008: 59). If one ascribes to some Habermasian notion/ideal of dialogue according to which the dialogue was public and, furthermore, recorded. I am not saying that that is wrong but merely trying to point out that such a starting point may divert us from seeing some of the important mechanisms of media events. I do, however, agree with Hervik when he argues that Prime Minister Anders Fogh Rasmussen's refusal 'to meet with the Muslim ambassadors [early in the unfolding of the affair] from a neo-conservative perspective is not a blunder but part of fight to beat the opponent' and that it was unwise (Hervik, 2008: 75). It is true that a conflict frame is highly linked to liberal pluralism and its ideal of a plurality of voices rather than attempts at consensus through dialogue. Although liberal democracy indeed may be argued to have established itself as a contemporary ideological consensus there is, however, always a range of positions available on the market of opinions. Within the world of newspapers and journalism this has meant a shift from ideological differences towards a market differentiation based on shifting systems of values. But whether this forecloses more nuanced frames that favour more balanced views can hardly be determined on an overall level but will depend on the specific case and context.

I disagree with Hervik's underlying assumption that if the Prime Minister had interpreted the event 'correctly' he would have been able to see that his refusal was 'wrong'. This is, after all, politics, and pointing out, as Hervik (2008: 70) does with undertones of illegitimacy and conspiracy, under the sub-heading 'The Neo-conservative Bond', that Fogh Rasmussen and *Jyllandsposten* were somehow swayed by the American neo-conservatives only goes so far in furthering our understanding of the affair as a media event. Such a view does not pay enough attention to the fact that media cater to a range of political positions linked to views and tastes some of which are very different from those held by academics unthreatened by globalisation. One might wish that this was not so but that is hardly going to change the situation.

Since new media technologies have diversified former publics into smaller units based on a range of audience characteristics that cut across national, cultural, ethnic and religious boundaries it is hardly surprising that the cacophony of voices representing everything from private individuals to heads of states and international organisations did not coalesce into a coherent dialogue in Denmark let alone on a global scale. With the emerging media landscape as well as flows of people the cartoon affair will hardly be the last major media event that cuts across more and more media platforms as well as cultural boundaries. Such events may in one sense be a response to diversification itself because these offer opportunities for re-imagining belonging along national lines as well as other foundations of communities. This was certainly the case in the cartoon affair. It may also be, as this chapter has tried to argue, be because such media events constitute necessary occurrences for a continuous realignment of media, politicians and audiences along values clusters deemed to be central in various and conflicting ways.

References

Bødker, H. (2007), 'Politik som trykte liv' [Constructing Lives, Constructing Politics], *Journalistica*, vol. 1, no. 2, 15-29.

Dahlgren, P. (2006), 'Doing Citizenship: The Cultural Origins of Civic Agency in the Public Sphere', *European Journal of Cultural Studies*, vol. 9, no. 3, pp 267-86.

Eide, E., Kunelius, R. and Phillips, A. (2008), 'Contrpuntal Readings' in Eide, E, Kunelius, R. and Phillips, A. (eds) *Transnational Media Events – The Mohammed Cartoons and the Imagined Clash of Civilizations*, Gothenburg: Nordicom.

Elmelund-Præstekjær, C. and Wien, C. (2008), 'Mediestormens politiske indflydelse og anatomi' [The Political Influence and Anatomy of the Media Storm], *Nordicom Information*, pp. 19-28.

Hervik, P. (2008), 'Original Spin and Its Side Effects' in Eide, E, Kunelius, R. and Phillips, A. (eds), *Transnational Media Events – The Mohammed Cartoons and the Imagined Clash of Civilizations*, Gothenburg: Nordicom.

Hjarvard, S. (2006), 'Religion og politik i mediernes offentlighed' [Religion and Politics in the Public Sphere] in Lisbeth, C. (ed.), *Gudebilleder – Ytringsfrihed og religion i en globaliseret verden* [Pictures of God – Freedom of Expression and Religion in a Globalised World], Copenhagen: Tiderne Skifter.

Kunelius, R. and Nossek, H. (2008), 'Between the Ritual and the Rational' in Eide, E, Kunelius, R. and Phillips, A. (eds) *Transnational Media Events – The Mohammed Cartoons and the Imagined Clash of Civilizations*, Gothenburg: Nordicom.

Pedersen, O., Kjær, P., Esmark, A., Horst, M. and Meier Carlsen, E. (2000), *Politisk journalistic* [Political Journalism], Arhus: Ajour.

Powers, S. (2008), 'Examining the Danish Cartoon Affair: Mediatized Cross-Cultural Tensions?', *Media, War and Conflict*, vol. 1, no. 3, pp. 339-59.

Schantz, H. (2008), *Modernitet og religion* [Modernity and Religion], Aarhus: Aarhus University Press.

Schultz, I. (2006), *Bag nyhederne* [Behind the News], Copenhagen: Samfundslitteratur.

Seidenfaden, T. and Larsen, R. (2006), *Karikaturkrisen – En undersøgelse af baggrund og ansvar* [The Caricature Crisis – an Investigation of Background and Responsibility], Copenhagen: Gyldendal.

Chapter 5

The AKP Government in Turkey: Politics, Democracy and the Media

Jeffrey Haynes

The issue of the relationship between Islam and democracy is often debated, even if a definitive answer seems unreachable. Turkey is frequently seen as a positive example of the compatibility of Islam and democracy. This is particularly the case following recent democratic reforms and the experience of 'moderate' government, following the election in 2002 and re-election in 2007 of Prime Minister, Recep Tayyıp Erdoğan, and his 'post-Islamist' party,[1] the Justice and Development Party (Adalet ve Kalkınma Partisi – AKP). The AKP government appears to accept liberal democracy, although some claim the party's espousal of democracy is pragmatic and functionalist, not really a 'true' commitment.

This chapter focuses on internal and international factors that influence the AKP government's stance on liberal democracy. I explain that the ruling AKP government appears to have a rather limited understanding of democracy: as a set of representative institutions and a free electoral system. The chapter then examines pro-democracy pressures coming from the European Union in the context of the political role of the media. It also examines the serious rift between 'secularist' and 'Islamic' media in Turkey, and the implications for the country's democratic development. The conclusion is that while there are clear signs of an institutional commitment to democracy developing in Turkey, some important dimensions are lacking or at least still in short supply, including: civility and tolerance. These are significant obstacles to be overcome before we can envisage development of a recognisable *liberal* democracy in Turkey.

Politics in Turkey: From Atatürk to the AKP

The Republic of Turkey connects Europe and Asia, bridging a divide between (mainly) Muslim Asia and (mainly) Christian Europe. Sharing a border with several Muslim countries – Iraq, Iran, and Syria – Turkey is also a member of NATO, an organisation dominated by the United States and other Western countries. While the Muslim population of Turkey amounts to 99 per cent of the overall

---

1   The AKP is referred to ideologically in various ways: 'Islamist', 'Islamic', 'post-Islamist'. Its own preferred label is 'conservative democratic' (Turunc, 2007).

inhabitants,[2] the country emphatically rejected Islamic rule in 1923 in favour of an emphatically secular government. Now, however, Turkey's current government – led by a party with roots in political Islam, the Justice and Development Party (AKP) – finds itself caught on the horns of a dilemma. On the one hand, Western governments are, to varying yet significant degrees, suspicious of political Islam in office, a concern of course highlighted in recent years following 9/11 and the subsequent 'war on terror'. On the other hand, Turkey has an increasingly vocal Islamic constituency at home that dislikes Turkey's growing closeness towards what some see as a 'Christian club', the European Union (Gül, 2004; Walker 2004). The dilemma is that, despite decades of aggressive secularisation, Islam maintains a strong social (and to a degree, political) position among many Turks. It is this sense of adhesion to Islam which provides the AKP with much of its impressive electoral support. However, the country's political culture has been dominated for decades by a pronounced secular constituency, whose prominent groups are to be found in both civilian and military circles. How should the AKP proceed in office: defer to the demands of its supporters and many of those who vote for it and reintroduce aspects of Islam into public life or stick to the secular path which has not only dominated the country's development for over 80 years but has also brought Turkey within sight of EU membership?

In recent years, popular demands for more Islam in public life has seriously conflicted with the country's strongly pro-secular orientation laid down in the 1920s by the founder of the Turkish republic, Mustafa Kemal Atatürk (1881-1938). Since then, Turkey's political history has reflected two key aspects: (1) a strongly secularising and centralising state, and (2) the military's political domination. Turkey first democratised in 1950 but in the six decades since then the military has made periodic, dramatic political intrusions.[3]

Transition from military rule in 1983 exemplified the degree to which outgoing military regimes in Turkey consistently set the terms of their departure from power. Post-1983 constitutional amendments eradicated some legacies of military rule, including the ban on political activity by former politicians and on cooperation between political parties and civil society organisations, including trade unions and professional organisations. In addition, other constitutional exit guarantees, such as the president's power to block constitutional amendments, automatically expired in 1989. On the other hand, the progress of civilianisation – and hence democratic consolidation after 1983 – arguably had less to do with formal constitutional change than with informal practice and adaptation. The point is that, despite Turkey's current status as a 'partly free' country in Freedom House

---

2   Most Turkish Muslims are Sunnis, although around 20 per cent are Alevis of the Twelver Shia sect. The remaining 1% of the population includes Christians, Jews, and Bahais.

3   Turkey has had four military coups: in 1960, 1971, 1980 and 1997. The most recent was described as a 'soft coup', when the generals edged from power a government they considered Islamist, by using both public and behind-the-scenes pressure.

terminology, implying that the political system is characterised by a fair degree of democracy, the military retains high political salience in Turkey, which may put in doubt the country's long-term democratic consolidation. In sum, the long term structural effect on politics of aggressive secularisation and military significance has significantly influenced the country's political culture and made it difficult to develop an emphatically democratic regime. We shall illustrate this later in a discussion of the role of competing media – 'secular' and 'Islamic' – in the country's current process of democratisation.

The roots of the military's political involvement can be traced back to before the founding of the modern state of Turkey in 1923, to the time of the Ottoman empire (1293-1922). Since Turkey's founding, there has been nearly a century of often aggressive modernisation and secularisation, initially dominated by the leadership of a military hero, Mustafa Kemal 'Atatürk' ('Father of the Turks'). For 15 years, until his death in 1938, Atatürk aggressively imposed western-style civil law in Turkey. The new republic also inherited from the Ottoman empire a strong, centralised and highly bureaucratic state which Atatürk proceeded to mould to his own vision. Believing that Turkey's indigenous traditions – including, Islam – were unequivocal expressions of backwardness, Atatürk believed that national progress would come by emulating, absorbing and reproducing 'European' cultural values and political institutions. This dual ideological perspective was henceforward promulgated in state policies and programmes, defended not only by the politically powerful armed forces but also by an array of increasingly entrenched civilian secular interests.

The armed forces long enjoyed almost total control over their own processes of recruitment, training and promotion, resulting in the creation of a specific military culture facilitating the development of a specific role within Turkish society: the *über*-secular defender of Atatürk's revolution. The armed forces' institutional autonomy made it impossible to manipulate the military for political purposes from outside its ranks. In recent years it demonstrated a profound ability to maintain its cohesion and organisational integrity – a period when Turkish society itself became increasingly fragmented into competing classes, ethnic entities, religious groups, and ideological factions. Its political clout was demonstrated by the fact that the armed forces could – and did – close down political parties which it believed to be 'extremist' – that is, either too religiously oriented, too ideologically radical, or too separatist in orientation, for example, those connected to Kurdish interests. In addition, the military top brass periodically purged the officer corps with the aim of rooting out those suspected of sympathising with Islamist groups or Kurdish rebels.

National leaders, supported by the military, have also long shown little concern for the wishes of the national legislature[4] which has resulted in a lack of horizontal accountability between the leader and the legislature. Consequently, civilian

---

4 The Grand National Assembly of Turkey (Turkish: *Türkiye Büyük Millet Meclisi – TBMM*), usually referred to simply as *Meclis* – 'the Parliament').

political leaders have on occasion sought to make policy by decree – following discussions with senior military figures. In sum, Turkey's political culture and the legitimacy of successive regimes has been strongly moulded by the heavily politicised armed forces. As a result, Turkey is a limited democracy which has failed in recent years to make clear democratic progress.

Political Participation and Institutions

A cohesive political party system is often associated with democratic sustainability. Turkey offers an example of a party system that began with just two parties for the first contested election in 1950. However, over time, party numbers grew, a consequence of increasing political polarisation and ideological division. By the end of the 1990s, there were more than 30 parties, with ideological concerns ranging from those represented by right-wing, ultra-nationalist parties, through various Islamist groups, to those on the extreme left. By 2008, however, the number of 'major' and 'minor' political parties had fallen to 'only' 23.[5]

Since the 1970s, Turkey's party system has been characterised by volatility, fragmentation, and ideological polarisation (Ozbudun, 1996: 124). Volatility is exemplified by sudden and significant changes in the share of the votes that leading main parties acquire from one election to the next. Fragmentation is reflected in relatively high numbers of parties appearing in parliament (seven after the 2007 elections). Ideological polarisation among parties in parliament is reflected in parties such as the Great Union Party (Conservative Turkish nationalism) and the Democratic Society Party (Kurdish independence). The appearance of ideologically polarised parties is symptomatic of wide societal and political divisions not only found among the parties but also in the state bureaucracy, universities, schools, media and police. This is a symptom of an important transformation in the Turkish system over time: a sharpening left-right ideological dimension that encouraged the military to return to power in 1980, leading to the temporary cessation of democracy. The division endured although now it is more accurately characterised as a three-way split between 'secular', 'religious' and 'sub-national' (that is, Kurdish) interests.

How to explain Turkey's sharp ideological division? It seems certain that the loss of political efficacy for centre parties was exacerbated by the country's serious fiscal, social, and economic difficulties and pervasive state-level political corruption, which appeared to encourage some people to look to extremist

---

5   Major parties are defined as political parties that received more than 10 per cent of the votes in the latest general election (22 July 2007) and/or are represented in parliament. Minor parties are defined as political parties that have fulfilled the requirements of the Supreme Electoral Council (*Yüksek Seçim Kurulu* in Turkish, abbreviated as YSK) and their names were listed in the ballots. There are currently six 'major' parties and 17 'minor' parties, http://www.columbia.edu/cu/lweb/indiv/mideast/cuvlm/turkparties.html, accessed 28 April 2009.

solutions. Economic problems placed new limits on the largesse that parties were able to distribute among their supporters. This was a serious blow to their chances of picking up votes (Ozbudun, 1996: 130). The drift from the moderate parties in the 1980s and 1990s was also encouraged by the fact that most of Turkey's political parties were strongly centralised organisations, highly dependent on access to government patronage, dominated by their top leaders who were rarely challenged from below. The consequence was that Turkey's parties have not generally developed as bone fide, representative electoral vehicles whose purpose is to represent various societal interests. Instead, they primarily function as clientelist networks through which government resources are channelled to supporters. Parties tend to neglect essential organisational work, concentrating instead on media appeals and image-building with the help of professional public-relations experts. The result is that local party organisations are often dominated by small groups of activists whose power comes from the fact that they control access to senior leaders. Party organisations have tended to be loose, with membership records not well kept and branches only really springing into life at election times. The point is that such parties do not fulfil the necessary role of cohesive parties and are not, as a result, conducive to democratic consolidation.

The military government tried to overhaul the party system by manipulating electoral laws. In 1983, it introduced a statute proclaiming that a 10 per cent national threshold – and even higher constituency thresholds – was necessary for parties to take seats in parliament. The hope was that this would lead to the elimination of the most intensely ideological parties, leading instead to a 'manageable' system of two or three parties. However, there continued to be a weakening of the politically moderate centre–right and centre–left, with a rise in popularity both of nationalist, separatist and Islamic parties. For example, in the 1995 elections, the Welfare Party (*Refah Partisi*), then the main Islamic grouping, achieved 21.4 per cent of the vote, the ultra-nationalist NAP gained 8.2 per cent, and the Kurdish nationalist HADEP managed 4.2 per cent. According to Ozbudun (1996: 124), this result 'boost[ed] the combined extremist vote share to one-third and raised the possibility that Turkish democracy [was] facing a systemic challenge'. It also reflected the fact that some parties, including the Islamist *Refah*, put in much care and attention to grassroots organisation, a strategy which paid off in electoral success (Haynes, 1998: 141-6).

Turning to civil society, a lack of consultation by government and societal consensus about the way forward has meant that policies are rarely supported by most societal interest groups, consequently facing heavy societal resistance and often being unimplemented. Opposition is not only focused in the burgeoning numbers of political parties, but also in Turkey's relatively robust civil society. Groups within civil society, many of which are focused in the country's powerful trade union movement, tended to be characterised by a relatively high degree of organisational independence, and supported in their struggles with the state by the relatively strong and independent judiciary.

Following its electoral triumph in 2002, five years later in July 2007, the ruling AKP won an overwhelming victory – with nearly 47 per cent of the total votes (in 2002 they won with just over 34 per cent of the vote) – in free and fair parliamentary elections with the participation of 14 parties. Recep Tayyıp Erdoğan was re-elected as prime minister.[6] The result paved the way for the party's presidential candidate, Abdullah Gül, to win election in August 2007, despite strong objections from both military and secularist opposition.[7]

In sum, Turkey's party system has not over time been conducive to democratic consolidation. It is fragmented, volatile, and ideologically polarised. Parties are very often the personal vehicles of senior leaders. This does not encourage the development of essential representational and organisational structures linking leaders and supporters. Instead, clientelistism is the glue that holds the system together. Parties, such as the AKP, that do energetically recruit supporters at the grassroots have been most successfully electorally.

Democracy, the European Union and Islam

In his book, *The Crescent and the Star: Turkey Between Two Worlds* (2001), Stephen Kinzer examines social and political tensions in Turkey encouraged by the country's bid to join the European Union (EU). He explores the cult of modern Turkey's founder, Kemal Atatürk, and the country's historical background rooted in Islam. Kinzer also examines Turkish oppression of the Kurds, as well as the long struggle to free Turkey's government from the grip of the military. Finally, he highlights an issue of both regional and international significance: can Turkey survive as a secular state in the Islamic world? If not, what are the chances of other modernising Muslim countries – for example Indonesia, Morocco and Tunisia – being able to make the transition to European-style modernity?

Turkey reached an important turning point on 17 August 1999. On that day, more than 18,000 Turks were killed in a massive earthquake. The inadequacy of the state's response to the earthquake led millions of Turks to question the country's entire power structure. This was because the authorities had allowed thousands of death trap buildings to be constructed, and then stood by impotently when there was no disaster plan to put into operation when many of them collapsed (Kinzer, 2001).

----

6   Following the resignation of an AKP member of parliament in September 2008, the breakdown of seats in the 550-seat national legislature was as follows in November 2008: AKP: 338 (61.5% of seats), Republican People's Party (CHP): 98 (17.9%) ; Nationalist Action Party (MHP): 70 (12.7%); Democratic Society Party (DTP): 21 (3.8%); Democratic Left Party (DSP): 13 (2.5%).; Independent: 5 (1%); Freedom and Solidarity Party (ODP): 1 (0.2%); Grand Unity Party (BBP): 1 (0.2%); Vacant: 3.

7   http://www.freedomhouse.org/inc/content/pubs/fiw/inc_country_detail.cfm?year=2008&country=7508&pf, accessed January 2009.

In addition, powerful forces of globalisation are also affecting Turkey's political culture. This is manifested in the continuing controversy about the country's bid to join the EU. Coincidentally, the EU announced that Turkey was an official candidate for membership, in the same year as the traumatic earthquake (1999). A wave of ecstatic self-congratulation washed over the country, accompanied by solemn newspaper commentaries declaring it the most important event since the founding of the Turkish Republic in 1923. But the EU then laid out the conditions under which Turkey could become a member, and the military and its civilian (secular) allies balked. To repeal limits on free speech, grant every citizen the right to cultural expression, subject the military to civilian control, resolve social conflicts by conciliation, allow citizens to practice their religion as they see fit – suggestions like these froze the generals into immobility.

EU membership was the touted reward – *if* Turkey both democratised and made progress towards an acceptable, interlinked democratic and human rights regime. Currently, Turkey's political system is judged by Freedom House to be 'partly free', as Table 5.1 shows. The qualifying adjective ('partly') is awarded because the country is only slowly emerging from many decades of strong military involvement in politics and its democratic credentials are not yet unimpeachable. To encourage greater democracy, the EU seeks to apply both political and economic conditionality.[8] While Turkey, on the periphery of Europe, has long aspired to join the EU, for years the country's relatively poor human rights record gave the EU a defensible reason not to progress Turkey's membership application. Since the early 1990s, however, Turkey's democratic and human rights record has demonstrably improved, as Table 5.1 indicates[9] – to the extent that EU membership may now be a realisable ambition. Note however that as long ago as 1973, Turkey was awarded the same 'partly free' rating by Freedom House as it did in 2007.

There is however another important factor to note regarding current EU–Turkey relations. Following 9/11 in particular, many EU governments believe that it is better to have Muslim Turkey in the EU rather than, potentially, part of an anti-

---

8　Yilmaz defines conditionality as the 'effectiveness, visibility and immediacy of external punishments and rewards'. The EU has employed conditionality since the 1980s to achieve certain foreign policy goals – including, good governance, democratisation, better human rights, the rule of law, and economic liberalisation – in numerous transitional democracies and non-democracies (Yilmaz 2002: 83).

9　The American non-government organisation, Freedom House, reported that 'Turkey [had] registered forward progress as a result of the loosening of restrictions on Kurdish culture. *Legislators made progress on an improved human rights framework, the product of Turkey's effort to integrate into European structures.* At the same time, political rights were enhanced as the country's military showed restraint in the aftermath of a free and fair election that saw the sweeping victory of a moderate Islamist opposition party' (http://www.freedomhouse.org/template.cfm?page=22&year=2002&country=2309). In 2007, in addition, Turkey 'received an upward trend arrow for holding free and fair parliamentary elections' (http://www.freedomhouse.org/template.cfm?page=22&year=2007), accessed January 2009.

Table 5.1   Democracy in Turkey, 1973-2007

Year	Political rights (PR)	Civil liberties (CL)	PR + CL average	Freedom rating
1973	2	4	3	Partly free
1977	2	3	2.5	Free
1983	4	5	4.5	Partly free
1987	2	4	3	Partly free
1993	4	4	4	Partly free
1997	4	5	4.5	Partly free
2003	3	4	3.5	Partly free
2007	3	3	3	Partly free

Source: http://www.freedomhouse.org/template.cfm?page=15.

western 'axis of evil' characterised by extremist Islam. Partly as a consequence, in early 2003, the European commission recommended that aid to Turkey should be doubled – from €0.5bn to €1.05bn – in 2004-6. This can be seen as a calculated attempt both to encourage Turkey's AKP government to refrain from military intervention in Iraq as well as concrete encouragement to continue with domestic political and human rights reforms that would hopefully bring the country 'closer' to Europe (Osborn 2003). During 2007-2013, aid was scheduled to amount to nearly €800 million a slight fall on 2004-2006, but still a considerable sum underlining Europe's commitment to democratising Turkey (Ayvaz, 2008).

Some senior European figures were, however, strongly and openly opposed to Turkey's membership bid. For example, in September 2004, Frits Bolkestein, then the EU single market commissioner[10] and former leader of the Dutch Liberal Party, warned that 'Europe's Christian civilisation' risked being 'overrun by Islam'. In addition, he claimed, the EU was in danger of 'imploding' in its current form if 70 million Turkish Muslims were allowed to join. Thus, according to Bolkestein, Turkey's entry could undermine Europe's 'fragile' political system, ending all hopes for the continent's integration. Bolkestein claimed in a speech at Leiden University, the Netherlands, in September 2004, that demography was the 'mother of politics', that is, 'while America had the youth and dynamism to remain the world's only superpower, and China was the rising economic power, Europe's destiny was to be "Islamised"'. Quoting the Orientalist American author Bernard Lewis, Bolkestein warned Europeans that in a few decades Europe could

---

10   A spokesperson for the European Commission stressed that the Dutch commissioner 'was speaking in a personal capacity', http://www.rferl.org/featuresarticle/2004/09/ fdc6f2b0-c615-4ee1-a913-ca182c355a43.html, accessed April 2009.

become an 'extension of North Africa and the Middle East'. He also compared the EU to the former Austrian-Hungarian empire, which included so many different people from various cultures that it eventually became ungovernable. Bolkestein did however imply that a closer relationship between Turkey and 'Europe' would be desirable – under certain conditions:

> Although a secular state, Turkey is still rooted in Islam. As such she could spearhead a cultural continent with its Arab neighbours and thus become the main actor of a culture with its own identity but with whom others can share common humanist values. This idea does not oppose close and friendly association and collaboration with Europe; instead, it could foster a common front against all forms of fundamentalism ('Turkey-European Union').

Cardinal Joseph Ratzinger (since April 2005, Pope Benedict XVI) appeared to agree with Bolkestein. In an August 2004 interview with the French newspaper *Le Figaro*, Ratzinger commented on Ankara's application to join the EU. He claimed that 'Europe is a cultural and not a geographical continent. Its culture gives it a common identity. In this sense, Turkey always represented another continent throughout history, in permanent contrast with Europe'. It would be wrong, he believed, to equate the two sides for 'mere commercial interests' as it 'would be a loss to subsume culture under the economy'. Like Bolkestein, Ratzinger urged Turkey to assume leadership of the Muslim world, spearheading dialogue with the West (Kay, 2005).

Such controversial interventions encouraged a robust Turkish response. In December 2004, Turkey's then foreign minister (now president) Abdullah Gül claimed the 'carrot' of EU membership had been a key component of Turkey's 'process of political and economic reform that has been remarkably successful and has received widespread popular support'. Gül also claimed that Turkey was continuing to demonstrate strong and sustained commitment to internal political, social and economic restructuring that merited recognition by both the European and global community. Moreover, he averred, the numerous requirements for membership had now been addressed and thus fears expressed by figures such as Bolkestein appeared unwarranted. According to Gül, Turkey's Muslim identity would neither be a handicap nor 'political time bomb'. Instead, 'positive EU-Turkey relations will show that shared democratic values and political unity prevail, sending the message that a "culture of reconciliation" within Europe is at hand' (Gül, 2004).

The EU Commission was at the time of the interventions of Ratzinger and Bolkestein working on a report on the issue of Turkish accession to the Union. The EU enlargement commissioner, Gunther Verheugen, put forward a broadly positive verdict in numerous interviews. He suggested that by 2004 Turkey met various basic tests for EU membership, including a free market economy and pluralist democracy, conditions that had progressively strengthened since 2002. Moreover, the death penalty has been abolished and the Kurdish language recognised (Walker, 2004). In 2005, EU accession talks finally began with the intention of finding a *modus operandi* for Turkey to join the Union. But because of the controversy about Turkey's application, the talks were likely to be lengthy, without certainty of success.

Overall, however, there is no single picture of Turkey within the EU. Instead there are several, competing, images. On the one hand, Turkey is believed to constitute an essential part of European heritage, going back to Greco–Roman times and early Christianity. On the other hand, Turkey is believed to epitomise an extra-European fundamental strangeness, characterised by past hostilities, helping create an aspect of a negative but nonetheless common experience. Viewed through the lens of these preconceived images, the interpretation of current phenomena varies considerably. However, the interior developments in Turkey since 2007, including the notable election triumph of the AKP, have strongly increased the awareness in the European Union that Turkey does not really correspond to only one of the more or less popular images, but that the country is actually beset by various, sometimes conflicting, political, societal and cultural currents.

The AKP in Power: Relations with the Media

Domestic political developments in Turkey have widely been interpreted in the European media as reflective of a fundamental power struggle between 'secularists' and 'Islamists', characterised by controversies surrounding various issues, including (1) the presidential elections in 2007, won by the AKP candidate, Abdullah Gül (2) the first concrete measures to reform Article 301 of the Turkish penal code – which forbids reference to the genocide of Armenians in 1914 – from three to two years imprisonment, and (3) the AKP government's decision to no longer ban headscarves from universities (although overturned by the constitutional court in July 2008). Most recently, in July and October 2008 respectively, there was the closure case against the AKP (the Supreme Court eventually agreed by one vote [6-5] not to close the party, although it did deprive it of a considerable part of its public financing)[11] and official charges against a shadowy group known as Ergenekon,[12] as the latest and most extreme manifestations of this struggle. Just as the possible closure of the ruling party would have been a unique case in Turkish history, the charges filed against numerous personalities believed to wish to overthrow the present government, were also regarded as unprecedented actions

---

11   The charge against the AKP to be a 'centre of anti-secularism' not only threatened the existence of the governing party but was also combined with an attempt to forbid the continuous political engagement of more than 70 of its members, including Prime Minister Recep Tayyip Erdoğan and President Abdullah Gül.

12   'Ergenekon' or the 'Ergenekon network' is an alleged clandestine ultra-nationalist organisation in Turkey with ties to the country's military and security apparatus.

against a so-called 'deep state', whose existence was allegedly revealed by the Ergenekon conspiracy.

In very general terms, the continuing power struggle between 'secularists' and 'Islamists' is also widely considered to reflect a polarisation within Turkey between the 'new' Anatolian middle class (many of whom are regarded as 'Islamist' in the sense not only that their cultural roots are in Islam but also that their religious beliefs are central to their success in business), strongly supportive of the AKP since its foundation in 2001, and the 'traditional' Kemalist 'secularist' establishment. This constituency is mainly represented electorally by the Republican People's Party (Turkish: *Cumhuriyet Halk Partisi* or CHP) and in societal terms by the military. This polarisation implies that a monolithic image of Turkey is no longer appropriate – if it ever was.

Another blow to the monolithic image of Turkey came in January 2008, when the Turkish daily newspaper, *Sabah*, reported that the AKP government was 'preparing a reform which would allow foreigners to own 50 per cent of private broadcasters rather than the current 25 per cent'.[13] The existing law was said to be an obstacle in the 2007 sale of media firm ATV-Sabah (owners of *Sabah* newspaper). After several foreign firms unsuccessfully showed interest, ATV-Sabah was eventually sold for the minimum auction price of US$1.1 billion to local conglomerate Calik Holdings, owned by Ahmet Calik, an associate of Prime Minister Erdoğan. The sale was largely financed by two massive loans from state-owned banks, and included the daily *Sabah* (circulation 400,000),[14] the second largest national private television network, ATV, and several periodicals. *The Star*, a daily with a circulation of about 100,000, was sold earlier to another local group. Until its sale, *The Star*, too, had been critical of the government. Overall, the sales significantly boosted a steadily growing sector, often referred to as Turkey's 'religious media'. This sector already included the mass circulation daily *Zaman* (over 500,000 copies daily), and a host of smaller newspapers and private television stations.

A few weeks later, in May 2008, KanalTurk, the most fiercely antigovernment national television channel in Turkey, was sold to Akin Ipek, also an associate of the prime minister, Recep Tayyıp Erdoğan, for around US$30 (40 million Turkish lira) (*Milliyet*, May 15 2008). Together these sales consolidated a growing shift

---

13   The pro-business AKP had tried to reform the law on foreign ownership in 2005 but the bill was vetoed by the former president. Current President Abdullah Gül is a former member of the AKP and has a track record of approving legislation passed by the AKP-dominated parliament, see http://www.reuters.com/article/mergersNews/idUSL128096820080112, accessed March 2009.

14   The daily circulation of all 20 major national newspapers is about five million copies a day, in a population of more than 70 million. Hilmi Toros, 'Media-Turkey: Messenger Comes Under Attack', 7 October 2008, http://ipsnews.net/news.asp?idnews=44153, accessed March 2009.

in the balance of power in the Turkish media from opponents to supporters of the ruling AKP.

Tuncay Özkan, a 41-year-old journalist founded KanalTurk in 2004.[15] Both Özkan and his television station played a significant role in organising a series of mass public protests against the AKP's attempts to appoint Abdullah Gül to the presidency in the spring of 2007. Özkan was concerned that Erdoğan was seeking to control Turkey's flow of information through a dual strategy: (1) encouraging AKP supporters to enter the media, and (2) buying off the criticisms of mainstream – that is, 'secularist' – newspapers and television channels by not only offering lucrative state contracts to their owners but also promising them privileged access to privatisation deals. The result was that many among the thousands of demonstrators at rallies that erupted throughout Turkey in early 2007 regarded both the government and the mainstream press as equally culpable: the former ignored the protests and the latter under-reported them. The rallies had a key slogan: 'Biz Kac Kisiyiz?' ('How many people are we?'), that was also used as the name of the main website for the protests, www.bizkackisiyiz.com.tr (Jenkins, 2008).

Many people in Turkey regarded Özkan's accusations as hypocritical, given that he also 'sold out' to a known ally of the prime minister and his party. Yet, this apparent hypocrisy does not necessarily undermine the veracity of Ozkan's accusations. Many Turks would concur with the view that domestic press coverage is not only influenced by media owners' personal political sympathies but also by the possible impact of news items on their other business interests. This is not to suggest however that owners' individual control is so great that they personally endorse such decisions as a matter of course; it is instead far more likely that in many cases, such interference comes from zealous editors who, wishing to play it safe, directing or moulding coverage in a certain direction and not others.

For example, in June 2001, prior to the coming to power of the first AKP government, the then Interior Minister Sadettin Tantan, a man known to be strongly opposed to corrupt practices, launched an investigation against allegations of bribery involving some of his cabinet colleagues. He was quickly ousted from his job at the behest of the then Prime Minister, Mesut Yilmaz. At this time, the most powerful media mogul in Turkey, Aydin Doğan, was lobbying the government to increase his business interests through expansion into the energy sector, dominated by state ownership. Several prominent columnists on the mass circulation daily *Milliyet*, owned by the Doğan Group, wrote articles criticising Tantan's dismissal, the editor refused to publish them for fear of antagonising Yilmaz (*Milliyet*, June 7, 2001). 'More recently, after agreeing to give the Doğan Group an exclusive interview, Erdoğan was somewhat surprised when the journalists who came to his office were accompanied by a team of businessmen anxious to discuss the Doğan Group's bid for a privatisation tender' (Jenkins, 2008).

---

15   Özkan moved all stations to his new TV channel Kanal Biz. He was detained in September 2008 in the Ergenekon investigations.

Despite such issues, the Turkish media market, which is both expanding and lucrative, is highly attractive to investors. Turkey is characterised not only by a large and young population, but also by high – albeit recently declining – recent annual economic growth.[16] Companies which expressed an interest in ATV-Sabah, eventually sold to AKP associate, Ahmet Calik, included the Rupert Murdoch-owned News Corp. NWSA.N and Europe's largest commercial broadcaster RTL AUDK.LU (Ross-Thomas, 2008).

There are no reliable figures for the market shares of individual television channels. There are, however, robust statistics for newspaper circulation. Until relatively recently, the Doğan group controlled around 75 per cent of total circulation in Turkey, and its flagship daily, the mainstream – that is, secularist/nationalist – *Hurriyet*, was the country's best-selling newspaper. Recent statistics published by a Turkish media monitoring organisation, Dorduncu Kuvvet (or 'The Fourth Estate'), suggest that now the Doğan Group's share of total newspaper circulation has fallen to around 50 per cent, while that of newspapers sympathetic to the AKP has risen to around 40 per cent (Tunc, 2004; Jenkins, 2008).

Excluding sports dailies, Turkey's total daily newspaper circulation stands at around six million for a population of around 70 million ('Newspaper sales exceed six million mark').[17] According to figures published by Dorduncu Kuvvet for the week ending May 11, 2008, the best-selling daily newspaper in Turkey was *Zaman* with 860,000 copies, of which 845,000 are subscriptions. *Zaman* is run by followers of the exiled Islamic preacher Fethullah Gülen. Although Gülen has avoided endorsing any political party, *Zaman* is an outspoken supporter of the government and several AKP ministers are known to be very close to the Gülen movement (Jenkins, 2007; Krespin, 2007). *Posta*, a stable mate of *Hurriyet*, comes second with 645,000. *Hurriyet* is third with 532,000, while *Sabah*, recently purchased by Ahmet Calik, stands at 410,000. Significantly, *Zaman*'s English language sister newspaper, *Today's Zaman*, is now Turkey's best-selling English language paper with 4,500 copies. *The Turkish Daily News*, which for many foreigners was their window on Turkey for over 45 years and which is now also owned by the Doğan Group, sells only 2,850 copies a day. In other words, a pro-AKP newspaper already dominates the English language press in Turkey.[18]

The issue of media ownership and attendant questions about circulation and influence find focus in the relative significance of the 'secularist' versus 'Islamist' media and their differing ideological positions. This issue is not of importance

---

16   Global Economic Perspectives, http://turkeyeconomy.blogspot.com/search?updated-max=2008-08-18T05%3A35%3A00-07%3A00&max-results=5, accessed 28 April 2009.

17   Total readership is, however, certainly considerably higher, however, as many institutions and companies subscribe to a newspaper that is then read by more than one employee.

18   All figures from Dorduncu Kuvvet, www.dorduncukuvvetmedya.com, accessed March 2009.

only to media ownership questions but is also related more generally to the state of democracy in Turkey:

> Mainstream Turkish media loves to be alarmist about the creeping Islamization of Turkey. Especially since the conservative AKP (Justice and Development Party) came to power in 2002, fear mongering about the shariah imposers has become the main theme of the secularist press. Some fear that we will soon become another Iran. Others worry that we will turn into another Malaysia (which doesn't sound too bad, actually). Even the non-delusional secularists, which make up a tiny minority, are deeply concerned about the rise of Islam (Akyol 2008).

The reference in the quotation to 'mainstream' Turkish media is an allusion to the 'secular' media in the country. Many sections of Turkish media critical of the government say Prime Minister Recep Tayyip Erdoğan is bent on silencing them through intimidation – or controlling them through purchase. At stake is said to be the very existence of an independent media, beyond the control of Erdoğan's AKP government. The polarisation between the two was made clear in a recent 'row between Prime Minister Erdoğan and media mogul Aydin Doğan, who owns more than 50 per cent of the Turkish media as well as a substantial part of the country's banking and energy sector, guarantees gigantic media and capital support for any possible contender to Erdoğan' (Kalyoncu, 2008).

Some commentators claim that this was symptomatic of Erdoğan's 'war' against the secular media, including the media empire, the largest in Turkey, of billionaire Aydin Doğan.[19] Doğan owns the eponymous Doğan Yayin Holding A.S., controls six national dailies including the second most popular daily, *Posta* (circulation 645,000), two top TV networks including the all-news CNN Turk, and a group of periodicals. All of these pursue a secularist agenda.[20]

---

19   Doğan Yayin Holding A.S., through its subsidiaries, operates primarily in the media sector not only in Turkey, but also elsewhere in Europe, including Russia. The company engages in newspaper, magazine, guide, and book publishing; television and radio broadcasting; printing; news agency; foreign trade; and distribution and courier businesses. It is also involved in advertising, retail, internet publishing, music and entertainment, factoring, telecommunication, real estate, payment systems, logistics, and insurance businesses, as well as operating as an internet service provider (ISP). The company was founded as Miltas Milliyet Basim Malzemeleri Ithalat ve Ticaret A.S. in 1980 and changed its name to Milliyet Yayin A.S. in 1981. Later, it changed its name to Doğan Yayin Holding A.S. in 1994. The company is based in Istanbul, Turkey. Doğan Yayin Holding A.S. is a subsidiary of Doğan Sirketler Grubu Holding A.S. (http://investing.businessweek.com/research/stocks/snapshot/snapshot.asp?symbol=DYHOL.IS, accessed April 2009.

20   The second largest company is ATV-Sabah, which is made up of assets seized by a state body from the Ciner Group in 2007 and which was sold to Ahmet Calik in December of that year. Third largest is the media business of unlisted conglomerate Cukurova, which, it is claimed, is looking to sell a stake in its media assets.

In September 2008, Doğan's news outlets reported on the so-called Lighthouse case in Germany, which highlighted serious corruption charges against associates of Turkey's prime minister. The German-based, Turkish-run charitable foundation was accused of fraud and embezzling funds from Turkish workers and of siphoning millions of Euros to media and others close to the AKP in Turkey. Several members of the foundation were eventually found guilty. In mid-September 2008, a court in Frankfurt, Germany, jailed three managers from the charity's German branch, Deniz Feneri, for directing €18.6 million euros (US$26 million dollars) raised from the Turkish community in Germany into private companies (*The Economist*, 2008). Several people based in Turkey, including head of Turkey's media watchdog, Zahid Akman, were implicated as the masterminds, amid claims that the charity, whose founders are close to the government, might have funnelled funds into the prime minister's AKP. The Lighthouse case came within weeks of the resignation of Mehmet Yasar Ozturk, parliamentarian from the central Anatolian province of Yozgat and a deputy leader of the AKP over opposition-led allegations, also widely reported by the Doğan media, of bribery in a real estate transaction ('Turkey-press scan September 26').

Prime Minister Erdoğan achieved power in 2002 on an anti-corruption platform (in Turkish, the acronym AKP means 'white' or 'clean') (Bekdil, 2008; *The Economist*, 2008). He publicly accused Doğan of orchestrating a media campaign against him as revenge for his failure to obtain preferential treatment from the government for his other business interests, mainly in real estate. Denying the accusations, Doğan said Erdoğan was trying to muzzle the independent media. While Erdoğan sought to encourage Doğan into not reporting the case, Doğan showed that he was not prepared to be intimated by Erdoğan and spent days covering the Deniz Feneri (Lighthouse) fraud case (*Today's Zaman*, 2008). In the process, Doğan's media uncovered other corruption scandals involving leading AKP figures. Erdoğan is said to have 'told his supporters not to buy newspapers owned by Doğan Media Group and not to watch news channels owned by him either' (van der Galien, 2008).

The International Press Institute, the World Association of Newspapers, and the World Editors Forum informed Recep Tayyıp Erdoğan in a joint letter that 'the state's duty is not to silence critical reports, but to provide the media an environment where it can perform without fear of oppression' (Toros, 2008). The issue is likely to be mentioned in an imminent status report by the European Union – due in November 2008 – on Turkey's controversial bid to become the first full Muslim-majority country member of the EU. The EU was concerned about the Erdoğan/Doğan spat, not least because it appeared to show that the necessary degree of tolerance to make democracy work was still lacking in Turkey. The head of the EU delegation in Turkey, Marc Peirini, said in September 2008 that the EU was monitoring the situation between Erdoğan and Doğan. According to Peirini, 'We talk to both sides. The [EU] commission will make its final judgment at a political level' (Pierini quoted in Camlibel, 2008). He also said that judgement on the Deniz Feneri fraud case would distort the progress report that evaluates the country's one year performance on progress for alignment with the Acquis. In addition, Pierini stated that in order to have an effective democracy and to have the Copenhagen criteria fulfilled, what is needed is both the ballot box, which already exists in Turkey, and co-existence between different lifestyles. 'You need to have dialogue between the political forces and in a way of some form of modernization for the co-existence between different lifestyles because, obviously, that does not come automatically from elections. You have elections, you have a certain result, but you still have a problem of co-existence' (Marc Pierini, quoted in *Milliyet*, 26 September).

Conclusion

In November 2008, Erdoğan and his AKP controlled parliament single-handedly (338 of the 550-seat chamber, 61.45 per cent). The party also controlled Turkey's executive branch of government, and had a strong ally in the form of the president, Abdullah Gül, a founding member of the AKP. This was the first time that the presidency had been occupied by a non-secularist.

After years of inconclusive democratisation, Turkey seems to be at a political impasse. It seems most unlikely however that overtly authoritarian government would return to Turkey in the short-term, not least because this would make the possibility of EU membership recede into the distance. According to Ozbudun (1996: 126), there is a strong 'commitment to democracy at both elite and mass levels'. On the other hand, it has so far proved impossible to institutionalise democracy in a manner commensurate with democratic consolidation. While a high proportion of citizens vote in elections – well over 80 per cent on average in the seven national-level parliamentary elections since 1983 – the choices they make have not necessarily helped the cause of democratisation, as they tend increasingly to vote for parties that are regarded by their political enemies as actually or potentially extremist, including in recent years, the AKP (Günes-Ayata, 1994).

Democratic *persistence* is not the same thing as 'the genuine stability that flows from [democratic] consolidation ... Stability requires not merely a passive acceptance of the system, because there is no better alternative at the moment, but a positive belief in the moral value of democracy in principle' (Diamond, 1996: 77). This state of affairs is lacking in Turkey. The situation reflects the importance of both structural and contingent factors. Regarding the former, the long-term political influence of the armed forces has been an impediment to democratisation since the military has taken upon itself the role of political guardian since the republic's founding. The result has been that democratic progress has been continually circumscribed by the willingness of the military to intervene politically, if necessary to circumvent political outcomes sanctioned by the ballot box, such as the electoral victory of *Refah Partisi* in 1995 (overthrown in a military 'soft' coup two years later). The position of the military remains untouchable: It has overthrown four elected governments since 1960, two of them for being 'too Islamist'. It has made it known that it will step in if the secular order is seriously threatened.

The importance of contingency can also be noted in Turkey's recent political history: in particular, both economic downturns and the continuing desire for EU membership have helped to shape political developments over time but not, however, as yet decisively. Among the remaining institutions beyond AKP's control, academia and the judiciary are still packed with secular appointees of former presidents, but this situation will not last forever. As time goes by, attrition will mean that replacements will be required. The job of choosing them will fall to President Abdulah Gül, although his status as head of state now makes him apolitical.

Conservative practices applied by several AKP-led municipalities, including in Istanbul an alleged alcohol ban in some parts of the city and violence against shopkeepers selling it, made headlines in newspapers in Turkey in 2008 (*Radikal*, 2008). Was this the beginning of the end of secularism in Turkey? Would it encourage the military to act again to throw the popularly elected AKP from power? If so, what would this mean for the country's EU membership bid?

Marc Pierini, head of the EU delegation in Turkey, said the EU was closely watching such incidents and was proposing an ombudsman system to regulate the coexistence of different lifestyles in Turkey. 'But still, probably this is one way, of course, not the only one, but one way to regulate different lifestyles without crisis all the time. *This is a very delicate balance that Turkey has to find. We are well aware that there are different trends in the society but, at the same time, democracy is to organize these...So we are watching*' (emphasis added; 'EU monitors the debate between Dogan and Turkey's ruling AKP').

References

Akyol, M. (2008), 'Turkey is getting more secular, not religious', *Turkish Daily News*, 25 September.

Ayvaz, T. (2008), 'Turkey to receive 495 million euro pre-accession EU aid', *Turkish Daily News*, 18 July.

Bekdil, B. (2008), 'Lesser than white, greater than green', *Turkish Daily News*, 24 September.

Camlibel, C. (2008), 'EU on tenterhooks over domestic tension in Turkey', *Turkish Daily News*, 25 September.

Diamond, L. (1996), 'Democracy in Latin America: degrees, illusions, and directions for consolidation', in T. Farer (ed.), *Beyond Sovereignty: Collectively Defending Democracy in the Americas*, Baltimore, MD: The Johns Hopkins University Press.

Economist, The (2008), 'Less than white?', 18 September.

'EU monitors the debate between Dogan and Turkey's ruling AKP' (2008), *Turks. US Daily World EU News*, 25 September, http://www.turks.us/article.php?stor y=20080925092756683, accessed April 2009.

Galien, van der, M. (2008), 'Erdogan's war on media: EU is watching', 26 September, http://www.poligazette.com/2008/09/26/erdogans-war-on-media-eu-is-watching, accessed April 2009.

Gül, A. (2004), 'Turkey's Muslim identity did not prevent Turkey's intense relations with Europe', 16 December, *Zaman Online. First Turkish paper on the Internet*, http://yaleglobal.yale.edu/display.article?id=5041, accessed March 2009.

Günes-Ayata, A. (1994), 'Roots and trends in clientelism in Turkey', in L. Roniger and A. Günes-Ayata (eds), *Democracy, Clientelism, and Civil Society*, Boulder, CO: Lynne Rienner.

Haynes, J. (1998), *Religion in Global Politics*, London: Longman.

Jenkins, G. (2007), 'AKP forming closer links with the Gulen movement', *Eurasia Daily Monitor*, 4, 217, http://www.jamestown.org/edm/article.php?article_id=2372611, accessed April 2009.

Jenkins, G. (2008), 'AKP Strengthens its hold on the Turkish media', *Eurasia Daily Monitor*, 5, 93, http://www.jamestown.org/edm/article.php?article_id=2373064, accessed April 2009.

Kalyoncu, M. (2008), 'A critical decision – Turkey's chief EU negotiator and the AK Party government's fate', *Today's Zaman*, 10 October 2008.

Kay, J. (2005), 'Pope Benedict XVI's political resume: theocracy and social reaction', 22 April, *World Socialist Web Site*, http://www.wsws.org/articles/2005/apr2005/pope-a22.shtml, accessed April 2009.

Kinzer, S. (2001), *The Crescent and the Star: Turkey Between Two Worlds*, New York: Farrar Straus Giroux.

Krespin, R. (2007), 'The upcoming elections in Turkey (2): The AKP's Political Power Base', The Middle East Media Research Institute, 19 July.

Milliyet (2008), 'EU: We are closely following the conflict, 26 September.

'Newspaper sales exceed six mln mark', *Turkish Daily News*, 13 February 2007, http://www.turkishdailynews.com.tr/article.php?enewsid=66030, accessed March 2009.

Özbudun, E. (1996), 'Turkey: How far from consolidation?', *Journal of Democracy*, 7, 3, 123-38.

Radikal (2008), 'Alcohol Ban Expands To More Restaurants In Istanbul', 25 August.

Ross-Thomas, E. (2008), 'Turkey eyes reform of media ownership law', 12 January, *Reuters Business and Finance*, http://www.reuters.com/article/mergersNews/idUSL128096820080112, accessed April 2009.

Today's Zaman (2008), 'Three convicted in Deniz Feneri case', 25 September.

Toros, H. (2008), 'MEDIA-TURKEY: Messenger Comes Under Attack', *IPS Inter Press Service*, http://ipsnews.net/news.asp?idnews=44153, accessed April 2009.

Tunc, A. (2004), 'In quest of fair journalism in the cyberspace: A comparative look at the American and Turkish online media watchdogs', http://www. dorduncukuvvetmedya.com/dkm/print.php?sid=3191, accessed April 2009.

'Turkey-European Union' (2004), *AsiaNews.it*, 8 September, http://www.asianews. it/view.php?l=en&art=1442, accessed April 2009.

'Turkey-press scan September 26th' (2008), http://www.newstime7.com/ haber/20080926/Turkey-press-scan-September-26th.php, accessed April 2009.

Turunc, H. (2007), 'Islamicist or democratic? The AKP's search for identity in Turkish politics', *Journal of Contemporary European Studies*, 15, 1, 79-91.

Walker, M. (2004), 'Walker's world: Turkey's effect on Europe', *The Washington Times*, 6 October.

Yilmaz, H. (2002), 'External-internal linkages in democratization: Developing an open model of democratic change', *Democratization*, 9, 2, 67-84.

Chapter 6

The Political Rhetoric
of the Vatican: Aims and Strategies
of the Holy See as a Transnational Actor

John Bradley

Introduction

The Vatican is often overlooked when books or papers are written about transnational actors.[1] This chapter seeks to redress that oversight by considering the Holy See's important position in global religion and international politics. With over a billion baptized members,[2] the Catholic Church[3] is the largest Christian denomination, and the Vatican also has a unique status, with the Pope serving as both the leader of a church and a head of state. With its substantial network of diplomatic missions, as well as media outlets such as its own international radio station and newspaper,

---

1   The Catholic Church has not been completely ignored in this context: On the subject of the Catholic Church as a transnational actor, Ivan Vallier's compelling account (1971) is most instructive. Though dated, this essay lays the foundation for subsequent work on the subject: 'Forced to give up temporal political responsibilities, the transnational center of the church has gained more freedom to assert general stands on controversial issues and ethical problems. Through these processes, the church has moved up the hierarchy of social control toward a systemic position as a global pastor. At the same time the center has had to yield more autonomy and flexibility to its major field units' (Vallier, 1971: 499-500). The more recent study by Jeff Haynes (2001), asserts that the Catholic Church 'has been influential in some national contexts in helping undermine the hegemony of authoritarian governments'(143), whilst Samuel Huntington sees the Catholic Church as the prototype transnational actor (1973: 359). Keohane and Nye (1971) mentions the Catholic Church in similar terms, and the framework laid out in this essay is extremely useful for the study of this topic. More recently, the collection of essays *The Catholic Church and the Nation State* (Manuel, Reardon, Wilcox, 2007) is enlightening. This book is the most up to date account of the Church's approach to international politics. Most pertinent is the essay by Lisa Ferrari: 'The Vatican as a Transnational Actor'.

2   Many of these are not practising (i.e. do not attend Church regularly). For more detailed statistics refer to the *Annuario Pontificio 2008* (Libreria Editrice Vaticana, Citta Del Vaticano).

3   I will refer to the Catholic Church as 'the Church'. I am not making any claims, theological or otherwise by doing this, it is simply to avoid repetition.

and a comprehensive web-presence, the Holy See has a sizeable global presence. Nevertheless, the Church is much more than just the heavily centralised presence of the Vatican, and I will seek to explain how the involvement of many interdependent actors, coupled with the tiny geographical size of the Vatican City State, and small cadre of personnel employed therein, means that the Vatican is rarely able to exert influence on its own. In fact, even with the involvement of the many spokes of the Church itself, the Vatican relies on maximising its influence through diffusion, acting behind the scenes, and influencing more powerful international actors.

In this study I will begin by looking at the Church as a transnational actor, first by briefly setting it in a theoretical context, and then by looking at the structure of the Church, and how that lends itself to forging a cohesive transnational agenda. I will then look more specifically at how the Church seeks to influence specific international issues: here, after a brief introduction, and a discussion of the theological backdrop to the Church's international activity, I will begin by addressing how the influence of the Pope shapes the transnational aims of the Church. I will then continue to illustrate how the Church seeks to exert transnational influence with two further examples. The first will be the Vatican's role during the Lebanese Civil War (1975-1990). I will look at how the Vatican used its diplomatic presence, both from within the Vatican diplomatic service, and from the ranks of the international episcopate, to attempt to exert influence in Lebanon. The second case study will look at Vatican Radio, looking at its global reach and how it seeks to influence world affairs. I will conclude that the Vatican, and indeed the wider Catholic Church seeks to be influential in international politics and in the media, with varying degrees of success.

The Catholic Church as a Transnational Actor

There is now a reasonable academic consensus that transnational actors do have an impact on international politics (Risse, 2002: 255). Some scholars go further, for instance Zurn (2002) suggests that the transnational 'society world' has made the current order of international relations obsolete. Ruggie (1993) avers that political, social and economic boundaries have ceased to be confined within nation states. However, I am not directly addressing this particular theoretical argument. I am tentatively accepting the scholarly consensus that transnational actors do have an impact on world politics, and seeking to understand *how* the Church, as a transnational actor, seeks to achieve this. Nevertheless, as Clark and Chan (1995) argue, it is impossible to sustain a unifying theory on the impact of transnational actors, so I must proceed with caution.[4] I propose that the political action of the

---

4   Looking specifically at the Catholic Church, there is a growing consensus that international non-governmental organisations affect world politics (cf. Boliand Thomas, 1999; Checkel, 1997). Realist theorists argue that influence from transnational actors on powerful states equals international influence, and so that influence is dependent on

Church depends on the interdependence of various parts of the Church, which all subscribe to the same overarching rhetoric, which is grounded in the history and long-established structures of the Church. It is this interdependence, coupled with a rigid hierarchy and code of obedience that, along with its geographical spread, maintains the Catholic Church's influence in world affairs. The political rhetoric is designed to show the Catholic Church as a trusted, stabilising influence on world affairs. Through the bishops' manifest loyalty to the Pope, the liturgical uniformity, and the capacity for Church leaders from all over the world generally[5] to 'sing from the same hymn-sheet' on issues such as abortion, the political rhetoric of the Catholic Church, and particularly the Vatican, is a potent force.

The Catholic Church defies easy classification (using simple models)[6] as a state, an inter-governmental organisation, or a non-governmental organisation (NGO).[7] Whereas the European Union might fall between the first two, the church seems to relate to the first and third, and may even cover aspects of the second: 'The fact that the Church can be partially understood either as a NGO, or as a state, but fully understood in neither category, reflects the differences in ecclesiastical and secular epistemologies. The Church straddles two categories of political personhood because those categories were formulated by academic analysts looking at secular institutions' (Ferrari, 2007: 32-33). The Church's role as a transnational NGO and a sovereign entity, particularly through its myriad of diplomatic missions, helps to promote its transnational programme. It is important here to pause to relate the odd genesis of the Vatican City State, and how it is viewed internationally. The Vatican State was created as a result of the Lateran Accords of 1929, which were made

---

the policy goals of those states. However, these states are reliant on transnational actors to an extent, as they rarely have a consistent policy on international issues (e.g. human rights), as the amount of time and resources they can devote to these issues is dependent on the domestic situation. Indeed, Risse-Kappen (1995) argues that states are, in a way, dependent on international non-governmental organisations, especially now that the UN provides a forum for them to meet and to promote policy. Therefore, there is a debate in the transnational actor theory, which is looking at whether 'easy' access to a state aids the policy goals of transnational actors. Constructivism is illustrative on this point: easy access does not always lead to success. This is because the policy of a given transnational actor needs to 'resonate' with pre-existing collective identities and beliefs of the representatives/ population of the state involved.

5   For a significant exception to this, one can look at the 'Liberation Theology' movement which has flourished from the 1950s to the present in Latin America. Many bishops who were part of *Conselho Episcopal Latino Americano* (Latin American Episcopal Conference) stood in opposition to the Pope on issues surrounding social inequality in particular. Nevertheless, the Vatican has sought to curb the influence of this movement by appointing more conservative bishops. See here Rowland, C. (ed), 2007. *The Cambridge Companion to Liberation Theology*, Cambridge: Cambridge University Press.

6   Other, more nuanced state models might be applicable here, cf. Ayubi, N. (1995) *Over-stating the Arab State: Politics and Society in the Middle East*, London: I.B. Tauris.

7   Cf. Ferrari, 2007.

with Italy and established a sovereign state under the jurisdiction of the pope, in order that he could avoid political interference in the operation of the Church. Of course the 700-900 population of the Vatican is dwarfed by the presence of over a billion Catholics worldwide. Indeed, therein lies the Holy See's influence: through the exercise of its 'moral capital', rhetoric and symbolism, the Holy See ensures that via the worldwide Catholic population, and its influence on Catholics in secular office, the Vatican (tiny as it is) is always heard, even if it is not fully heeded (cf. Ferrari, 2007).

Although the Vatican plays a strong coordinating role in the transnational efforts of the Catholic Church, when looking in more detail at the dynamics of the Church, one sees that much of the Vatican's influence comes from the other components of the Church. It is certainly the case that 'central policy' and theological objectives come from the centre, and the official line of any bishop should in theory be in step with the Vatican position. In theory, a bishop has full autonomy over his diocese, with the Pope's role being to dismiss him if his actions are out of line. However, in practice the Vatican has a much tighter hold over the episcopate than that. To start with, the Congregation of Bishops, in the Vatican, chooses all Bishops via a 'terna' of three names submitted by the local Nuncio (who in turn is overseen by the Secretariat of State). This decision is usually only rubber-stamped by the Pope, but if it is an important appointment (São Paulo, New York, Paris, Sydney, for example), then the Pope will take a close interest. The second reason is that a bishop is likely to be summoned to the Vatican for talks long before a burgeoning disagreement reaches the stage of dismissal or excommunication (the former almost never happens as a bishop is encouraged to resign; the latter is vanishingly rare). The reason that the Vatican can wield this influence over bishops is that there is a close relationship between bishops and the Vatican: all bishops must visit Rome, tour the departments of state and visit the Pope every five years; and if a bishop is controversial in the interim he is summoned to Rome, and interrogated (for want of a better word).[8]

The case of Lebanon has some fascinating differences to normal policy in this area. As a historically independent Eastern Church, which recognises the primacy of the Pope, the Maronite Patriarch is elected by his brother Maronite bishops (both inside and outside of Lebanon). The Patriarch then appoints his own bishops. Nevertheless, these appointments must be rubber-stamped by the Pope, as a show of deference to his spiritual authority. The extent to which a bishop can act independently is hard to assess. In theory he can be as independent as he likes. In fact, in terms of foreign policy statements, a bishop who disagrees with the Pope (say over the American-led war in Afghanistan)[9] is going to cause much

---

8   An example of this is the summoning of Cardinal Bernard Law to Rome, in 2002, in the midst of the Archdiocese of Boston's paedophilia scandal unfolding. Law later resigned.

9   Cf. Allen, J., 2001 'At synod, church leaders disagree on war' in *National Catholic Reporter*, 11 November: http://www.natcath.com/NCR_Online/archives/110201/110201d.

less annoyance within the Vatican than one who unilaterally changes a single word in the Roman Liturgy. The Pope is unlikely to dismiss a bishop the way a CEO might sack an employee, because a bishop remains a bishop, even if sacked, and a 'rogue' bishop is a terrifying prospect for the Church, as he can ordain priests and start his own schismatic Church.[10] What is clear is that there is a delicate balancing act of authority that exists within the Church, and why it is hard to pin down exactly where that authority lies when international policy is formed and enacted.

Moving to the other constituent parts of the Church, and how they interact is much more straightforward. All of the Vatican Congregations and Councils come under the authority of the Pope, who deputises responsibility for each one to a Cardinal Prefect. These Cardinal Prefects can become very powerful (as happened to an extent with Josef Ratzinger[11] as Prefect of the Congregation for the Doctrine of the Faith [CDF]), but this is rare, as the Pope can simply dismiss a Prefect at any time, and give him a lesser job (which often happens).[12] Also closely related to the Vatican are the following: (1) Catholic charities – as they tend to follow Vatican dicta when making public statements. The major exception to this is when discussing condoms as a way of combating AIDS, when some Catholic charities struggle to follow the official Vatican line on this issue.[13] (2) Influence on Catholic countries – this tends to be via conservative Catholic politicians, who maintain the Vatican line (cf. opposition to abortion in recent debates on the issue amongst local politicians in Mexico City).[14] (3) The media outlets of the Catholic Church – notably Vatican Radio, L'Osservatore Romano and Catholic Television. These are all essentially mouthpieces of the Pope, and rarely (if ever) criticise him, or the Vatican. The next constituent part is the religious orders of the Church, for instance the Jesuits, Dominicans, Franciscans and Benedictines.[15] These show a

---

htm, accessed 19 October 2008.

10   As the example of Lefebvre shows, this is a complicated issue. Archbishop Lefebvre was a senior prelate who took the lead-role in opposing the changes in the Church associated with the Second Vatican Council. He founded the traditionalist 'Society of St. Pius X' in 1970, and shortly before his death he consecrated four bishops, against the direct orders of Pope John Paul II, thereby incurring automatic excommunication. Cf. Laisney, F. (ed.) (1998) *Archbishop Lefebvre and the Vatican, 1987-1988* Kansas City: Angelus Press, for the relevant documents with an explanation from a Lefebvre supporter.

11   Later Benedict XVI.

12   Cf. Disagreements between Benedict and Michael Fitzgerald, which led to the latter being moved from his position as prefect at the Council for Interreligious Dialogue to being Nuncio to Egypt.

13   Cf. approach of 'Catholic Aid for Overseas Development' (an English charity) http://www.guardian.co.uk/society/2005/feb/05/internationalaidanddevelopment.aids, accessed 19 October 2008.

14   http://news.bbc.co.uk/1/hi/world/americas/6586959.stm, accessed 19 October 2008.

15   The Jesuits offer an excellent case study of how stormy the relationship between Popes and orders can become. The Jesuits swear personal allegiance to the Pope, *but* they elect their own 'Father-General', and he has so much influence in Rome, that he is known

large degree of autonomy, and many of the clerics disciplined by the CDF in recent years have been Jesuit scholars.[16] They also have international networks to rival that of the Vatican's string of nunciatures, and often run important educational institutions.[17]

Case Studies

All of these different components of the Church broaden the potential sphere of influence of the Catholic Church considerably. It is a mistake to treat the Catholic Church as equalling the Vatican: that is as a centralised and unitary religio-political actor. It is better, instead, to view it in terms of complex inter-dependence where the influence of the Catholic Church is gained through using manifold and multifarious channels. Thus the transnational network of the Catholic Church can be viewed as starting with the Pope, the Vatican and its diplomatic machinery at the top, episcopal conferences next in the order of precedent, followed by individual dioceses, and finally parishes. A clear example of the Catholic Church wielding its influence as a transnational actor was at the United Nations 1994 conference on Population and Development. The Clinton administration in the United States was confident that it could push through its favoured document, which included a 'pro-choice' stance on abortion. In fact 90 per cent of the document was approved at the conference. The Vatican, however, mobilised Catholic and Muslim countries to derail the last 10 per cent, which contained the pro-choice language favoured by Clinton (Ferrari, 2007: 33).

It is not really possible to look at the Catholic Church as a transnational actor, without considering it both as a religio-theological actor and as a political actor: in this sense, it is unusual amongst churches and religions due to the existence of the Vatican City State. There is always a mélange of the theological and the political in its foreign policy. It is particularly important to pay close attention to the role of Vatican II[18] in shaping the Church's approach. Four documents in particular are important here: Firstly *Dignitatis Humanae*[19] which underlined the primary interest of the Church in religious freedom, which remains an important policy in its global mission, particularly in countries where Christians are persecuted;

---

as the 'Black Pope' (a reference to the colour of his robes). The orders are independent of the episcopate, and so can often 'cause more trouble' for the Vatican.

16   For instance, the Jesuit scholar Jacques Dupuis was investigated by the CDF over his book *Toward a Christian Theology of Religious Pluralism*.

17   e.g. Université Saint-Joseph de Beyrouth.

18   The Council of all the world's Catholic bishops, held in Rome 1962-1965.

19   http://www.vatican.va/archive/hist_councils/ii_vatican_council/documents/vat-ii_decl_19651207_dignitatis-humanae_en.html, accessed 23 October 2008.

Secondly, *Gaudium and Spes*[20] which brought in the significance of social issues and global justice (and though this led to the local Church wielding more influence before, it did not detract from the central role of the Vatican in defining the Church's policy). This document made it clear that the Catholic Church sees its role not just as a religious one, but in promoting social justice to people of all religions and none. Thirdly, *Nostra Aetate*,[21] which was the Council's document on interreligious relations, which gave a special place to Jews and Muslims amongst followers of other religions; and finally, *Lumen Gentium*,[22] which spoke of the salvific mission of Christ and the Church. This last document is important as it reemphasises the primary role of missionary work in the Church's international policy.

The Role of the Pope in Shaping Policy – The Example of Islam

A central contextual consideration is the impact of the views of different popes on the foreign policy and dialogical approach of both the Vatican and the wider Catholic Church. The example of the attitudes of the two most recent popes towards Islam is instructive, as it goes some way to explaining why the current pope, Benedict XVI, has had a more turbulent relationship with Muslim leaders. John Paul II displayed great charisma, and made use of his quasi-celebrity status to bring attention to causes close to his heart. One of those causes was a firm commitment to dialogue with Muslims. Troll (2000) suggests that John Paul II was extremely diplomatic, and because he was so eager not to upset serene relations he perhaps avoided being too explicit in his statements, whilst always remaining optimistic (Troll, 2000: 238-44). As well as Lebanon, he engaged in peace initiatives in Bosnia, Iraq, and Jerusalem. He also spoke to large crowds, for instance to 80,000 Muslim young people in Casablanca in 1985, when he spoke with great respect and asked the youths to treasure their faith and heritage. In his dialogue with Muslims, he stressed the promotion of peace, the providing of a realistic response of faith to the spiritual malaise of modern life, witness of respect for God and religion, joint service of humanity, and common ideal of a society (cf. Arinze, 1987). Many Muslims publicly mourned the death of John Paul II. Rwanda's mufti, Saleh Habimana, declared that 'the death of the pope is the disappearance of a hero of recent times', and President Mohammad Khatami of Iran, a Muslim cleric, flew to Rome for the funeral in an unprecedented sign of respect.

---

20   http://www.vatican.va/archive/hist_councils/ii_vatican_council/documents/vat-ii_cons_19651207_gaudium-et-spes_en.html, accessed 23 October 2008.
21   http://www.vatican.va/archive/hist_councils/ii_vatican_council/documents/vat-ii_decl_19651028_nostra-aetate_en.html, accessed 23 October 2008.
22   http://www.vatican.va/archive/hist_councils/ii_vatican_council/documents/vat-ii_const_19641121_lumen-gentium_en.html, assessed 23 October 2008.

With the current pope, the attitude of Benedict XVI to the entrance of Turkey into the EU is instructive. The Vatican has consistently opposed the entrance of Turkey, and would see such a move as detrimental to the 'Christian roots' of Europe. At various times, Benedict has addressed the interpretation of the Second Vatican Council, and advocated understanding it not as a 'revolution', but as a 'deepening' – comments which have been interpreted as him wanting to reduce the momentum of the dialogical process. Justo Lacunza Balda, the former head of the Pontifical Institute for Arabic and Islamic Studies agrees, saying that criticism has been focused on the lack of reciprocal goodwill gestures in many Muslim countries: 'Humanly speaking, it is of course important to see some payback' (cf. Williams and Cooperman, 2005). An example of a senior figure close to Benedict who has spoken on this subject is Cardinal Camillo Ruini, the former vicar for Rome, who has been especially vociferous on the issues of reciprocity and religious freedom. Indeed, the document *Dominus Iesus*,[23] which was prepared in 2000, by the Congregation for the Doctrine of the Faith, under Ratzinger's presidency, is concerned that interreligious relations should not be understood on the model of ecumenism – that is a search for doctrinal agreement. Benedict has been concerned that such an approach may encourage syncretism, 'in which the goal becomes blending elements of various faiths into a kind of New Age pâté agreeable to modern tastes' (Allen, 2006). This attitude towards Islam from the very centre of the Catholic Church, has led to increased suspicion towards the Church from many Muslims globally, and can only have contributed to the violent reaction to his 2006 speech in Regensburg.[24]

The Lebanese Civil War

As evidenced by the Council documents listed above, when considering the Catholic Church as a political actor in the Middle East, the stance of the church towards other religions becomes exceedingly important. Notably here, its approach to Islam and Judaism is instructive. This is bound up intractably with the more political issues of the defence of Christian communities in the Middle East (Catholic and non-Catholic); its interests in Israel and the Palestinian Territories (especially

---

23   http://www.vatican.va/roman_curia/congregations/cfaith/documents/rc_con_cfaith_doc_20000806_dominus-iesus_en.html, accessed 25 October 2008.

24   In 2006, the Pope made a speech at Regensburg University in Germany, which was widely criticised by Muslim leaders, after he quoted Emperor Manuel II, Paleologos of the Byzantine Empire as saying: 'Show me just what Muhammad brought that was new and there you will find things only evil and inhuman, such as his command to spread by the sword the faith he preached'. 'Benedict said "I quote" twice to stress the words were not his and added that violence was "incompatible with the nature of God and the nature of the soul"'. BBC News Website, 14 September 2006 'Pope's speech stirs Muslim anger' http://news.bbc.co.uk/2/hi/europe/5346480.stm, accessed 20 October 2008.

Jerusalem), and its advocacy of peace initiatives. An example of the Church's work in this regard in the Middle East might be that of its mediating role during the Lebanese Civil War (1975-1990). The Vatican has committed considerable resources to Lebanon, and its approach is fundamentally guided by the goal of fostering peaceful coexistence between Christians and Muslims as a way of saving the Christian community. Although it has had a turbulent relationship with sections of the Maronite community, it has retained their respect.

During the civil war, the Catholic Church was in a unique position as it could comprehend the inter-Christian and inter-Maronite rivalries in more depth than state-actors, due to its relationship with the patriarchate and its expert local knowledge of the Christian communities through the Nuncio and other clerics. Interestingly, the Vatican also exercised a slight hold over the Christian, particularly Maronite community as there was, in the early years of the war, an assumption that the Vatican would take the side of the Maronite cause. However, this position of respect was eroded somewhat, as the Vatican continued to denounce the idea of partition during the 1980s, when many Maronites saw it as the only way out of the war. Although this position soured relations with the Maronites in the end, there is a strong argument to be made that the influence the Vatican had on the Maronites regarding partition was significant. The Holy See may well have had leverage in Israel at that time: the Israeli government had been lobbying for recognition by the Holy See for decades, and the prospect of this was an incentive for them to cooperate with the Vatican, until 1993 when the 'fundamental agreement' was signed, and diplomatic relations were established.[25] It is important to remember also, that the Holy See had, and still does have, a large network in Israel/Palestine: mostly through religious communities overseeing the Holy Places.

During the Lebanese Civil war, in addition to its interventions with successive United States' administrations, the Holy See coordinated its efforts with the American Catholic Hierarchy, and major international actors such as France and the US paid close attention to exhortations from the Holy See (cf. Irani, 1994: 187). In 1975 Cardinal Paolo Bertoli led a Vatican mission to Lebanon to try and find a means of dialogue between the conflicting parties, meeting many people, from the President of Lebanon to Yassir Arafat. The following year, Monsignor Mario Brini led another mission which focused on pastoral and humanitarian considerations before Bertoli returned in 1978. This trip involved information gathering and attempts to convene a summit of religious leaders as well as to bring some reconciliation to the Maronite factions. In 1980 the Holy See's top diplomat, Cardinal Agostino Casaroli, the Secretary of State, visited Lebanon on a trip that was pastoral in nature. Some parties in Lebanon had unrealistic ideas about how much the Holy See could achieve: believing that the Pope and his envoys could bring the factions together and the war to an end. In fact hopes were so high that Casaroli had to tone down what people believed could be achieved by the Papacy and its diplomatic missions.

---

25   Cf. Marshall, 2004.

During the Lebanese War, the fundamental objective of the Holy See was to save Lebanon as an independent state in order to protect the Christian presence not only in Lebanon but throughout the Middle East. The Holy See opted to act as a mediator and conciliator among the various groups, underlining the limits inherent in the spiritual nature of its mission (cf. Irani, 1986, ch. 3). Concretely, Cardinal Bertoli's 1975 mission led to institutional reforms that were long overdue (ibid.). In 1980 a Vatican mission was successful in reconciling factions of the Maronite community, though not the Maronites with the Lebanese in general (Irani, 1994: 182). The regular mention of the Holy See and its influence in speeches by politicians such as Bashir Gemayl (ibid: 184) is testament to their authoritative role. By the end of the 1980s, the influence of the Vatican in Lebanon was severely compromised as it has lost the confidence of many Maronites. However, by this time Cardinal Terence Cooke, and later Cardinal John O'Connor of New York were working to influence American policy, both through visits to Lebanon and having the ear of President Reagan (ibid: 187). Finally, the enormous humanitarian effort of the Holy See may have assisted Western policy (ibid) as it reduced resentment towards Western involvement, and due to the nature of the structure of the Church, lessons learned in humanitarian missions could be passed via the Nuncio or other clerics, to the Vatican and thence into international political circles.[26] Therefore we see, in the Church's involvement in Lebanon, the involvement of all the components of the Church mentioned above: from the Pope, and the Vatican administration, to local bishops and religious communities.

Vatican Radio

I have now looked in some detail at the structural workings of the Vatican diplomatic machinery, and an example of how (along with the other arms of the Catholic Church) it can enhance the role of the Church in world affairs. The second example I have chosen in order to demonstrate the global reach and influence of the Church are its media outlets. Primary amongst these is Vatican Radio.[27] Vatican Radio began broadcasting in 1931, and Marconi himself helped to set up the station, indeed, Vatican Radio is the oldest transnational broadcasting network in the world. By 1939, it was broadcasting in nine languages, and in January 1940,

---

26   $6.7 million was distributed by the Pontifical Mission for Palestine in 1987 alone – cf. Martino, 1989: 77.

27   Also notable is L'Osservatore Romano, the semi-official Vatican newspaper. Publishes in nine languages and distributed in 129 countries, circulations figures are kept secret, but it is known that they are not big enough to prevent the newspaper making significant annual losses. It has been compared to the old Soviet mouthpiece 'Pravda' as it does not publish dissent, and is essentially the Pope's uncritical mouthpiece. Cf. http://query.nytimes.com/gst/fullpage.html?res=9D00E5DA1331F930A15751C1A960958260&sec=&spon=&pagewanted=all , accessed 17 October 2008.

according to the stations own reports, it was the first radio station to denounce Nazi concentration camps. Indeed, between 1940 and 1946, 1.25 million messages were broadcast via Vatican Radio from families to prisoners by war between 1940 and 1946. Goebbels was so infuriated by Vatican Radio during World War II that he swore to destroy it (Moreau, 1993: 3). In the 1980s, Vatican Radio was at the forefront of John Paul II's mission to the oppressed Catholics of Eastern Europe: in April 1981 for example, Vatican Radio reported violence against seminarians and priests in Czechoslovakia (Matelski, 1997: 57). Vatican Radio was one of the only transnational services that could overcome Soviet jamming, and was thus a vital tool for the alliance of countries and organisations who were opposed to Soviet domination in the region. Through Vatican Radio, for instance, John Paul II was able to express his support for the 'Solidarity' Union, and help to keep its spirits high (ibid: 59-60).

Today, Vatican Radio has lost some of the raison d'être that came with the struggle against oppressive regimes in Eastern Europe. But with forty-five broadcast languages in 2008, including Arabic and the main Chinese languages, Vatican Radio is still reaching oppressed Catholics throughout the world. Nevertheless, it remains something of a propaganda machine: with a diet of papal masses, papal statements and devotional readings, it rarely criticises the Church. In addition to this, it is almost impossible to assess listener figures, although it is cited often by the world's media, which is another important indicator of influence (Matelski, 1995: ch. 8), and also receives an enormous amount of post from all over the world (96,000 items in 1990 alone – cf. Moreau, 1993: 24). Today, Vatican radio employs nearly 500 people, from 50 different nations. It is technically advanced and broadcasts via shortwave, medium wave and FM, as well as via satellite. Using native journalists around the world to gather news, Vatican Radio clearly has incredible global reach. With a conservative agenda on issues such as euthanasia and abortion, this network is a powerful tool for the Church to promote its point of view on social as well as religious issues, with almost every person in the world as a potential listener.

Conclusion

The self-identity of the Church is constructed to a great extent by the power given to it by its one billion members worldwide – the words of the Pope would have little impact, if there were only him and three other Catholics in the world. The soft-power, strong diplomacy and lack of (for instance) armed forces, mean that co-operation, rather than an atavistic idea of necessary conflict is most likely to prevail within the Church. The unique structure of the Catholic Church, based in a sovereign state, but impossible to define by that state, is reflected also in its global agenda. The tension between humanitarian concerns that transcend religion, and consciousness of an evangelical mission defines the Church's transnational agenda to a great extent: it has taken a great humanitarian interest in Lebanon, but of course is concerned with maintaining the Christian presence there; Vatican Radio deplores totalitarianism and human rights abuses, but has the agenda of wanting to see its listeners in China able to practise Catholicism without hindrance.

A good case in point of this 'tension' in the Church's global agenda is that of Christian–Muslim dialogue. On the one hand, the Catholic Church's diplomatic efforts go beyond Christian–Muslim dialogue. This could be seen as a common interest in moral values, for instance opposition to abortion, secularism and atheism. But on the other hand, interfaith dialogue and diplomacy seem to be related: in the Middle East, Vatican diplomacy is primarily geared to safeguard the presence of the Christian minority, and those of Christian migrant labourers. In this regard the Vatican has a hard task – particularly in Iraq, Lebanon and Palestine. But it also wants to use it to deal with issues outside of the Middle East, such as the rising Muslim population in Europe and what that entails.

It is only through the uniformity of the message which comes from the Catholic Church that it remains such an influential transnational actor. The *numbers* of Catholics in the world alone would not count for much, if there were a *perception* that they mostly ignored proclamations made by their bishops, or by the Pope. But the Vatican uses the extraordinary structures of the Church to maintain a loose control over the 'message' that the global church propagates. By giving out messages of certainty, for good or bad, the Catholic Church helps to maintain the confidence of its followers. Indeed even if they do not follow the instructions of prelates, there is a widespread perception by those outside the Church that the prelates *are* listened to. Countless examples act as evidence for the continued interest of the world in the Catholic Church. The Church has observer status, for example, at the United Nations and the Arab League; statements made by the Pope on subjects as wide ranging as other religions, and whether a war is legitimate, are leapt upon by press reporters; major public events (commemorations, tragedies) often involve Church leaders leading a nation in grief or celebration; Catholic bishops banning political candidates from receiving communion led to widespread commentary and debate. It is evident, therefore, that the Vatican – and indeed the wider Catholic Church – seeks to be influential in international politics and in the media, with varying degrees of success. Further study of the Holy See as an actor in these areas would be pertinent and valuable, and contribute to a better understanding of how the Catholic Church continues to impact on international affairs, both religiously and politically, with its unique mixture of tradition, diplomacy, experience and rhetoric.

References

Allen, J.L. (2004), *All The Pope's Men: The Inside Story of How The Vatican Really Thinks*, New York: Doubleday.

—— (2006), 'Behind the Changes at the Interreligious Council', *The National Catholic Reporter* 5 (24), 17 February 2006, http://nationalcatholicreporter. org/word/word021706.htm, accessed 17 June 2008.

Arinze, F. (1987), 'Interreligious Dialogue at the Service of Peace', *Islamochristiana* 13, 1-8.

Ellis, K.C. (ed.) (1987), *The Vatican, Islam and the Middle East*, Syracuse: Syracuse University Press.

Bach, A. (2004), *Religion, Politics, Media in the Broadband Era*, Sheffield: Phoenix Press.

Boli, J. and Thomas, G. (eds) (1999), *Constructing World Culture: International Nongovernmental Organizations Since 1875*, Stanford: Stanford University Press.

Checkel, J. (1997), 'International Norms and Domestic Politics: Bridging the Rationalist/Constructivist Divide', *European Journal of International Relations* 3, 473-95.

Clark, C. and Chan, S. (1995), 'Multinational Corporations and Developmentalism', in Risse-Kappen, T. (ed.), *Bringing Transnational Relations Back In: Non-State Actors, Domestic Structures and International Institutions*, Cambridge: Cambridge University Press.

Ferrari, L. (2007), 'The Vatican as a Transnational Actor', in Manuel, P.C., L.C. Reardon and C. Wilcox (eds), *The Catholic Church and the Nation-State: Comparative Perspectives*, Washington, DC: Georgetown University Press.

Hanson, E.O. (1987), *The Catholic Church in World Politics*, Princeton: Princeton University Press.

Haynes, J. (2001), 'Transnational Religious Actors and International Politics', *Third World Quarterly* 22 (2), 143-58.

Hehir, J.B. (1987), 'The Catholic Church and the Middle East: Policy and Diplomacy', in Ellis, K.C. (ed.), *The Vatican, Islam and the Middle East*, Syracuse: Syracuse University Press.

Huntington, S.P. (1971), 'Transnational Organizations in World Politics', *World Politics* 25 (3), 333-68.

Irani, G. (1986), *The Papacy and the Middle East*, Notre Dame, Indiana: Notre Dame University Press.

—— (1994), 'The Holy See and the Conflict in Lebanon', in Kent, P.C. and J.F. Pollard, *Papal Diplomacy in the Modern Age*, Westport, Connecticut: Greenwood Press.

Kent, P.C. and Pollard, J. (1994), *Papal Diplomacy in the Modern Age*, Westport, Connecticut: Greenwood Press.

Keohane, R.O. and Nye, J. (1971), 'Transnational Relations and World Politics: An Introduction', *International Organization* 25 (3), 329-49.

Kreutz, A. (1990), *Vatican Policy on the Palestinian-Israeli Conflict*, Westport, Connecticut: Greenwood Press.

Manuel, P.C., Reardon, L. and Wilcox, C. (eds) (2007), *The Catholic Church and the Nation-State: Comparative Perspectives*, Washington, DC: Georgetown University Press.

Marshall, J.B (ed.) (2004), *The Vatican-Israel Accords: Political, Legal and Theological Contexts*, Notre Dame, Indiana: Notre Dame University Press.

Martino, R. (1989), 'The Holy See and the Middle East', *American–Arab Affairs* 29, 75-85.

Matelski, M. (1995), *Vatican Radio: Propagation by the Airwaves*, Westport, CT: Praeger Publishers.

Meyer, B. and Moors, A. (eds) (2006), *Religion, Media and the Public Sphere*, Bloomington: Indiana University Press.

Moreau, P. (1993), *Radio Vaticana 1931-1991*, Città del Vaticano: Tipografia Poliglotta Vaticana.

d'Onorio, J.B. (2000), *La Diplomatie de Jean Paul II*, Paris: Les Éditions Du Cerf.

Philpott, D. (2000), 'The Religious Roots of Modern International Relations', *World Politics* 52 (2), 206-45.

_____ (2004), 'Christianity and Democracy: The Catholic Wave', *Journal of Democracy* 15 (2), 32-46.

Reese, T.J. (1996), *Inside the Vatican: The Politics and Organization of the Catholic Church*, Cambridge, Massachusetts: Harvard University Press.

Risse, T. (2002), 'Transnational Actors and World Politics', in Carlsnaes, W., T. Risse and B. Simmons, *Handbook of International Relations*, London: Sage.

Risse-Kappen, T. (1995), 'Introduction', in Risse-Kappen, T. (ed.), *Bringing Transnational Relations Back In: Non-State Actors, Domestic Structures and International Institutions*, Cambridge: Cambridge University Press.

Ruggie, J. (1993), 'Territoriality and Beyond: Problematizing Modernity in International Relations', *International Organization* 47, 139-74.

Street, N.L. and Matelski, M. (eds) (1997), *Messages from the Underground: Transnational Radio in Resistance and In Solidarity*, Westport, CT: Praeger Publishers.

Sweeney, F. (ed.) (1970), *The Vatican and World Peace*, Gerrards Cross: Colin Smythe.

Troll, C.W. (2000), 'Catholic Teachings on Interreligious Dialogue. Analysis of some Recent Official Documents, with Special reference to Christian Muslim Relations', in Waardenburg, J. (ed.), *Muslim-Christian Perceptions of Dialogue Today: Experiences and Expectations*, Leuven: Peeters.

Vallier, I. (1971), 'The Roman Catholic Church: A Transnational Actor', *International Organization* 25 (3), 479-502.

Williams, D. and Cooperman, A. (2005), 'Vatican is Rethinking Relations with Islam', *Washington Post* 15 April 2005, http://www.washingtonpost.com/ac2/wp-dyn/A55208-2005Apr14?language=printer, accessed 13 June 2008.

Zurn, M. (2002), 'From Interdependence to Globalization', in Carlsnaes, W., T. Risse and B. Simmons, *Handbook of International Relations*, London: Sage.

Chapter 7

Populism and Security in Political Speechmaking: the 2008 US Presidential Campaign

Michael Higgins

Introduction

The issue of security has been a prominent feature of the US political landscape since the attacks of 9/11. Not surprisingly, then, issues of security, trust and credibility were raised throughout the 2008 US election presidential campaign. In the latter stages of his presidency, George W. Bush had been engaged in portraying his two terms as a successful period as national protector, keeping the US safe from further terrorist attack. Both the policy and the rhetorical strategies of the Bush administration coalesced around an emphasis on 'homeland security'. As well as producing a dominant way of asserting political legitimacy, this put in place an administrative framework within which elected legislators had to situate themselves, including the candidates for the 2008 presidential election. Although they engaged in these debates in quite different ways, it is significant that all but one of the candidates for 2008 participated in the policy framework of homeland security. Prospective Democrat President Barack Obama sat on the *Senate Committee on Homeland Security and Governmental Affairs*, while his prospective Vice-President Joe Biden sat on the *Senate Subcommittee on Terrorism, Technology and Homeland Security*. Outside of the committee setting, while Obama avoided supporting Bush's most controversial security measures, prospective Republican President John McCain voted for the *Patriot Act* in 2001 and in 2006, and for the *Homeland Security Department Appropriations Act* in 2006 (Council on Foreign Relations, 2008). McCain's prospective Vice-President Sarah Palin's record on security is less established, through a simple consequence of having spent less time in political office and remaining in state governorship. We will go on to see, however, that Palin's contribution to the Republican tactic of articulating security with national self-interest offered some telling insights into the communication of politics.

While the overall rhetoric of security has been directed inward, prioritising a concern with 'home', it has included a significant exclusionary strand. Rees (2009: 108-9) emphasises that this concern with homeland security established a regime of shared practice that allowed Washington to strengthen some of its international partnerships (such as the UK) while temporarily marginalising certain, troublesome others (most notably France and Germany). In spite of the emphasis placed on Washington's short term squabbles with a number of longer-term allies, Rees (2009: 109) points out that implementation of the resultant policy initiatives on matters such as airport security and the pooling of intelligence, require a level of international cooperation that stretches beyond the rhetoric. However, the contention here will be that while the notion of 'homeland' holds out a virtuous arrangement for all national administrations that adopt similar codes of governance, the concentration on domestic well-being extends into the realm of economic and ideological interest.

In any event, security was a key selling point for the Republican ticket. This issue was framed, on the one hand, around personal credibility. The McCain campaign developed their approach to security and national safety, by drawing upon McCain's history as a prisoner of war in Vietnam and his image as a maverick politician that has shown a willingness to take uncompromising decisions. While these were selling points in McCain's campaign for the primary elections of 2000 (see Wallace, 2008), in 2008 they had been emphasised by the release of McCain's ghost-written commentaries of courageous decisions *Hard Call* (McCain and Salter, 2007). The assertion of a link between the capacity to deal with security issues and political and personal experience was not an argument confined to the Republican campaign. In the Democratic primaries too, Hillary Clinton ran an advert asking whether it is she or Barack Obama that has the understanding to deal with a 3am call to the White House concerning an urgent matter of security. Also significant, however, was Obama's response that experience is of little use when it is disabled by dogmatism, in a strategy to assert a self-interested parochialism on the part of his opponents. As we will see, much of the election discourse of both sides centred on setting security concerns within various national or international parameters.

What the relatively inexperienced Sarah Palin contributed to the Republican rhetoric on security was to draw upon the rhetorical force of the 'homeland' in 'homeland security'. Palin operated to place the experience and credibility of McCain in a particular context, and to emphasise the national self-interests involved. She performs this role using strategies associated with the traditions of political populism, and an understanding of the modes of populist address in Palin's speeches help us to see how these boundaries of concern are established. Furthermore, these can be fruitfully compared alongside similar strategies in the speeches of Barack Obama, which we shall see are directed towards different ends.

Populism and Leadership

References to populism routinely drive debates around political culture, both in the academy and more broadly. According to Margaret Canovan's (1981: 261) book-length treatment, populism as expressed by the political classes is the drive to tailor ideas so that they appear to spring from 'the people' rather than any political, economic or bureaucratic elite. This stems from an association, laudable in itself, between political power and subaltern collective action. As Hannah Arendt (1998: 201) remarks 'the only indispensable factor in the generation of power is the living together of people'. At least in principle, populism is the art of negotiating and implementing policies that appeal to these collectives. Populism also draws upon an equally admirable insistence that 'public will' should have a bearing on political policy. 'The people' are therefore presented as the foremost agents of political change.

Of course, populism is only one means of fostering an illusion of collectivity and representativeness. In its meaningful form, the expression of populism depends upon the presence of a 'charismatic leader' and their claims to represent this 'popular will' against an unrepresentative system. Over the course of the presidential election, the main candidates were routinely assessed on their capacity to 'connect' with voters in particular ways: Obama through oratory skill, the promised change of mixed-race ethnicity and youthful vitality, and McCain by drawing upon his proven loyalty and courage, and maverick image. In her more recent work, Canovan (2002) acknowledges that populism is better understood as a series of political strategies than a political ideal, such that it offers a 'thin-centred' rhetorical basis for claiming political representativeness. What may be construed as the emptiness of the politician aligning themselves with the populace does not detract from the rhetorical force of its appeal, however, and even the most vacuous petitions to 'the people' offer what Abts and Rummens (2007: 408) describe as 'a central signifier which receives a fundamentally monolithic interpretation'. The populist address is simple and it tends to work. For all its emptiness, arguments against an effective populist strategy are positioned such that they seem to gainsay the popular will.

The effective populist address is also designed to avoid feeling especially political. The key terms of Obama's campaign, such as 'change', 'trust' and 'hope', the latter also taken up in Obama's (2006) political writing, are designed to evoke shared human potentiality rather than disputable political values. Regis Debray writes that what is offered is not so much the rancorous posturing of political division, as 'a fraternity that keeps us warm' (Debray, 1983: 142). The promise is that if you listen and believe, you will never be alone. In the past, this emphasis on inclusiveness and belonging is what has lent populism some degree of elasticity. Ernesto Laclau (1977) uses the concept of 'articulation' to illustrate how populist discourses can be conjoined with established sets of political beliefs expressing a variety of contradictory interests. In Laclau's vision, one in which he draws heavily upon Gramsci's (1971) notion of hegemony, the battle over populist legitimacy is more crucial to victory than any claim to political or ideological credibility. Populism therefore offers a means to forego acknowledgment of foundational political and economic interests. In short, populism presents an empty rhetorical style readily adaptable to whatever political agenda is at hand.

The Analysis of Populism

The focus of Regis Debray is on the use of pronouns in devising a populist address, and this has also guided the 'critical discourse analysis' of political language. Norman Fairclough (1989: 180) looks at the use of pronouns by Margaret Thatcher to claim solidarity with her listeners, 'to pass off her practices, perceptions and precepts as those of 'the people' in general'. Even elsewhere on the political spectrum, Fairclough (2000: 30) observes a strategy of inclusive pronominal usage in the speechmaking of ex-Labour Prime Minister Tony Blair that 'rests upon the constant 'commonsensical' equivalence of country, nation and business'. Higgins (2004), moreover, shows how the terms of even the most outwardly stable inclusive address can shift to accommodate whatever political agendas are at hand. While pronouns are every bit as useful for potentially non-inclusive illocutionary acts of political discourse such as promising or requesting, the populist utility of the pronoun is largely in keeping with what Brown and Gilman (1972) describe as their shift away from the expression of power differentials to that of a 'solidarity ethic'.

This analysis will look at the speechmaking of Sarah Palin, with a particular concentration on the acceptance speech for her nomination as candidate for the Vice-Presidency. The mechanism for looking at Palin's speech will be the straightforward one of examining patterns of pronominal usage. The first suggestion to emerge from the analysis will be that the clustering of pronouns enables us to comprehend the structure of the speech, as well as allowing us to see how the speech discharges its various purposes; including accepting the nomination, McCain and selling Palin herself. Partly, Palin's speech will prove to be an exercise in managing different personae, and Drake and Higgins (2006) argue that successful political speechmaking draws upon an ability to shift between 'frames' (Goffman, 1986): speaking for oneself at one moment, and expressing party loyalty the next. The suggestion here is that analysis of pronominal usage can show us how these shifts are managed. The second suggestion will be that Palin's use of pronouns gives us an insight into a particular form of political populism, such that she embodies a shift in populist address from the inclusive address of old, to one centred on the self and the experiential.

So if Sarah Palin embodies an interesting development of populism, in what terms is populism integrated into US political culture? In a history of the topic, Michael Kazin (1998: 12) gives the American brand of populism a number of characteristics. First, it is rooted in the Christian-protestant social mores of the US, drawing upon such metaphors as 'Judas, sin and redemption' to offer emotive expressions of loyalty, error and repair. It is also founded on a timeless notion of 'Americanism', as a 'creed for which independence had been won and that all genuine patriots would fight to preserve'. This is a doctrine that presents America as 'an isolated land of virtue whose people were on constant guard against the depredations of aristocrats, empire builders, and self-aggrandizing officeholders both within and outside its borders' (Kazin, 1998: 12).

Yet from the beginning, the viability of 'the people' to whom this popular sentiment is addressed has been in doubt. Kazin suggests that the original notion of 'people' was 'more incantation than description', borne of political fervor mixed with the religiosity of such accomplished rhetoricians as Adam and Jefferson. Amongst 'the people' so-addressed, the effectiveness of this reading would wear off during the first round of tax hikes, and the Massachusetts farmers, to name just one group, set out to question in whose name executive power was being exercised (Kazin, 1998: 13). Yet, Kazin (1998: 14) is keen to emphasise, even these early rebellions were founded on an interest-based 'producerism', determined to assert the rights of the small businessman against the state. What was being addressed, in other words, was the effectiveness with which the populist ideal was being pursued rather than the integrity of populism itself.

Palin on Palin, and Security

I turn now to the contribution Sarah Palin can make to our understanding of populism, and how she uses this in supporting the Republican agenda on homeland security. The introduction has already discussed the ways in which Palin is distinguishable from both McCain and the Democratic candidates by her lack of experience in the national legislator: a factor that was incorporated into the Republican campaign as evidence of a critical distance from 'Washington elites' together with their perceived special interests. It is also commonly accepted that the addition of Palin to the Republican ticket was an attempt both to attract women voters that might have opted for Hillary Clinton and to introduce youthful vitality and allure into the McCain campaign. If not for the extent of her grasp of core principles, therefore, there is ample evidence that Palin was chosen for the forms of rhetoric made possible by the terms of what Street (2003) describes as a public personae. And in the event, her impact upon many core Republican supporters has been significant; with much of the resulting praise directed towards her campaign speeches.

There are a number of possibilities available for us to analyse Palin's speechmaking, many of them relevant to debates around political populism. As Steven Pinker (2008) recently wrote in the *New York Times*, one way of explaining Palin's appeal amongst the Republican base is the folksiness of her speech style. She talks of 'kids' rather than 'children', routinely drops her g's, and uses what Pinker describes as 'cutesy near profanities like "darn", "heck" and "doggone"'. While these qualities are important towards understanding the political personae represented by Palin, there are other patterns in Palin's speech that give more precise insights into what Pinker describes as Palin's 'governing philosophy'; in particular, the manner in which she draws upon, asserts and manages a set of personal and professional credentials.

The speech that is of immediate interest is the one that marked Palin's appearance on the national political stage, where she accepted the nomination as prospective vice-president on the Republican Party ticket. I want to begin my discussion of this speech by making two points. First, there is a notable series of thematic clusters in Palin's use of the first person singular, which correspond to different phases in the integration of the speaker's public persona and experiential competence into the speech. Tokens of 'I' are contained within four stages of the speech, leaving prolonged passages of the speech – one in particular – in which there are none. These four phases are 'formal acceptance', 'credential claim', 'simple soul fallen amongst politicians', and 'concluding formal support'.

The first and fourth stages of the speech can be examined together, which are 'the formal acceptance' and 'the concluding formal support' phases respectively. These are the bookends of the speech in which Palin enacts the ritual of accepting the nomination for the Vice Presidency. This extract is from the speech's opening:

> (1) I accept the call to help our nominee for president to serve and defend America. I accept the challenge of a tough fight in this election... against confident opponents ... at a crucial hour for our country. And I accept the privilege of serving with a man who has come through much harder missions ... and met far graver challenges ... and knows how tough fights are won – the next president of the United States, John S. McCain.

As Max Atkinson (1984) points out, the art of political speechmaking is the choreography of applause, and even this formalistic opening uses well-worn techniques of political rhetoric. Specifically, Palin works 'I accept' into what Atkinson (1984: 57) describes as a 'three part list' designed to 'project' the name of her senior running mate, John McCain.

There follows a brief period in which Palin expounds upon the positive qualities of McCain. She uses what is still the developmental stage of the speech to assert the credentials of McCain as a guardian of national security. This is expressed first by means of an implicit claim on McCain's unstinting allegiance to nation, setting this against a mythical political establishment. Palin says: 'It was just a year ago when all the experts in Washington counted out our nominee because he refused to hedge his commitment to the security of the country he loves'. The theme is then developed through the affirmation of a direct link between McCain's innate qualities and his approach to current security policy: 'He's a man who wore the uniform of his country for 22 years, and refused to break faith with those troops in Iraq who have brought victory within sight'.

Palin then shifts into what can usefully be described as 'the credential-claim phase'. This is characterised by a period of switching between Palin evidencing her position as an 'ordinary' American in the 'just your average Hockey mom' mould, and Palin asserting her place as the engaged political advocate. Extracts 2, 3 and 4 function as assertions of ordinariness combined with feistiness on Palin's part; on the one hand, lending a tone of humility to her family status by deploying 'just' as a hedge designed to convey humility and ordinariness rather than downplay the message (extracts 2 and 3), while placing no such conditions on the description of her motive to action ('because I wanted to make my kids' public education better'). Extracts 4 and 5 demonstrate how Palin turns her claim of ordinariness into political advocacy, moving from the presentation of a 'message' to the quasi-contractual speech act of the 'pledge':

> (2) […] that is exactly the kind of man I want as commander in chief. I'm just one of many moms who'll say an extra prayer each night for our sons and daughters going into harm's way.
> And in April, my husband Todd and I welcomed our littlest one into the world, a perfectly beautiful baby boy named Trig. I grew up with those people.

> (3) I was just your average hockey mom, and signed up for the PTA because I wanted to make my kids' public education better.

> (4) To the families of special-needs children all across this country, I have a message: For years, you sought to make America a more welcoming place for your sons and daughters.

> (5) I pledge to you that if we are elected, you will have a friend and advocate in the White House.

A consistent characteristic of these claims to representativeness is the association between the experiences of Palin's background with the responsibilities of her political career. Extract 2, for example, calls explicitly upon the audience's knowledge of Palin's own special needs child. Similar links between down-home representativeness and the possibilities of political advocacy continues through these following extracts:

> (6) When I ran for city council, I didn't need focus groups and voter profiles because I knew those voters, and knew their families, too.

> (7) Before I became governor of the great state of Alaska, I was mayor of my hometown.

The bearing of Palin's experience might well be opened to debate – most notably the implication that techniques for encouraging citizen engagement in the capital of Alaska would function just as well at a national level – but the rhetorical force of the comparison stems from Palin's strategic separation of the technical and exclusionary lexicon used in extract 6 to describe the back-stage activities of political elites – referring to 'focus groups' and 'voter profiles' – and extract 7's positive framing of the elected positions that Palin has occupied.

The next section of the speech, which follows on almost immediately, may be described as the 'simple soul, fallen amongst politicians' phase. Having already constructed an opposition between the honest McCain and a craven political establishment, this is the section of the speech in which Palin draws upon her own homespun credentials to develop a contrast between her and those she had previously named as 'experts in Washington' and that she and the Republican strategists describe as the 'Washington elite':

> (8) And I've learned quickly, these past few days, that if you're not a member in good standing of the Washington elite, then some in the media consider a candidate unqualified for that reason alone.

> (9) But here's a little news flash for all those reporters and commentators: I'm not going to Washington to seek their good opinion – I'm going to Washington to serve the people of this country. Americans expect us to go to Washington for the right reasons, and not just to mingle with the right people.

> (10) While I was at it, I got rid of a few things in the governor's office that I didn't believe our citizens should have to pay for. That luxury jet was over the top. I put it on eBay. I also drive myself to work. And I thought we could muddle through without the governor's personal chef – although I've got to admit that sometimes my kids sure miss her. I came to office promising to control spending – by request if possible and by veto if necessary.

Palin expresses this, first, in terms of a conflict in political interest which, in extract 8 casts her as the naïve interloper and, in extract 9, as the outsider determined to hold fast to their own values. In extract 10, she goes on to express this role of the outsider in a mocking denial of the material excesses of central government. Taken together, all of these extracts draw upon what John Wilson (1990: 62) describes as the claim to sincerity implicit in the use of 'I' in political speeches. Also, by pretending to eschew the normal strategies of political research, not needing a 'focus group', Palin consolidates her claim to be an ordinary person having to engage with the political classes as a painful duty, but while remaining one of the people supposedly represented.

Outside the frame of her political speeches but within the professional contexts that Goffman (1971) would describe as 'front stage' and in public view, Palin expresses this role in a performance of easy and informal courtesy. An illustrative example of this was Palin's handshake with her Democratic counterpart Joe Biden prior to their televised debate, where she asked, in a pseudo-private exchange only just audible over the applause, 'Can I call you Joe?'. Also, the claim expressed in extract 3 that Palin is 'just your average hockey mom' proved to be a resilient item of political shorthand, successful in combining an apparently common touch with an investment in what Angela Smith (2008) highlights as the moral grounding of the politicians' family. Much of the subsequent press coverage of Palin's speech picked up on and emphasised this 'hockey mom' sobriquet. Palin too returned to the description in a image-enhancing display of levity designed to mitigate her aggressive role in the Republican campaign, where she constructed a question and response joke around the name for the benefit of a Republican audience: 'What is the difference between a hockey mom and a pitbull? Lipstick'. Not only a genuinely ordinary and homespun representative, then, but feisty, determined and uncompromisingly protective as well.

Palin therefore engages in a mode of rhetoric carefully designed to generate sympathetic popular sentiment amongst what she and her party see as a core constituency. John Street (2003) discusses such political strategies as these in terms established by P. David Marshall's work on the operation of celebrity. The status of the celebrity, Marshall (1997: 204) argues, is built upon an 'affective function' with the audience – not only to appeal to the audience but to cultivate an emotive response and attachment within them. Street suggests that his drive for an affinity with the audience governs the selling of political personalities every bit as much as other public personalities. Accordingly, strategies are conceived across the realms of both politics and entertainment to market personalities as knowable and appealing. Kathleen Hall Jamieson (1996: 517) describes political advertising as an attempt to make candidates recognisable and distinctive, and 'expose their temperaments, talents and agendas for the future in a favourable light'.

Such that Palin asserts her position as the everywoman that chance and commitment has taken to the political stage, she represents a political personality that has been fashioned along populist lines. Palin's public persona is built around the contours of her own domestic background and concerns for the interests of those close to her. Her claims to ordinariness are concretised by references to her family (extract 2), her disabled child (extract 4) and what she presents as a gut empathy with the regular US voter (extract 5). All of this operates in parallel with an explicitly stated mistrust of the Washington-based system of government (extract 8) and a determination to visit the benefits of her common sense upon what she presents as a Washington elite (extracts 9 and 10). In this way, Palin's lack of experience in the administration of security is presented as lending a uniquely sincere dimension to her faith in McCain's competence to manage national security.

Where Palin's expressed concern with the interests of the US everywoman is most significant in policy terms is where she situates security within the context of a defined set of material interests. These are patterns that serve to emphasise the 'homeland' component of homeland security. The following two extracts are drawn from the latter part of Palin's speech, in which her patterns of pronominal usage shift outward, extending first to an inclusive 'we' and the shifting again towards the listening audience as 'you':

(11) To confront the threat that Iran might seek to cut off nearly a fifth of world energy supplies, or that terrorists might strike again at the Abqaiq facility in Saudi Arabia, or that Venezuela might shut off its oil deliveries, we Americans need to produce more of our own oil and gas. And take it from a gal that knows the North Slope of Alaska: we've got lots of both.

(12) What exactly does [Obama] seek to accomplish, after he's done turning back the waters and healing the planet? The answer is to make government bigger, take more of your money, give you more orders from Washington, and to reduce the strength of America in a dangerous world.

In extract 11, Palin draws upon the supposed folk-knowledge of the ordinary Alaskan (albeit from her position as state governor) to respond to a series of asserted international threats, from Iran, Venezuela and the enemies of Saudi Arabia. This 'we' that is under threat is first named explicitly as the US electorate ('we Americans') and then reasserted in terms of implied shared ownership ['we've got lots of both']. It is in extract 12's direct address to this electorate that Palin expands upon the theme of a US-under-threat (from a 'dangerous world'). She, on the one hand, lists a series of emaciating developments that would inevitably result from an Obama administration (the growth of external control and the lessening of personal wealth), while at the same time deploying 'you' to impose an opposition between electorate themselves and the order-givers of Washington.

Having offered some reflections on the construction of Sarah Palin and its significance, it is useful to note these populist strategies are common across the election campaign; in particular, in the speeches of Barack Obama, since highlighted for their persuasive and inspirational qualities (Sanders, 2009: 235). In a number of important respects, any comparison between Palin and Obama will appear to be strewn with difficulties. For one thing, their speeches are influenced by the different positions they hope to take within the executive, with the differences in expressive freedom and power these bring. Palin is at least partially impeded from presenting herself as an agent of political change by her position as prospective Vice President rather than President, and we have seen that she ameliorates this by foregrounding her claim to be an outsider. Obama, on the other hand, is obliged to present himself as enactor of the Democratic political agenda. Yet, for all these key points of distinction, the relationship between Palin and Obama is an important one. Palin was recruited to the Republican ticket to give voice to the party's attacks on Obama, allowing McCain to retain the demeanour of the statesman he had established in the 2000 presidential primaries, generous to all and above politicking (see Wallace, 2008). Although McCain's avuncular detachment was to be compromised as poll ratings began to recede, specifically in the October televised debate, McCain's lines of attack had already been ventriloquised by Palin: in particular, that Obama had associates with terrorist and anti-American connections. Taking the role that Obama occupied for the Democrats, there is an important sense in which Palin was therefore used as a primary definer of the Republican campaign, setting the terms of the Republican agenda.

In common with Palin, a survey of the use of personal pronouns in Obama's nomination acceptance speech shows the extent of the emphasis on his own background and the competence his own experiences give him to serve. In that speech, Obama even acknowledges that the narrative behind this rhetoric is becoming well-worn with the line 'Four years ago, I stood before you and told my story'. Although the clusters of pronominal usage are less pronounced in Obama's speech than in Palin's, where they were separable into distinct phases, there are a number of similarities. Specifically, and to use the terminology adopted for Palin, Obama includes a prolonged formal acceptance phase, and a brief 'simple soul fallen amongst politicians' phase. However, what distinguishes Obama's speech from Palin's is Obama's extensive use of the inclusive pronoun to refer to the American people.

But before we look at any extract from Obama's speech, it is worth dwelling on the terms and significance of this mode of inclusivity in Palin's speechmaking. While Palin overwhelmingly uses inclusive personal pronouns to refer to herself, her family, her administration, and those presumed to be in communion with the Republican Party, extract 11 highlighted the one passage in which she deploys 'we' in a manner that includes the US people. This is the passage that carries on that nationwide address:

(13) Our opponents [the Democrats and media] say, again and again, that drilling will not solve all of America's energy problems – as if we all didn't know that already. But the fact that drilling won't solve every problem is no excuse to do nothing at all. Starting in January, in a McCain-Palin administration, we're going to lay more pipelines ... build more new-clear plants ... create jobs with clean coal ... and move forward on solar, wind, geothermal, and other alternative sources. We need American energy resources, brought to you by American ingenuity, and produced by American workers.

When it is viewed in the context of extract 11, it is clear that the final inclusive pronoun in this extract is designed to include the US electorate as a whole, having been established by the immediately-preceding specification 'we Americans'. The first two tokens of 'we' and the initial 'our' refer to a Republican administration – on the basis that only they will have the power to act to 'lay more pipelines' – but are sufficiently ambiguous to extend to the listening audience and US population (who are invited to assent to the laying of such pipelines). On the basis of extract 13, it is also apparent that the nation addressed has the common bond of material concerns, as in 'we need', as well as the material possessions of extract 11's 'we've got'. Crucially, these are presented as interests that are best served by the energy policy approved by Palin and the Republican Party, thereby collapsing together national belonging, material interests, and an affinity with core Republican beliefs.

This use of a strategic inclusivity to respond to environmental issues has not been confined to the presidential campaign. This following extract is taken from a speech Palin gave in October 2007 to a local chamber of commerce in her capacity as Governor of Alaska:

(14) More and more we're being challenged to balance the need for development with the need to protect our natural resources.

Just as in extract 13, where one of the pronouns refers to the administration, so there is some ambivalence here in whether the 'we' is that of the nation, the Alaskan people, or the competent authorities. While it is a plausible explanation to see this as an example of what Harvey Sacks (1992: 713) describes as an 'organisational pronoun' that has the effect of both depersonalising action and emphasising institutional duty, what might be read as a tactical uncertainty between an inclusive versus an exclusive 'we' results, in this case, in nation, administration and Republican Party being presented as one.

Obama on America and Safety

We can turn now to Obama's nomination acceptance speech for the Democratic presidential nomination. In this speech, Obama uses inclusive pronouns far more frequently than Palin, spreads them more evenly through the speech, and deploys them in a quite different way. These are two extracts:

> (15) Instead, it is that American spirit – that American promise – that pushes us forward even when the path is uncertain; that binds us together in spite of our differences; that makes us fix our eye not on what is seen, but what is unseen, that better place around the bend.

> (16) America, we cannot turn back. Not with so much work to be done. Not with so many children to educate, and so many veterans to care for. Not with an economy to fix and cities to rebuild and farms to save. Not with so many families to protect and so many lives to mend. America, we cannot turn back. We cannot walk alone. At this moment, in this election, we must pledge once more to march into the future. Let us keep that promise – that American promise – and in the words of Scripture hold firmly, without wavering, to the hope that we confess.

What is again notable is the relative indeterminacy of this inclusiveness. The 'we' that pledges to 'march into the future' may either be interpreted exclusively (to mean Obama and his proposed administration), or inclusively (to encompass the whole American people) (Fairclough, 1989: 127-28). The most likely interpretation – aided substantially by the repeated invocation 'America, we cannot turn back' – is that this is a national 'we'. Even though, as John Wilson (1990: 33) argues, this warming embrace is routinely predicated upon a more chilling threat to national and therefore 'our' well-being, Obama's address is purposefully centred on an abstract and yet socially progressive idea of American belonging, centred on his evocation of politically-inspired 'hope'; consistent through the Democratic campaign merchandise and Obama's (2006) own political writing. In terms of the shared techniques of choreographing audience response (Atkinson, 1984: 108), and in a way that is consistent with extract 16's assertion of political beliefs and shared morals over explicit material interests, Obama's mode of inclusiveness can be placed in the oratory tradition of Martin Luther King. Obama's style is partly that of a man seeking political converts, and who produces what Montgomery (2000) describes as an unbounded 'we' designed, at least in terms of the rhetoric, to reach across national boundaries.

However, when Obama turns to the issue of security, a set of concerns he recasts as 'threat' and 'safety', he uses pronouns in a quite different way:

> (17) That's not the judgment we need. That won't keep America Safe. We need a President who can face the threats of the future, not keep grasping at the ideas of the past.

> (18) We are the party of Roosevelt. We are the party of Kennedy. So don't tell me that Democrats won't defend this country. Don't tell me that Democrats won't keep us safe. The Bush-McCain foreign policy has squandered the legacy that generations of Americans – Democrats and Republicans – have built, and we are here to restore that legacy.

In extract 17, 'we' is contained with the category of those within the political constituency of the American President, and operates as a direct appeal to the national body politic. Included in this is an implicit attack on his electoral opponents: they are, it is implied, grasping at the ideas of the past. In extract 18, however, Obama sets about defending his own security credentials by occupying a role as representative and defender of the Democrat Party, using an exclusive form of 'we' in order to express this illocutionary position. That is, the dominant pattern to emerge from Palin's rhetorical use of pronouns is to implicate the national body within her rhetoric on security, and to align this with a set of political beliefs and material concerns. Where Obama discusses security, on the other hand, the dominant theme is an evocation of his own party's history of trustworthiness and dependability. In sum, Palin's discourse on security is founded upon a mythical 'American people', and sets them against an aloof and wrong-headed state machine, whereas Obama seeks to defend the possibilities of the responsible and diligent state.

Conclusions

Palin and Obama pursue similar rhetorical strategies, such that they draw upon their own backgrounds to establish both the experiential credibility to speak, and to cultivate an affinity with the listening audience. As Willner (1984) points out, fostering the illusion of both of these characteristics and others are defining qualities of the charismatic politician across political traditions. Palin, however, deploys a populist approach to her treatment of security and other issues, one that articulates her down-home representativeness with particular political and economic interests. Jeffrey Scheuer (2001) argues that the easy simplicity of populism suits the right-wing more than other points on the conventional political spectrum. Alain Badiou (2008), for example, argues that the discourse of French President Nicolas Sarkozy depends upon a link between right-wing political populism and the generation of irrational fear. Or to take a still more pertinent example, Robert Putnam (2001) claims that the self-interested materialism often associated with elements of the political right is better served by an unrelenting focus on the self and the actual over the politics of possibility and the more abstract notions of community that this entails. Sarah Palin embodies a style of political rhetoric that draws vitality from her own material interests and beliefs, and who in turn projects her own ordinariness and representativeness onto those very interests. The Republican version of populism, manifest in the figure of Palin, is one that accords with Kazin's (1995) historical description as setting the interests of the common folk at odds with those of the governmental and business elites, but in this case channelled quite specifically through her own experience and homespun wisdom.

While the choice of Palin and her subsequent public profile was partly a response to the perceived elitism of Obama – in her speech she says 'it's easy to forget that this is a man who has authored two memoirs but not a single major law or reform' – the persona of Palin draws deeply from a well of 'anti-intellectualism' in the US. However limited the constituency for these innate suspicions of learning and the establishment, Richard Hofstader (1964) traces them to the crafted simplicity and suspicion of central authority embodied in the Founding Fathers, and that Jude Davis (2006) has mapped onto George W. Bush and other contemporary political figures. But for all that, the rhetoric of Sarah Palin offers important lessons for many of the established views of populism beyond the future possibility of another major figure in the US executive perceived as lacking intellectual weight. In turning the politics of personalisation towards a system of rhetoric based upon the interests of the self, Palin represents a form of populism peculiarly suited to the political right, and provides evidence of a need to think again about the strategies of populism in communicating politics on those issues that draw upon broader concerns.

Acknowledgements

I am grateful for the input of Angela Smith of the University of Sunderland and Martin Montgomery of the University of Strathclyde.

References

Abts, K. and Rummens, S. (2007), 'Populism versus democracy', *Political Studies*, vol. 55: 405-424.

Arendt, H. (1998), *The Human Condition*, 2nd edition, Chicago: Chicago University Press (originally published in 1958).

Atkinson, M. (1984), *Our Masters' Voices: The Language and Body Language of Politics*, London: Routledge.

Badiou, A. (2008), *The Meaning of Sarkozy*, London: Verso.

Brown, R. and Gilman, A. (1972), 'Pronouns of power and solidarity', in P.P. Giglioli (ed.) *Language and Social Context*, Harmondsworth: Penguin (originally published in 1960).

Canovan, M. (1981), *Populism*, London: Junction.

Canovan, M. (2002), 'Taking politics to the people: populism as the ideology of democracy', in Y. Mény and Y. Surel (eds) *Democracies and the Populist Challenge*, New York: Basic Books.

Council on Foreign Relations (2008), 'Issue tracker: the candidates on homeland security', [Online], Available: http://www.cfr.org/publication/14763/candidate_on_homeland_security.html, accessed 27 February 2009.

Davies, J. (2007), 'Stupid white men: towards a political mapping of stupidity', *Research in English and American Literature*, vol. 23: 189-210.

Debray, R. (1983), *Critique of Political Reason*, London: New Left Books.

Drake, P. and Higgins, M. (2006), 'I'm a celebrity, get me into politics: the political celebrity and the celebrity politician', in S. Holmes and S. Redmond (eds) *Framing Celebrity: New Directions in Celebrity Culture*, London: Routledge.

Fairclough, N. (1989), *Language and Power*, London: Longman.

Fairclough, N. (2000), *New Labour, New Language?*, London: Routledge.

Goffman, E. (1971), *The Presentation of Self in Everyday Life*, Harmondsworth: Penguin.

Goffman, E. (1986), *Frame Analysis: An Essay on the Organisation of Experience*, Boston: Northeastern University Press.

Gramsci, A. (1971), *Selections from Prison Notebooks*, London: Lawrence and Wishart.

Higgins, M. (2004), 'The articulation of nation and politics in the Scottish press', *Journal of Language and Politics*, vol. 3: 463-483.

Higgins, M. (2008), *Media and Their Publics*, Maidenhead: Open University Press.

Hofstader, R. (1964), *Anti-intellectualism in American Life*, London: Jonathan Cape.

Jamieson, K.H. (1996), *Packaging the Presidency: A History and Criticism of Presidential Campaign Advertising*, 3rd edition, New York: Oxford University Press.

Kazin, M. (1998), *The Populist Persuasion: An American History*, revised edition, Ithaca: Cornell University Press.

Laclau, E. (1977), *Politics and Ideology in Marxist Theory: Capitalism, Fascism, Populism*, London: Verso.

Marshall, P.D. (1997), *Celebrity and Power*, Minneapolis: Minnesota University Press.

McCain, J. and Salter, M. (2007), *Hard Call: Great Decisions and the Extraordinary People Who Made Them*, New York: Twelve.

Montgomery, M. (2000), 'Discourse, identity and nationalism', in M. Coperías Aguilar (ed.) *Culture and Power: Challenging Discourses*, Valencia: Universitat de Valencia.

Obama, B. (2006), *The Audacity of Hope: Thoughts on Reclaiming the American Dream*, New York: Crown.

Obama, B. (2008), 'Full text of Barack Obama's acceptance of the Democratic nomination for president', http://www.guardian.co.uk/world/2008/aug/29/uselections2008.barackobama2, accessed 9 October 2008.

Palin, S. (2007), 'Speech to Juneau Chamber of Commerce Annual Dinner', 27 October, http://gov.state.ak.us/speeches-58442.html, accessed 2 October 2008

Pinker, S. (2008), 'Everything you heard is wrong', *New York Times*, 4 October.

Putnam, R.D. (2001), *Bowling Alone: The Collapse and Revival of American Community*, New York: Simon & Schuster.

Rees, W. (2009), 'Securing the homelands: transatlantic co-operation after Bush', *The British Journal of Politics and International Relations*, vol. 11: 108-121.

Sacks, H. (1992), *Lectures on Conversation: Volume 1*, Oxford: Blackwell.

Sanders, K. (2009), *Communicating Politics in the Twenty-First Century*, Basingstoke: Palgrave Macmillan.

Scheuer, J. (2001), *The Sound Bite Society*, New York: Routledge.

Smith, A. (2008), 'Son of the manse or new man? Gordon Brown as reluctant celebrity father', *British Politics*, vol. 3: 556-575.

Street, J. (2003), 'The celebrity politician: political style and popular culture', in J. Corner and D. Pels (eds) *Media and the Restyling of Politics*, London: Sage.

Times Online (2008), Full text of Sarah Palin's speech to Republican Convention, http://www.timesonline.co.uk/tol/news/world/us_and_americas/us_elections/article4671886.ece, accessed 1 November 2008.

Wallace, D.F. (2008), *McCain's Promise*, New York: Back Bay.

Willner, A.R. (1984), *The Spellbinders: Charismatic Political Leadership*, New Haven: Yale University Press.

Wilson, J. (1990), *Politically Speaking: The Pragmatic Analysis of Political Language*, Oxford: Blackwell.

Chapter 8

Towards a Theorisation of the Link Between Media, Religion and Conflict

Lee Marsden and Heather Savigny

Underlying the compelling case studies in this book have been a series of theoretical concerns about the nature of contemporary political discourse, and the way in which the media conflate, interpret, present and re-represent religion and conflict. At the heart of each chapter is an awareness of a set of complex interactions between media, religion, conflict within (and in the case of religion also outside of) a neoliberal environment. In order to make sense of these complex processes, this final chapter is devoted to teasing out some of these theoretical concerns. We are arguing that while these three categories may be treated elsewhere as analytically distinct, they are ontologically intertwined, and so we are seeking to produce an analytical framework which maps this analytical and ontological terrain. In so doing we suggest there are underlying tensions in the relationship between the media, religion and conflict, and we seek to offer a framework which enables a reflection upon the contingent nature of this interaction. Underlying all the chapters is a concern with the relation between structure and agency. As such, we begin by providing an overview of structuration/the structure/agency debate and within this highlight the importance of the role of ideas. We then move to consider each of the three analytic categories (media, religion and conflict) in turn, and the links between them, through this framework and conclude by suggesting a framework of analytic integration.

Overview of the Conceptual Issues Underpinning the Case Studies

Each chapter in its own distinctive way has made a contribution to understanding the myriad ways in which the relationship between the media, religion and conflict takes place. While these chapters can be viewed as studies in their own right, what they also enable us to do more broadly, is reflect upon the way in which we might analyse the relationship between media, religion and conflict, all of which takes place in a political context.

As briefly noted in the introduction, we use the terms media, religion, conflict and politics as generic labels, but these also have particular meanings. As we are seeking to highlight, the interactions between these are complex, and so in order to present as clear an analytic frame as possible we adopt the following definitions:

Politics: While recognising that politics can refer to all forms of interaction where power relationships take place (so both in the personal sphere as well as the public) in this chapter we revert to a formal, traditional definition and use the term politics and political system to refer to the formal mechanisms of the state. This encompasses both the domestic workings of the state, such as that of politicians, executive, legislature and bureaucracy and the state as an actor in the international arena which can also be represented by world leaders. We also acknowledge that within this formal definition there is the existence of a set of political ideas which underpin behaviour.

Media: When we refer to the media, again while we recognise the existence of a plethora of media forms (such as books, films, magazines, mobile phones) and media content whereby politics can be played out (such as entertainment media) we use the term 'media' to mean traditional media forms whose content has a news agenda, so we are referring mainly to broadcast and print media.

Religion: Where we refer to religion, although a theological perspective would draw attention to the belief in a supernatural power as driving behaviour, we adopt the conventional IR/Political science approach which more broadly defined relates to the behaviour of communities prescribed by religious leaders, sacred texts and traditions. As with politics, however, this allows for the acknowledgement of a set of ideas and values which inform action and behaviour.

Conflict: Where we use the term conflict we take this term to refer to disputes within and between states and more broadly to refer to a struggle between opposing forces, ideas and interest which may or may not lead to violence. This highlights the existence and significance of a sense of 'otherness'. The notion of conflict is both reliant on the existence of an 'other' and at the same time can lead to a reinforcement of that sense of 'other'. In brief, conflict arises where there is an incompatibility or mutual exclusiveness leading to contestation in the aspirations and desires of actors.

As with all forms of social science, there are a number of ways in which to reflect upon the relationship between these differing aspects, and each requires a different starting point. Clearly, there are tensions within political systems about the sets of ideas which underpin them and if we accept that the relationship between media, religion and conflict is played out in a broader political context, then it is important to reflect upon some of the tensions both between and within this arena (for example, as drawn out in the discussion of the 'left' by Cohen). We have also seen the importance of the role of the media in political society and the way in which the media themselves have played a role in endorsing the political conflation of religion with forms, and as sources, of contemporary conflict (as Lewis et al. in this volume have highlighted). The media have also played a role as re-presenters of conflict (Gaber et al.) as well as their interaction with political elites providing a source of conflict (Bødker; Ettinger and Udris). We have also seen the tensions between religion and politics providing the starting point of analysis (Haynes) and the way in which religious actors seek to play a political role (Bradley). At the same time attention has been drawn to the way in which religion has provided the context within which political action has taken place which in turn has been played out through the media (Higgins). What we are seeking to do is highlight the complexity of these interactions, which we seek to conceptually map below.

Structure and Agency

The first conceptual issue which becomes immediately apparent is the relationship between structure and agency. While the aim here is not to seek to refine the structure/agency debate (not least as it has been done far more eloquently elsewhere see for example, Hay, 2001) but to use this debate as a 'problematique' for mapping some of the complex processes at stake within this book.

The structure/agency debate has taken a number of directions. Some have sought to present this as a 'problem' requiring a solution. Others represent this as a 'problematique'; as a mechanism through which to problematise and theorise the world around us. It is this latter approach that we adopt within this chapter. Clearly debates about structure and agency are not new to the fields of sociology, political science or international relations, indeed, Marx's maxim that 'men make history but not in circumstances of their own choosing', highlights the historical and ongoing nature of this concern. The issue here is neither to seek a 'solution' nor to determine which came first, the structure or the agent, and as such which should be privileged in analysis and explanations, rather we contend, this debate provides us a means through which to understand the contingent nature of the interactions between media, religion and conflict.

The 'problem' of structure and agency as outlined by Giddens in his structuration theory suggests that structures and agents are analytically separable. Structures are assumed to both constrain and facilitate action. Structures and agents are involved in a dialectical relationship, and neither remains static. That is, we can analyse structures and we can analyse an agent's interaction within structures, but these structures are not static and are constituted and reconstituted over time, as a consequence of an agent's interaction with them. As such agents act within, or action may be constrained by, structures, but crucially that (in)action within those structures serves to reinforce and reconstitute those structures. This reconstitution is dialectical and ongoing, so that those reconstituted structures then provide alternate courses of action, within which agents act (or not), and then reconstitute and reshape those structures (cf. Giddens, 1984). We build on this and draw on the work of Hay (1995; 2001) drawing attention to the mutually interdependent relationship (both analytical and ontological) between the two. In this way, we reflect upon structure and agency as a process, but with a particular emphasis upon the interaction between the two.

The 'strategic-relational' approach as developed in the work of Hay (1996) and Jessop (1990) suggests that action occurs within a particular structure or context. This context is *strategically selective* – that is, it favours certain strategies over others. Highlighting the fluid and contingent nature of interaction, this approach suggests that the interaction between structures and agents is not necessarily as equal as implied by Giddens and while, like Giddens' work, this illustrates how structures and agents can interact and transform each other, this strategic selection means that the pre-existing structure privileges certain strategies over others. So, for example, while the pre-existing structure of the media industry may be open to anyone who wishes to produce a newspaper, the prohibitive start up costs (for example, in terms of lack of access to existing channels of production and distribution) mean that very few individuals are actually likely to enter the market place. That is the media marketplace is structured as 'strategically selective': influencing who is likely to set up a newspaper. This does not mean it is impossible for any individual to set up a newspaper, but it is just much more difficult than it would be for an existing business in the media industry. In this way the structure of the media industry can be seen as both facilitators and constrainers of action.

A third dialectical approach to structure and agency takes account of the role of culture as a mediating layer in the relationship between structure and agency. As defined by Archer (1996) the premise is that structure and agency are still analytically distinct, but that culture plays a role in mediating between the two, adding another layer to social reality. The role of culture is also fluid and contingent and vacillates between being 'the superordinate power in society' akin to performing a hegemonic role, and being 'reduced to a mere epiphenomenon (charged only with providing an ideational representation of structure)' (1996:1). In this way, the introduction of culture enables us to reflect upon the layers which may influence an agent's view or perception of the structures within which s/he finds her/himself. That is culture embodies a framework, as a set of values and normalising ideas through which actors perceive the structures within which they are operating. For example, if we are to look at media organisations and their function in society, we do so through a cultural lens of an acceptance of the existence of liberal democratic capitalism. What this highlights is the importance of a consideration of the role of the ideational alongside the material. Accepting the critical realist position outlined above, we argue that ideas clearly play a role in the process of understanding, analysing and the construction of social reality. Following Hay (2001), we also accept that ideas play an important role in this process and we accept that ideas cannot be divorced from the material processes and contexts within which they emerge and become embedded.

In this brief summary there are a number of conceptual issues that we wish to draw attention to. First, the structure and agency debate provides us with a (relatively) simple mechanism through which to identify not only what is significant in analysis, but why this might be the case and the role of that conceptual or analytical category. Second, the structure/agency debate is not viewed here as a 'problem' or something which needs resolution in its own right. Rather, following Hay, we suggest it is a 'language by which ontological differences between contending narratives may be registered' (2001:3). In this way, the structure/ agency problematique provides us with the vocabulary and conceptual toolkit through which to reflect upon the interaction between structures and agents, rather

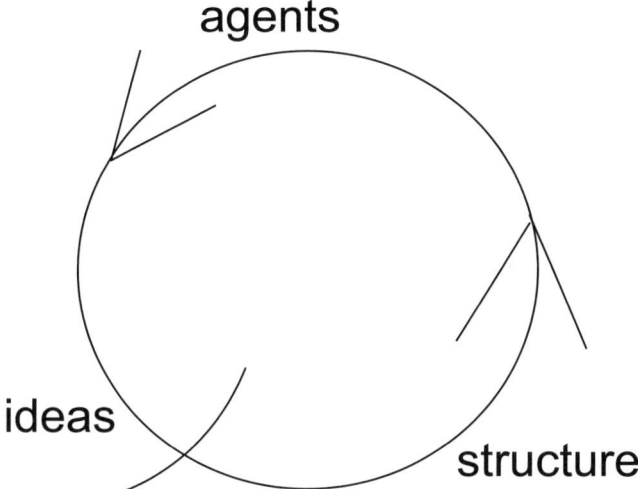

Figure 8.1   Dialectical interaction between agents and structures in which structures are perceived by agents through a lens of ideas

than establish causal solutions to explain political and social phenomena. It is this interaction which is of primary concern, as this interaction produces both intended and unintended consequences. This also provides us with a mechanism through which we can explore the complexities of the relationships between media, religion and conflict. Third, a strategic relational approach to the issue of structure and agency, enables us to us to think through why some strategies may be privileged over others and fourth, the introduction of the role of the ideational component (referred to hereafter as ideas) enables us to explore and think through why actors perceive these structures in the way that they do (diagrammatically represented in Figure 8.1)

Providing this conceptual basis we now move to explore the ways in which the analytical categories that have been the theme of this book can be analysed through the framework provided in the structure/agency problematique. We do this in the following three sections. The final section suggests that in order to understand the relationship and interaction between the three we need to analytically integrate them, providing for a more fluid account, reflecting an awareness of the contingent nature of this interaction.

The Media: Structure and Agency

As has been suggested throughout this book, the media have the capacity to act as both structures and agents. As has been made clear throughout, we accept that the media operate within a political context (either domestically or internationally), and this political context is characterised by political ideas and beliefs as well as the existence of political agents who perceive this structure through that lens of ideas (for example in the West, through a neoliberal framework). Our main concern in this section however, is to draw attention to the interaction between the media as a structure and the potential for the media to exhibit degrees of agency as mediated through a 'lens' of ideas.

Viewing the media as structure draws attention to the way in which media structures are situated and shaped by their political context. Political structures, in Western systems, position the media as businesses, open to competition and responsive to market demands (although this relationship is slightly different within public service broadcasting organisations). On a material level, this has taken the form of a proliferation of media forms, de-regulatory legislation and changes in patterns of media ownership (through mergers and acquisitions) producing a small number of media conglomerates with global production and distribution chains, all of which have served to increase market pressure as news media compete for audiences in a bid to retain profitability.

For some, competition is thought to lead to a more wide ranging and diverse media (Bagdikian, 1990). However, more recent empirical investigations have shown the opposite to be the case. Lewis et al. (2008) have noted the way in which the political economy of newsgathering is now characterised by a lack of journalistic sources, and an overreliance of journalists on official sources and PR rather than independent reportage. As the number of news gathering agencies decrease, so we witness more narrow, and less diverse coverage. Davies illustrates the difficulties of this through an interview with former *Sunday Times* reporter Philip Knightley who gives the example of *Newsweek*, the magazine which prided itself on world coverage, and which no longer has bureaus covering the Middle East, and is 'now covered by reporters working out of those two big Islamic news centres – London and Paris' (Davies, 2008: 100). Davies attributes this simply to the pressures of the market (this also has serious implications for the quality of information that we receive via our media sources). As traditional media face increasing competitive pressures from a proliferation of news sources, for example, 24 hour news provision and more notably from new media technologies which make news available for free, in order to stay in business, newspapers have responded by cutting back on staffing and increasing reliance on official sources and PR.

If traditional media forms are competing against free media content via new technologies, raising revenue from advertising becomes even more of a salient issue. But this need to gain revenue through advertising functions to structure the media industry in a particular way. As Gamson et al. observe 'media organizations use news and other programming as a commodity to attract an audience which they can then sell to advertisers' (1992: 377). In this way audiences are 'sold' to advertisers, and the primary aim becomes to attract an audience, not for media content per se, but for advertisers. As Herman and Chomsky (1988) observe, there is little incentive for media organisations to produce content which targets audiences with little or no buying power. This then privileges the role of advertisers, suggesting that an awareness of the demands of advertisers mean that some media and news content, that which is likely to encourage the public to adopt a 'buying mood' (Gamson et al., 1992), is more likely to be strategically selected than others.

If we also wish to consider the media, not simply as structurally determined, but as displaying an agential role, then almost immediately we can start to see some constraints. If media structures are governed by political and economic imperatives, this for example, constrains the opportunity for individual journalists and media outlets to engage in more critical journalism. In the vocabulary of the strategic relational approach, the media context thus selects a structure which downplays opportunities for critical journalism and content which may not produce consumers for advertisers which in turn means that dominant views and ideologies are largely reproduced rather than challenged. The underlying neoliberal democratic capitalism becomes the ideational lens through which media content is 'framed' and discourses reproduced. Moreover, we witness the role of owners and editors who seek to manipulate the media agenda to reflect their political interests (for example Murdoch's *News International Corporation*) and in this media owners, through their outlets can exhibit agential qualities and can play a role in structuring the news agenda. The interrelationship between journalists and politicians also provides a site of contestation and conflict whereby politicians seek to manipulate news agendas to positively present their own political line, and while they need news stories also seek to retain a commitment to espousing journalistic rather than political values. At the same time, strategic selectivity reminds us that the pressure for news stories coupled with a declining demand for newspapers and a shrinking number of news agencies, mean that the strategic selection is one which accepts and reproduces political PR, rather than sourcing alternative stories. As such, this exposes a series of tensions between the liberal theoretical demand for 'truth' and objectivity (suggesting the media have the capacity to display agency) and the tension of the demands of the market as the context and structure within which the media both operate.

Religion: Structure and Agency

Religion is the unusual analytic category in this book, as it plays the role of a structure, can display agency but also embodies a set of explicitly stated ideas and values. There are clear tensions when discussing the role of religion in contemporary society. To a certain extent these tensions have always existed and indeed the structure/agency debate can be seen to have its antecedents in theological debates around predestination and freewill (cf. Schmalzbauer, 2003). Religion operates as structure in its denominational or organisational role providing a context in which action takes place. Traditionally, religion provided the structure which underpinned social and power relations both within the church and within wider society, as identified by the founding fathers of sociology. Marx's approach to religion was entirely structural interpreting the function of religion as maintaining the status quo and keeping the proletariat compliant. Durkheim also acknowledges this role but further considered that religion was essential to enable society to function:

> Religion instructed the humble to be content with their situation, and, at the same time it taught them that the social order is providential: that it is God himself who as determined each one's share. Religion gave men a perception of a world beyond this earth where everything would be rectified; this prospect made inequalities less noticeable, it stopped men feeling aggrieved (Durkheim, 1972: 177).

In modern British and American society religion has become subordinate to secular institutions – however, the legitimation and moral underpinning of such societies rests on religious foundations. Durkheim's conscience collective remains dependent on religion and religious ritual (see Day, 2008). This can be seen in Western Europe where despite the decline in religious observance and belief the calendar and holidays are nonetheless determined by Christian practice and ritual. In Britain, the Church of England is the established religion with Archbishops automatically entitled to sit in the upper legislature chamber. The monarch is crowned by the Archbishop of Canterbury and is at once head of state and head of the church. All major national events including remembrance parades, the funerals of ex-prime ministers, the triumphs and failures of the country's military adventures are celebrated within a religious context.

In the United States where the constitution enshrines the separation of church and state in accordance with the intentions of the founding fathers religion is not simply confine to the private sphere. Religion as structure not only provides a moral and ethical compass for believers but also provides a shared narrative of a nation blessed by God in which the religious belief of politicians, especially a would be president, remains crucial in a country where it is conceivable for a black man or a woman but not an atheist to be elected president. As in Britain, the views of organised religion, continues to enjoy privileged access to political leaders and the media.

Modern society is distinguished by the secular state, where religion retains a privileged position in return for legitimating existing power structures within society, and can be called upon to reinforce shared ideals and nationhood. In traditional societies, including but not exclusively countries with Muslim majorities, the role of church, mosque or temple is more overt. Rather than appealing to secular values and institutions it is the shared values of the *hadith*, *Qu'ran*, sharia law, the *torah*, *halakhah*, or the Ten Commandments and Sermon on the Mount that provide structure. This can be recognised most clearly in the theocratic states of Iran and Saudi Arabia and in regions of Pakistan, Afghanistan, Somalia and Sudan where sharia law is practiced. Mary Maslak's observation of the Tharu community in Nepal provides a useful insight into religion as structure. She identified that it was the religious structure that provided the framework in which adults could function, and which determined power relations between genders. Religious ritual only involved men and this:

> ... creates and maintains a power structure that imbues them with the power to listen to the word of the gods and spirits, and to convey their interpretation of those words to women (Maslak, 2003: 163).

Clearly, in Maslak's example religion operates as both structure and agency. The community functions on a set of shared values/rituals (structure) but these are moderated and interpreted by men (agency), thereby reducing women's agency to actively influence decision making.

Religion exists as structure but is interpreted by agents, such interpretations by priest, rabbi or imam and religious actors external to the immediate place of worship reinforces the structure and becomes the conscience collective within religious communities. Further, religion displays agency when it demonstrates the capacity to shape contexts through religious leaders (agents) acting in the political sphere. Those religious leaders are not limited to church, mosque, synagogue or temple but also include writers, religious celebrities, evangelists, and religious organisational leaders. Such agents have the capacity to shape contexts beyond the local to the international. During the Iranian revolution and thereafter Ayatollah Khomeini achieved the overthrow of the Shah, the institution of theocratic government, inspired resurgence in radical Islamism, and was able to issue *fatwas*, including against Salman Rushdie, which had an impact on political processes in Britain and around the world.

The proclamations and actions of Osama bin Laden and Ayman al-Zawahiri on behalf of al Qaeda, have the capacity to inspire jihadists and to shape the political agenda of Arab and western governments. A series of spectacular attacks, combined with the capacity to kill western forces in Iraq and Afghanistan, covered extensively by the media, graphically illustrates how religious agency can determine media coverage, legislative decision making, security policy, and relationships between majority and minority communities within national boundaries.

In the United States, Christian Zionist organisations and pro-Israel Jewish lobbies, such as Christians United for Israel and the American Israel Public Action Committee, are able to shape US foreign policy on the Arab-Israel dispute through their ability to influence Congressmen, Senators, and, certainly under the Bush administration the White House itself. Religion acting as agency has also been instrumental in persuading governments in the United States to reduce the cost of antiviral drugs to combat HIV/AIDS in Africa, and provide billions of dollars in assistance to combat the disease. In the United Kingdom the Make Poverty History campaign to reduce global poverty had its roots in the Christian Jubilee 2000 campaign and was able to change government policy. Successive Popes have appealed to Roman Catholic congregations totalling over one billion people across the world, and where they have been unable to influence government policy on issues such as abortion or birth control have appealed directly to church members over the heads of governments. Pope John Paul II is credited with inspiring Poland's solidarity movement and becoming the catalyst leading to the collapse of communism in Eastern Europe. The effectiveness of religion as agency is that governments actively court religious leaders in order to elicit their support for policies, including going to war, and the media actively seek to report the latest proclamations of Pope Benedict, Archbishop Williams, Osama bin Laden, or Moqtada al Sadr.

Religion is, however, much more than just the expression of the political beliefs of religious leaders and the religious group. As Anthony King posits: 'religion refers to the collective consciousness of particular social groups, created and recreated in periods of exclusive interaction' (King, 2004: 139). Where King, following Durkheim, privileges the group over individual agency we assert that the group is significantly influenced by the individual agency of leaders. Whether there is a group or individual agency at work the significance is that both are manifestations of religious agency at work.

Structure and agency in religion are also interlinked as a set of ideas where religion provides a set of moral guiding principles which inform and motivate behaviour in a particular way. This normative impulse both prescribes and exhorts certain behavioural traits. In Christianity it might be applying the golden rule of doing unto others as you would have them do to you, and not breaking the Ten Commandments. In liberation theology it would be to apply a social gospel with a bias to the poor or in the prosperity doctrine of neo-Pentecostalism of giving in order to receive wealth from God. In Islam the injunction to jihad, the inner struggle to become a better, more spiritual person and to obey the Qur'an as interpreted by religious agents.

Secularisation has unsuccessfully sought to compartmentalise religion and politics, confining the former to the private sphere in order to enable economic progress without the moral constraint of religious belief, which has in the past and within Islam today lending money for profit, an essential component of capitalism. Today, in most of the world such artificial division between the secular and the religious has broken down or indeed was always overstated by parochial western sociologists. The relationship between the two remains in tension as Christianity in the West seeks to maintain its privileged status in face of competition from other faiths and secularists. Christianity, in common with other faiths is heterogeneous and its capacity to serve as structure and act as agent varies depending on the relative power of the branch of the faith being examined. Tensions may exist between secular political and economic power structures as when the Roman Catholic church in Latin America embraced liberation theology but today in much of the world growing churches have adapted well to neoliberal hegemony. This should not be surprising as churches seek to advance the needs of their own organisation and the close identification of Protestantism as a key component in the development of capitalism (cf. Weber, 1930; Tawney, 1938). In a real sense Christianity and neoliberalism are linked by an underlying philosophy.

There are greater tensions between Islam and neoliberalism especially following the US led invasions of Iraq, Afghanistan, and US support for Israel. While democracy may not be incompatible with Islam as evidenced by democratic governance for example in Turkey, Bangladesh, Indonesia and Malaysia and the tradition of *shura* (consultation), neoliberalism with its obsession with markets, flexible, portable land, insecure labour forces, and the expansion of global capitalism, probably is, if not with elites certainly where tensions exist between the demands of global capital against the demands of Islam as defined by religious leaders.

How then are such tensions played out in the media and what determines why some strategies are pursued rather than others? Whereas in this volume Haynes identifies a shift from the secular media to a more religious media in Turkey for the west in particular there is a strong secular bias in the media. This can be gleaned anecdotally from the surfeit of articles posted on the world wide web by religious individuals and organisations condemning the 'secular press' for failing to take them seriously and denigrating their beliefs. In John Schmalzbauer's (2003) survey of US journalism and academia he acknowledges the secular nature of the media but argues that many journalists and academics are increasingly comfortable with incorporating their religious sensibilities into their work. Although as he notes, some journalists and academics did make the point about being able to differentiate between advocacy and objectivity.

There is a fundamental incompatibility between the market pressures of modern media and sensitivity to religious issues. In a neoliberal political and economic environment in order to sell copy and advertising space the stories which sell are those involving power, influence, sensationalism and scandal. The imperative is to entertain, shock, surprise and excite audiences. In such an environment religion is able to offer a surfeit of stories which can fulfil this demand. The more controversial speeches and actions receive coverage and more moderate positions tend to be ignored as of no interest to readers. The opportunity to portray religious actors as hypocrites, through the moral impropriety of non-ethical share ownership, child abuse, sex scandals, homophobia, or holocaust denial is to good an opportunity to be missed. This is more easily achieved without ethical or moral considerations about the veracity of such stories troubling editors. This separation of a secular media and a religious 'other' can be overstated. Although a secular media might appear to sit in judgement on religion it actually seeks to use religion for its own purposes. Knowing that many of its audience are religious there is an unwillingness to deliberately alienate consumers. In the same way that politics and the church are assumed to be separated (but linked by underlying ideology) so the media and religion are assumed to be separate, although if the media and politics are underpinned by a commitment to neoliberalism, this also entails a commitment to the Christian principles that inform neoliberalism.

Western liberalism assumes a secular state, but, as noted in the introduction, while this secularisation may lead to a formal split between church and state; this separation is slightly more complex in the underpinning of contemporary liberalism of Christian values. While Christianity as a set of ideas is riven with conflict and opposing viewpoints, this opposition has remained largely separate from the state since the first amendment of the US Constitution ratified in 1791, constitutionally in the United States and *de facto* in liberal democracies elsewhere.

What we are suggesting then is that religion can be viewed as a structure both within and across societies. Given the secular nature of the contemporary state, in British and American societies, religious structures overlap with political structures but are not totally subsumed by them. While religious structures are subject to the legal jurisdiction of the states, nonetheless there is an aspect of religious structures which functions outside of the formal political sphere, which relates to the secular, private and spiritual dimension. Where there is overlap, religious leaders seek to act and effect change within the political sphere. While both political and religious actors perceive these structures through a lens of ideas, this lens is linked through an interlinkage of the Christianity which underpins neoliberalism and Christianity's adaption to the contemporary variant of neoliberalism.

Conflict: Structure and Agency

The structural realism of Kenneth Waltz was the dominant paradigm within international relations and security throughout the Cold War. In seminal texts including *Man, the State and War* and *Theory of International Politics* (Waltz, 1959; 1979) Waltz presented the world of international politics as characterised by anarchy, self-help and power balancing, where conflict and war were inevitable and hence the primary concern of the state. With the end of the Cold War this dominant paradigm came under sustained attack as liberal internationalism and liberal institutionalism portrayed a world no longer condemned to permanent conflict but one where economic interdependence, the democratic peace thesis and international institutions held out the prospect for a pacific future. Even in a Unipolar world, with the United States as global hegemon, asymmetric interdependence would reduce the impulse to war (Keohane and Nye, 1989). Yet the promise of a radically changed world has receded, if it ever really existed, states continue to dominate the international system, international organisations remain subordinate to national interests, states opt to either balance or bandwagon depending on regional sensibilities and self-interest, democracies are just as likely to go to war as non democracies, and where the global hegemony of the superpower is not balanced it will go to war in order to replace regimes not of its liking such as Iraq and Afghanistan. Although interdependence may lead to peace it is just as likely to lead to war, no less so in a neoliberal economic and political order (cf. Waltz, 2000).

The structure of the international system for realists and liberals remains anarchic, for Alexander Wendt, unlike Waltz, that structure is not a given but rather a social construct that can change for anarchy is what states make of it (Wendt, 1992). Wendt also challenged structural realism's emphasis on the causal power of structure (Wendt, 1987; 1999). Whichever theoretical standpoint is adopted and whether adherents consider conflict inevitable or not, conflict occurs and is mediated in the press and broadcasts. In the power politics of the Cold War the structure of an anarchic international system was sustained through the existence of an 'other', either communist or capitalist depending on which side of the bipolar divide you were situated. This structure determined the dominant paradigm of 'red threat' in which all conflict, including national liberation struggles in South East Asia and Latin America, were viewed through the prism of existential threat.

In the post-Cold war period the existence of an 'other' is constructed in order to be able to legitimate action in pursuit of a neoliberal agenda. The red threat is simply replaced by the Islamist threat, enabling neoliberal incursions to be made in states previously antagonistic to neoliberal economic and political systems. The media collude in such constructions and become part of the structure in some cases believing the 'other' presents a threat but often because a conflictual presentation of the 'other' plays to people's fears and hence sells newspapers and advertising space.

Conflict, however, is also something which can reshape and influence the structure (display agency) in terms of individuals (e.g. politicians) seeking to pursue overtly conflictual strategies – the decision by George Bush and Tony Blair to turn the 9/11 attacks into a war on terror and an opportunity to redraw the map in the Middle East through democratic imposition, reshapes pacific interdependence into conflictual neo-imperialism, where liberal internationalism or neo-conservatism pursue strategies that are more conflictual than the structural realism they claimed to have departed from.

Structures are not forever fixed, but, as Ken Booth points out they affect people's decisions but do not determine them. Individuals are not able to exercise complete freewill but act as structured agents (Booth, 2007: 216, 218). States, themselves can only be regarded as agents when: 'the agency of individuals in a representative capacity carries the allocative and authoritative resources of the state with it' (McSweeny, 1999: 150). The structure is able to change when the mediated agency of individual leaders determine to change the structure. When an African American president is elected does the structure determine how he is able to act in the international and domestic arenas? Will he be constrained by the structure to only act in predetermined ways thereby negating individual agency or does the power of new mediated ideas have the capacity to determine whether a US president will seek out and confront the 'other' or seek to reach out to others towards a pacific non confrontational world politics. Is it possible to move to the 'yes we can' of agency from the 'no we can't' of structure. Ken Booth sums up the dilemma succinctly when he posits that: 'Structures can't *conceive* new structures but human agents can even if they cannot *construct* them' (Booth, 2007: 217).

Whether conflict is understood through a realist/structural realist, liberal institutionalist or constructivist paradigm the structure/agency debate has contemporary resonance within the context of dominant neoliberalism and keeps alive the potential for agency to bring about change in the world system. In the

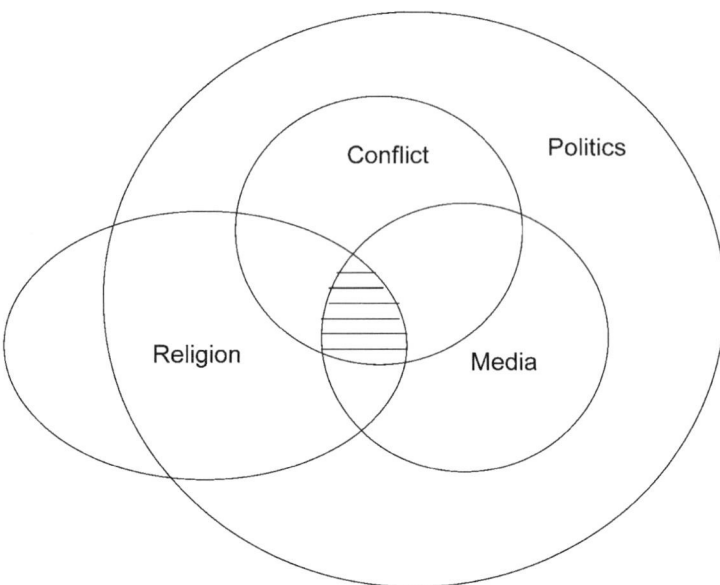

Figure 8.2   Dialectical and fluid interaction between media, religion and conflict in a political context. Analytical intersection represented by shaded area

mean time conflict underpins and constitutes structure and agency by presenting the 'other' as threat, 'us' as threatened, and the only conflict resolution to be found in the 'other' becoming 'us', through persuasion (religious, secular, political or economic conversion) or force. In such a process media and religion acquiesce or resist depending not on the merits or argument of the case but on their economic and political self interest.

Conclusion: Integrating Media, Conflict and Religion

The aim of this chapter has been to highlight both the complexity, and some of the underlying tensions which are inherent in the analysis, of the interaction between media, religion and conflict. As represented diagrammatically in Figure 8.2, what we have been seeking to highlight is that all three analytical categories have the capacity to reflect both structural and agential qualities and that structures are perceived by agents through an ideational lens. This interaction is dynamic and fluid, a process rather than a static event. Moreover, what we are seeking to show is that these categories overlap, constituting and reconstituting themselves and, in part influencing each other. What has been suggested is that the media have the capacity to operate as both structures and agents in the representation of the contemporary political context media and conflict. In this way, we are able to explore the role that the media (in its various forms) may play in setting the context through which religion and conflict are represented and interlinked in public discourse.

Analysing this interaction as a process reveals a series of tensions which may produce both intended and unintended consequences. In the political context, the discourse of an 'other' is one which is used by political elites to legitimate their actions both as states and within states. Religious debates tend to be played out in the media as conflictual and conflict and characterised by animosity rather than emphasising the shared values and understandings and opportunities for cooperation. This particular 'framing' of religion as conflictual (whether intended or an unintended) then serves to legitimate, or at least fails to challenge, the actions of political elites whose political strategies are premised upon the need for an 'other'. In a media structure where newsgathering capacity is reduced, reliance on official sources increases (Davies, 2008). As noted earlier, tensions then arise between the demands of the market and the demands of the democratic functioning of the media. The dominance of Western liberal democratic capitalism as a framework through which this tension is viewed enables the possibility to reflect upon conflict as a mechanism through which news can be 'sold' to audiences and audiences sold to advertisers. At the same time, however, this means that the discourse of 'otherness' remains unchallenged and is simply reproduced. In the post Cold War era, and particularly since the iconic imagery and subsequent events following 9/11, that discourse of 'otherness' has been polarised around religion as a source of conflict, which in turn has been used by political elites to legitimate political strategies, both within and between states.

Throughout this book we have argued that the media, religion and conflict are ontologically interlinked and that in order to understand one we must necessarily have an understanding of all three, in order to do this, we need to treat them as analytically interlinked and interdependent categories. In this chapter, the way in which we have sought to illustrate this is through reference to the structure agency debate as a mechanism of problematising this relationship and drawing attention to the interaction as the area of analysis. This conceptualisation underpins the preceding chapters which have through differing lenses sought to shed some light on an aspect of the interaction of media, religion and conflict, in a complex and turbulent political environment.

Bibliography

Archer, M.S. (1996), *Realist Social Theory: The Morphogenetic Approach*, Cambridge: Cambridge University Press.

Bagdikian, B. (1990), *The Media Monopoly* 3rd edition, Boston: Beacon

Bennett, W.L. (1988), *NEWS: The Politics of Illusion* 2nd edition, New York: Longman.

Booth, K. (2007), *Theory of World Security*, Cambridge: Cambridge University Press.

Day, A. (2008), *Religion and the Individual: Belief, Practice, Identity*, Aldershot: Ashgate.

Durkheim, E. (1972), *Emile Durkheim: Selected Writings*, edited by Anthony Giddens, Cambridge: Cambridge University Press.

Gamson, W., Croteau, D., Hoynes, W. and Sasson, T. (1992), 'Media Images and the social construction of reality', *Annual Review of Sociology*, 18, 373-93.

Giddens, A. (1984), *The Constitution of Society*, Cambridge: Polity Press

Hay, C. (1995), 'Structure and Agency' in G. Stoker and D. Marsh (eds), *Theory and Methods in Political Science*, London: Macmillan.

Hay, C. (1996), *Re-Stating Social and Political Change*, Buckingham: Open University Press.

Hay, C. (2001), 'What Place for Ideas in the Structure-Agency debate? Globalisation as a "Process Without a Subject"', available from http://www.raggedclaws. com/criticalrealism/archive/cshay_wpisad.html, accessed 1st April 2009.

Herman, E. and Chomsky, N. (1971), *Manufacturing Consent*, New York: Pantheon.

Jessop, B. (1990), *State Theory: Putting the Capitalist State in its Place*, Cambridge: Polity Press.

Keohane, R. and Nye, J. (1989), *Power and Interdependence*, New York: Harper Collins.

King, A. (2004) *The Structuring of Social Theory*, Abingdon: Routledge.

Lewis, J., Williams, A., and Franklin, B. (2008), 'A Compromised Fourth Estate?', *Journalism Studies*, 9 (1), 11-20.

Maslak, M. (2003), *Daughters of the Tharu: Gender, Ethnicity, Religion, and the Education of Nepali Girls*, Abingdon: Routledge.

McSweeny, K. (1999), *Security, Identity and Interests*, Cambridge: Cambridge University Press.

Schmalzbauer, J. (2003), *People of Faith: Religious Conviction in American Journalism and Higher Education*, Ithaca, New York: Cornell University Press.

Tawney, R.H. (1938), *Religion and the Rise of Capitalism*, Harmondsworth: Pelican Books.

Waltz, K. (1959), *Man, the State, and War: a Theoretical Approach*, New York: Columbia University Press.

—— (1979), *Theory of International Politics*, New York: University of Columbia Press.

—— (2000), 'Structural realism after the Cold War', *International Security*, 25 (1), (Summer), 5-41.

Weber, M. (1930), *The Protestant Ethic and the Spirit of Capitalism*, London: George Allen and Unwin Ltd.

Wendt, A. (1987), 'The Agent-Structure Problem in International Theory', *International Organization*, 41 (3), 335-70.

—— (1992), 'Anarchy is What States Make of It: The Social Construction of Power Politics', *International Organization*, 46 (2), 391-425.

—— (1999), *Social Theory of International Politics*, Cambridge: Cambridge University Press.

Index

Also of interest:

Religion, Conflict and Military Intervention
Edited by Rosemary Durward and Lee Marsden
ISBN 978-0-7546-7871-7